D1297210

WITHDRAWN

BELINSKY,

CHERNYSHEVSKY, and DOBROLYUBOV

SELECTED CRITICISM

891.709
M427br

BELINSKY,

CHERNYSHEVSKY, and DOBROLYUBOV

SELECTED CRITICISM

Edited,
and with an Introduction,
by Ralph E. Matlaw

INDIANA UNIVERSITY PRESS
Bloomington and London

First Midland Book edition published 1976 by arrangement with
E. P. Dutton & Co., Inc.

Copyright © 1962 by E. P. Dutton & Co., Inc.

All rights reserved
No part of this book may be reproduced or utilized in any form
or by any means, electronic or mechanical, including photo-
copying and recording, or by any information storage and re-
trieval system, without permission in writing from the publisher.
The Association of American University Presses' Resolution on
Permissions constitutes the only exception to this prohibition.
Published in Canada by Fitzhenry & Whiteside Limited, Don
Mills, Ontario

Manufactured in the United States of America

Library of Congress Cataloging in Publication Data

Matlaw, Ralph E., ed.
Belinsky, Chernyshevsky, and Dobrolyubov.

Reprint of the ed. published by Dutton, New York, which was
issued as no D96 of A Dutton paperback.

1. Russian literature—19th century—History and criticism—
Addresses, essays, lectures. I. Belinskiĭ, Vissarion Grigor'evich,
1811-1848. II. Chernyshevskiĭ, Nikolaĭ Gavrilovich, 1828-1889.
III. Dobroliubov, Nikolaĭ Aleksandrovich, 1836-1861. IV. Title.
PG3011.M33 1976   891.7'09'003   75-34729
ISBN 0-253-31155-1
ISBN 0-253-20200-0 pbk
1   2   3   4   5   80   79   78   77   76

CONTENTS

CAT May 25 '81

5-18-81 Pub. 4 25

80-6527

INTRODUCTION

THE SENSE of social responsibility, political commitment, and moral vision that informs Russian literature is in large part the product of a critical tradition established in the middle third of the nineteenth century. Belinsky, Chernyshevsky, and Dobrolyubov, men of widely differing temperaments and abilities, created an empirical doctrine of vast importance to the progress of Russian letters. In emphasizing the political implications of literature, largely at the expense of aesthetic criteria, its practitioners have at various times been known as "civic," "utilitarian," "sociological," or "radical" critics. In the Soviet Union they have retrospectively been opted as forerunners of Marxist-Leninist criticism, and renamed "Revolutionary Democrats." In addition to their places in literary history, they therefore also figure as cultural phenomena, with a vitality and importance rarely accorded to literary figures in modern times.

Vissarion Grigor'evich Belinsky, the most gifted and formidable Russian critic in the nineteenth century, the fountainhead of this tradition and the prototype for the figure that permeates mid-century Russian literature and dominates its attitudes, can be compared in stature and influence not so much with other prolific and influential critics and theoreticians of the nineteenth century, men like Sainte-Beuve and Taine in France, Friedrich Schlegel in Germany, and Coleridge in England, but rather with those men like Dr. Johnson or Boileau who do not at all resemble him in literary tastes and theories but who, like him, determined the cultural temper of a whole age. He was born in 1811, the son of a poor provincial doctor. He entered Moscow University in 1829, but was expelled three years later, officially "because of unsound health and also because of limited capabilities," but more likely for a very bad and somewhat inflammatory

viii   INTRODUCTION

play on the theme of serfdom. A liberal young professor of
European literature who founded the periodical *The Telescope*
offered him a post as reviewer. From 1833 until his death in
1848 from consumption aggravated by overwork, he poured
out a stream of reviews, articles, theoretical analyses, and
statements upon the appearance of every literary work of
any importance, with ever-increasing popularity among, and
adulation from, the liberal-minded youth of the day. In 1839
he moved from Moscow to St. Petersburg, reaching his most
important formulations in his annual reviews of Russian literature, particularly those for 1846 and 1847, which appeared
in the most influential of the liberal periodicals, *The Contemporary.*

Belinsky's career is associated with, and typifies, two important notions in Russian intellectual history. The first is the
rise of the "intelligentsia," a term, apparently of Russian
invention, that designates intellectuals of all persuasions
dedicated in one form or another to the improvement of life
in Russia, and so carries far greater ethical implications than
the mere word "intellectual." The second is that of the
raznochintsy, literally "persons of various classes," a term
applied to those members of classes other than the gentry,
usually the clergy or the minor and provincial professional
and bureaucratic classes, who sought to pursue a career other
than the one their background would normally indicate.
Frequently they became members of the intelligentsia, usually
after considerable privation. Unlike members of the gentry
such as Herzen or Turgenev, who could always turn to other
sources if necessary, they were entirely dependent upon
their intellectual labors, whether as tutors, journalists, or
writers, and from their position derived no small part of their
exaltation and indefatigability. While there were factions and
enmities within the intelligentsia, all its members were in
principle agreed on one point: opposition to the conditions
of life around them. Clearly connected with these conditions
is the intrusion of the *raznochintsy* into literature, until 1830
or so the exclusive purview of the gentry, who were all too
eager to avoid the imputation of professionalism. In style and
in tone a sharp shift may be observed, and no one better
exemplifies this change than Belinsky himself.

The background and development of this period form a
major part of one of Russia's most imaginative works, Herzen's
Past and Thoughts. Herzen's autobiography becomes the
cultural history of a period and the biography of its leading

members. There, too, occurs what has become the most
famous and memorable portrait of Belinsky. It begins with
a number of incidents illustrating Belinsky's shyness in social
situations, his intellectual and moral honesty, his modesty,
his constant battle to overcome his weakened state. Its central
part catches the real essence of the man and of his writings:

> But that shy man, that frail body, contained a mighty spirit,
> the spirit of a gladiator! Yes, he was a powerful fighter! He
> could not preach or lecture; what he needed was argument.
> If he was not contradicted, if he was not stirred to irritation,
> he did not speak well; but when he was touched to the quick,
> when his cherished convictions were challenged, when the
> muscles of his cheeks began to quiver and his voice trembled,
> then he was worth seeing. He pounced on his opponent like
> a panther; he tore him to pieces, made him look ridiculous
> and pitiful, and incidentally developed his own thought with
> extraordinary force, with extraordinary poetry. The discussion
> would often end with blood coming from the sick man's throat;
> pale, gasping, his eyes fixed upon the man with whom he was
> speaking, he would lift his handkerchief to his mouth with
> shaking hand, and stop, deeply mortified, crushed by his phys-
> ical weakness. How I loved and pitied him at those moments!

The fierce rhetoric of such an onslaught is conveyed in his
"Letter to Gogol," one of his last pronouncements, and one
that became Belinsky's testament and the gospel of liberals.
The compelling sense of urgency, the indignation and vitu-
peration that earned him the name "Furious Vissarion," or
"Raging Vissarion," are products of his total, uncompromising
belief in ideas and literature. He hated oppression and dogma
more than anything else—ironically, he has become sanctified
in the Soviet Union—and never shrank from the implications
of his theories or from renouncing and correcting them when
they proved unsatisfactory. Ultimately he was concerned with
the dignity of man, and his criticism was directed to that
final criterion. As a result of his passionate concern and of
his temperament, his literary judgments frequently foisted
upon works social criteria that, while commendable, do not
correspond to their authors' intention or to the work at hand.
Through his enormous influence on the reading public, he
unmade as well as made reputations, doomed authors to
oblivion, determined the interpretation (or misinterpretation)
of writers until the present time. Belinsky always sought to
distinguish the original from the merely imitative, the genuine

response from the artificial one, the valid from the meretricious. He recognized, elucidated, and encouraged almost every literary talent as soon as it appeared in those remarkable years that saw so many of Russia's great novelists and poets first breaking into print: Gogol and Lermontov, Turgenev, Goncharov, Dal', Nekrasov, Herzen, Dostoevsky, and Grigorovich, not to mention a host of lesser figures. Belinsky's is an enviable record in comparison to Sainte-Beuve's lack of enthusiasm when first confronted with Balzac, Stendhal, Flaubert, and Baudelaire.

Yet it was essentially those articles that presented the broad outlines of literature, rather than his analyses of individual works, that give him his eminence as the greatest of Russia's literary historians, for he had to a remarkable degree the faculty for seeing things (whether correctly or not) in broad outlines, organized according to a unifying scheme. Thus his first important work, the "Literary Reveries" of 1834, despite its gaps of knowledge and its prejudices, is the first significant attempt to show the nature of Russian literature, its development, its historical logic, and its achievement. And his last significant critical article, "Russian Literature in 1847," turns on the relevance of literature to the current scene and the notion of progress.

Belinsky's career is usually treated in three stages, though his influence depends primarily on a small part of his work in the last five, or even two, years of his life, when he had reached the broadest and most forceful formulation of his views, when he began to turn literary criticism into discussions of social movements—conceived in moral rather than in political terms—and when, by his relentless and vehement opposition to metaphysics and theology, to roseate and sentimental views, he affected the whole course of literary and critical realism in Russia. Belinsky began his career under the profound influence of German romantic and idealistic philosophy, proclaiming that literature is "the expression of the national spirit, the symbol of the inner life of a nation, the physiognomy of a nation," that insight is gained through imagination and poetic discovery, that art is an organic whole, and that "the poet thinks in images." At this stage, as indeed throughout his career, Belinsky asserted that art had first to be art, and could only then serve or express other interests. He distinguished between the "real" and the "ideal" by the formula "Realism deals with life, idealism with ideas," differentiating works in the first group (*Don Quixote, Onegin*)

from the second (*Faust, Manfred*). Art is connected with
real life, rather than with abstract beauty or theory. As the
"real" and "natural" gained ascendance in his scheme, as he
came more and more to demand "the closest possible resemblance of the persons described to their models in life," he
championed Gogol as a keen portrayer of Russian life, and
praised Gogol's followers, the so-called "natural" school, who
attempted to portray a character in his environment, for
using proper methods to depict crying injustices. As time
went on, he tended to place increasing emphasis on the real
and its implications, and to minimize the "ideal" and the
artistic. Thus after welcoming Dostoevsky's "realistic" *Poor
Folk* (which he misread as a work in Gogol's tradition), he
castigated Dostoevsky's first really original and important
work, *The Double*, by writing, "The fantastic belongs only
in lunatic asylums, not in literature. It is the business of
doctors, not of poets."

Belinsky's middle phase, the two brief years 1840–1841,
were a shock and embarrassment to his friends, and a source
of infinite misery to himself. For with that peculiar Russian
characteristic of carrying logical implications to impossible
extremes even when these are demonstrably absurd or
dangerous (which paradoxically is both the ultimate worship
of reason and its absolute denial), Belinsky now adopted the
Hegelian formula "All that is real is rational, all that is
rational is real" literally. He accepted the social order he had
so stanchly opposed before, and refused to fight its patent
injustices. During these years he wrote about the universal,
timeless themes, and on the fallacy of asking art to serve immediate ends. Finally he admitted his error and gratefully
if painfully returned to the underlying and motivating im-
pulse of his life and work: concern for the lives of human
beings, whose misery could not be explained away or assuaged
by any philosophical system or historical necessity. Thus in
one of the early works of the final phase, "The Discourse on
Criticism," he writes: "What is the art of our times? A judgment, an analysis of society, consequently criticism. . . .
For our time a work of art is lifeless if it depicts life only in
order to depict it, without a mighty subjective urge that
springs from the prevailing thought of the epoch, if it is not a
cry of suffering, or a dithyramb of rapture, if it is not a question, or an answer to a question."

He embarked at this time on a long series of articles on
Pushkin, and was the first Russian critic to assess Pushkin's

many-sided greatness. Belinsky keenly appreciated Pushkin's
art, though he also had drastic blind spots about some of
Pushkin's most perfect, but to Belinsky's mind trivial, works,
such as the *Tales of Belkin* and the jocular narrative poems.
(Belinsky and his followers were entirely devoid of humor.)
While Belinsky greatly admires Pushkin's psychological and
artistic skill, he now treats Pushkin as a purveyor of certain
truths about Russian life and its development, particularly
in the discussion of morality in *Eugene Onegin*. The correspondence between art and life has now become much
closer. The next step is clear: Pushkin reflects a bygone era,
and no longer adequately satisfies contemporary problems
and readers, who find Lermontov's works more interesting,
for they deal with current life. Gogol plays a central role in
this shift, moving from "ideals" (in Belinsky's peculiar sense)
to the copying of real life before him, introducing true
Russian matter into literature. Belinsky praises Gogol for
making the ugly and mean the subject of art, for introducing
types from lower social levels, in short, for introducing life
where previously only ideals reigned. Belinsky's wrath at
what he considered Gogol's betrayal and apostasy, the wrath
that he expressed in the famous "Letter," reached such
proportions no doubt precisely because Gogol was the most
gifted and important writer of the age. Parenthetically, it
must be stated that only at the end of the nineteenth century
did critics begin to question Belinsky's view of Gogol's
realism.

Belinsky's education was spotty; he had no languages; his
information and judgments were at times woefully deficient.
But he loved literature profoundly. He also had critical
genius, an immediate though far from infallible appreciation
for excellence. He was able at once to penetrate to the
essence of a work, to communicate it, to show its function
and importance in the context of the times. He was, as has
already been suggested, a man of complete honesty who
never hesitated to say what he thought. His critical practice
was to immerse himself in the work at hand until permeated
by it, and then to expound the meaning as it appeared to
him, largely through comments on extensive quotations. His
work gives the impression of being improvised, written at
white heat. It is prolix, ill organized, the style journalistic,
obscure, confusing, and often grating, but remarkably
vigorous and direct. It communicates the overwhelming excitement experienced by Belinsky himself, and lets the reader

follow, as it were, the steps in Belinsky's contact with the text and the resulting view. Very frequently in his working articles he merely exclaims rapturously at the veracity and beauty of a passage, and lets the text speak for itself. When this has been done, he will frequently launch into a discussion of the underlying merits and implications, as, for example, in the articles on Lermontov, where he dissects the pose of Pechorin, notes that *A Hero of Our Time* mirrors current dissatisfaction with life, and observes a profound despair at life beneath the posturing and mask of Lermontov's verse.

His review articles and summaries differ in method and in impact. Here he moves, particularly in the later ones, to generalizations about literary requirements and achievements, about literature's reflection of the social scene. Historically they are his most important works, though critically such ex-cathedra pronouncements do not show him to best advantage. He recognized, too, that his personality, his devotion and dedication to a moral vision, would ultimately be as influential as his written work. In fact the figure of Belinsky has become something of a legend, while his writings created a solid foundation for the "sociological" approach to literature, emphasizing that literature has a social function and that criticism's proper concern lies there rather than in the analysis of form.

II

The ten years that saw the flowering of German philosophical thought and the establishment of the intelligentsia have aptly been named "The Marvelous Decade" by one of its participants and its chief chronicler. The decade from 1855–1865, when so many of the masterpieces of Russian literature appeared, can only be called something like the "Civic Decade" as far as criticism is concerned. It is dominated by two figures who saw themselves as the heirs of the tradition bequeathed by Belinsky but who used literary masterpieces as springboards for their own views. These were Nicolay Chernyshevsky and Nicolay Dobrolyubov. They were influenced by the English utilitarians Mill and Bentham; they were profoundly affected by the new materialism and scientific outlook; they were much more committed to a specific political platform of the far left, and actively campaigned for political reform under the guise of literary criticism. Aesthetic values went by the wayside. To these two may be added the most radical of all, Dmitri Pisarev, the incarnation of the nihilist in thought, campaigning ultimately for what in the title of one of his more militant pieces was "The Destruction of Aesthetics."

The period is ushered in by the disaster of the Crimean War, the death of the repressive autocrat Nicholas I (which was greeted as an occasion for great celebration by many), the promise of reforms that culminated in the abolition of serfdom in 1861 and a series of further reforms. Growing political consciousness created a background where social problems and theories and tendentious "civic" criticism could flourish.

The most important figure of the period was Nicolay Chernyshevsky (1828–1899). The son of a priest, he was educated at a theological school and attended the University of St. Petersburg, publishing his Master's dissertation on *The Aesthetic Relations of Art and Reality* (1855). In it he argues that art is merely an inferior reproduction of reality and that its only function is to spread knowledge about reality. No one, Chernyshevsky claims, would ever hesitate in choosing between a real apple and a painted one. Aesthetic achievement is dismissed as mere sensual pleasure, and in- finitely inferior to beauty in real life. That same year he joined the staff of *The Contemporary*, the most liberal of the so-called "Thick Journals," monthly publications whose size engendered their name and which were devoted to economics, history, foreign affairs, philosophy, and literature. There he published his *Studies in the Gogol Period of Russian Litera- ture*, patterned after Belinsky's longer attempts to convey the literary history of an era. The *Studies*, however, are far more documentary in scope, and less concerned with aesthetic values than with the correspondence of literature to life. Here, as in his long articles on Pushkin, Chernyshevsky "cor- rected" Belinsky's views by fitting the same literary works into his own theoretical frame. He wrote a number of critical articles before relinquishing the literary department to his brilliant protégé Dobrolyubov in order to devote himself to the economic and political sections. In 1862 he was ar- rested as the leader of the radicals. Before his exile to Siberia in 1863, an event that established him as the martyr of the radical cause, he wrote, in the Peter and Paul fortress, a work entitled *What Is To Be Done? (From Stories About the New Men)*, a didactic novel conceived as an antidote to the unsuccessful revolutionary depicted in Turgenev's *Fathers and Children*. Here, in a work that can barely pretend to literary merit, he developed his ideas of science, reason, rationalism, man's acting for his own advantage, the doctrine of environment, of man's perfectibility and striving toward a harmonious, phalanstery-like community. The novel had an enormous vogue as a guide to radical youth, and has become a prototype for much Soviet fiction. Only in 1883 was Chernyshevsky allowed to return to Astrakhan, but he never came closer to the capital than Saratov, where he died in 1889.

Chernyshevsky had some keen insights into literature and into problems of language. His most perceptive criticism occurs in a short article on Tolstoy. In reviewing the *Sevastopol Sketches* (1856), he was the first to note that Tolstoy was a psychologist who describes "the psychic process itself, its forms, its laws, . . . the dialectics of the soul." Tolstoy is able to do more than communicate the mystery of the soul. He can dissect the movement of the soul, analyze it, explain it to the reader. Ironically, this man who had little use for literature first used the term "interior monologue" in an important passage of this review, applying it to that which passes in the mind of the dying soldier. Chernyshevsky also compares Tolstoy's descriptive art to that of the painter who catches the flicker of light on rustling leaves. Thus he grasped immediately two salient features of Tolstoy's art: his psychological finesse and his concern with fleeting states, that is, with change. But most of Chernyshevsky's articles can hardly be considered as literary criticism at all. His most famous article, "The Russian at the *Rendez-vous*," ostensibly a review of Turgenev's elegiac story *Asya*, becomes an attack on the indecisiveness and weakness of Russian liberalism. The story develops into an instructive warning not to vacillate or hesitate, but to attain the goal. He dismisses Turgenev's poetic rendering of frustrated love with the typical and often quoted passage: "Forget about them, those erotic questions! They are not for a reader of our time, occupied with problems of administrative and judiciary improvements, of financial reforms, of the emancipation of the serfs."

Even in an English translation, the enormous differences between Belinsky and Chernyshevsky are manifest. Belinsky's vocabulary is heavily tinged with terms common to romantic and Hegelian philosophy; Chernyshevsky's, with scientific and sociological jargon of the mid-century. Belinsky's seriousness and excitement are communicated in the very inelegance of his prose; Chernyshevsky's turgid prose and heavy-handed irony convey pedantry and indifference to human problems. His meandering sentences frequently remain incomplete or incorrect, his logic specious. Belinsky repeats his central ideas in article after article; Chernyshevsky is incredibly repetitious even within so short a scope as the article on Tolstoy. Whatever the enormous significance of Chernyshevsky's dissertation in providing the philosophic basis for subsequent "radical" criticism, it clearly shows him to be a Philistine. His literary criticism reflects the discomfort of a man who would rather be dealing with ideas in a purer state than that possible in artistic garb.

Chernyshevsky did some pioneering work on Russian prosody in the process of defending Nekrasov's use of the rhythms and meters of folk poetry. He claimed that in Russian, trisyllabic feet are more natural (hence "nearer to prose" and "better") than bisyllabic, a concept that was later to play a considerable role in freeing Russian poetic forms. But his importance ultimately does not rest on these minor pieces within his voluminous production. He was, and remains, the central figure in Russian radical thought of that era, and its theoretician in many fields. In literature, too, he did yeoman service, by codifying and exemplifying the utilitarian function of literature.

The second figure, Nicolay Dobrolyubov (1836–1861), was, like Chernyshevsky, the son of a priest, and received his education at a theological seminary and pedagogical institute. He wrote much more extensively on literature than his predecessor and mentor had, but fundamentally had just as little concern for art, and in his capacity as literary critic he reviewed many works in the social sciences. In 1857 he assumed the post of critic for *The Contemporary*, thereby freeing Chernyshevsky for work in other fields. Again like Chernyshevsky, he felt that literature is merely words that can reflect but cannot change reality. At times, however, he felt that literature might be "an auxiliary force, whose importance lies in propaganda." Dobrolyubov's important addition to the literary theories of his predecessors is that of "social types." Dobrolyubov writes primarily about characters in literature, treating them as real beings when he does not use them for mere polemics. The rationale is that "in these [living] images the poet may, imperceptibly even to himself, grasp and express an inner meaning long before his mind can define it. It is precisely the function of criticism to explain the meaning hidden in these images." In one of his last essays, on Dostoevsky's *Insulted and Injured,* an essay that shows greater concern for formal problems, he modified his view so far as to recognize that "the poet creates a whole, finds a vital link, fuses and transforms the diverse aspects of living reality."

Dobrolyubov's fame rests on four essays that deal with literary themes. Their titles are significant, for they indicate Dobrolyubov's polemical intention: "What is Oblomovitis?" (on Goncharov's *Oblomov*), "When Will the Real Day Come?" (on Turgenev's *On the Eve*), "The Kingdom of Darkness" (on Ostrovsky's plays about coarse bigotry and superstition among the old Moscow merchants), and an incredibly obtuse review of Ostrovsky's *The Storm* called "A Ray of Light in the Kingdom of Darkness."

The most important of these is clearly "What is Oblomovitis?" which in a sense creates, though it pretends to bury, "the superfluous man." Looking over thirty years of Russian literature, Dobrolyubov claims a striking discovery about Russian literary heroes. Using Goncharov's Oblomov as his starting point, he generalizes about the pattern of vacillation, weakness, egotism, and inactivity ostensibly shared by such figures as Griboedov's Chatsky, Pushkin's Onegin, Lermontov's Pechorin, and Turgenev's Rudin. The literary character is judged for his failure in the real world—not the world of the novel—for literature, after all, is only a reflection of the real world. Oblomov thus becomes "Oblomovitis," a disease common to Russians, whose roots lie in the moral and social corruption of society. Dobrolyubov uses the book as a springboard to the "real" world; and once he has explored the ills of that world, he projects them back onto the novel without, unfortunately, dealing with the novel itself or even analyzing its main character. Oblomov is merely a repellent nonentity, a symbol of the disease produced by the institution of serfdom.

The essay is important in the unfortunate practice of discussing literary characters as if they had real existence. Dobrolyubov is rigorous in this pursuit. He traces the literary ancestry of the heroine, primarily in order to elaborate on the development of Russian women in the past thirty years. He even denies Oblomov's foil, the efficient and active Stolz, a place as a figure in a novel of Russian life, for Stolz comes of a German family. Yet Dobrolyubov also notes that the portrait is abstract and not quite successful.

Similarly, Turgenev's *On the Eve* is the springboard for a discussion of Russian revolutionary possibilities. While it is perfectly obvious that Turgenev made Insarov a Bulgarian because the censor would never have passed a book depicting a Russian revolutionary, Dobrolyubov finds that this character can act because his cause is directed at a foreign oppressor, while a Russian would have to struggle against internal ills. Insarov is not a Russian, and hence is technically disqualified by Dobrolyubov, who nevertheless finds his "indomitable loyalty to an idea" interesting. The real point of the essay is implied in the title: When will the day come when a Russian revolutionary can be depicted? Needless to say, for Dobrolyubov this clearly presupposes his existence in real life.

In no other article did Dobrolyubov stray so far from his text as in his analysis of Ostrovsky's *The Storm*. He read this gloomy play about a pitiful, ignorant, superstitious woman in an oppressive milieu as a kind of joyous glorification of the best in the Russian spirit. The heroine, Katerina, commits adultery, and later, in fear of the tortures of afterlife and in despair at her situation, commits suicide. Dobrolyubov saw in Katerina an "instinctive consciousness of her inalienable right to love, happiness, and life," and in her death an inspiration to readers, an assertion that tyranny, as represented by the microcosm of the merchant family, would no longer be countenanced. It is a prime example of exalted feelings and laudable sentiments making for very poor criticism.

Had Dobrolyubov not died at so young an age, he might well have developed into a major critic. He was very gifted, and for all his concern with political implications had considerable sense of literature, in part evident in the verse he wrote. To be sure, it is "civic verse," and not of striking quality, but it testifies to a deeper involvement with art than his theoretical formulations would lead one to expect.

*   *   *

In some ways a more interesting figure, and the most radical of all, is Dmitri Pisarev, who incarnates the mid-century realistic temperament in what Turgenev called its "nihilistic" phase. He drowned in 1868 at the age of twenty-eight (there is some suspicion that he committed suicide), after spending a number of years in prison for having published radical propaganda. A member of the gentry, with considerable sensitivity to language and form, he deliberately affected a crude and coarse approach. He campaigned for the "Destruction of Aesthetics," asserting that a pair of shoes was better than a Shakespearean tragedy, for the former could be worn, while nothing could come of the latter. Even "radical criticism" was dismissed; in "Pushkin and Belinsky," the most vicious of his articles, he disposes of Pushkin as a frivolous poet without an adequate sense of social consciousness, and just as crudely dismisses Belinsky for having wasted his time by taking Pushkin's work seriously and commenting on it.

Pisarev's is essentially an anarchical mind, expressed at the extreme of utilitarianism. He refused to grant value to any manifestation that has no social consequence, and rejoices at the decline of letters. His review of *Crime and Punishment* ignores the novel in order to discuss poverty as the cause of crime. *War and Peace* is for him a senseless glorification of the old aristocracy, a waste of time. But Pisarev's reputation began with a rebuttal to Dobrolyubov's views of Oblomov, and his best work deals with the definition of the "new man" adumbrated by Chernyshevsky. Pisarev's most solid work is his review ("The Realists") of Turgenev's *Fathers and Children*, where he gave an acute analysis of Bazarov's character and significance. He saw, through what was more an act of insight into himself than an act of critical genius, the essence of his temperament and of the aspirations of his contemporaries, and he projected it clearly. In his iconoclasm, in his violent, independent, and sometimes imaginative sallies, he stands somewhat apart from the tradition of Belinsky, Chernyshevsky, and Dobrolyubov, though he clearly has many points in common with it.

The tradition begun by Belinsky was thus extended and codified by Chernyshevsky, Dobrolyubov and, to a far lesser extent, Pisarev. It was by no means the only critical camp. It would be instructive to compile a collection of essays by such figures as Maykov, Druzhinin, Grigoryev, Strakhov, and others who are more interesting as critics and who have been unjustly neglected, indeed, who have not even been reprinted. Yet it is clear that the tradition discussed here was the more important one in the nineteenth century, affecting the attitudes and interests of a large portion of the reading public and of lesser writers. The most important determinant of this direction was the practice and perhaps even more the figure of Belinsky. For all his crudity and critical errors, he served as a reminder and an inspiration for the deep moral and social importance of art. His followers, men of smaller stature, committed to more immediate aims and more doctrinaire methods, played a more important political role. They emphasized the philosophical, ideological implication of art at the expense of the aesthetic, but in the process created a type of criticism that for the first time dealt systematically with the relation between literature and society. Such criticism, of course, has by now been extensively practiced, and underlies the work of critics as disparate in mind and sensitivity as V. L. Parrington and Edmund Wilson. In Russia the tradition itself was continued, adapted to changing needs and views, and modified by men like N. K. Mikhaylovsky, G. Plekhanov, Lunacharsky, and others. Its final, logical metamorphosis is "Socialist Realism," the prescriptive Soviet doctrine that literature and art must depict reality while simultaneously showing man in the progress toward a better, socialist life.

RALPH E. MATLAW

V. G. BELINSKY

NOTE

Belinsky's articles are presented here in the translation that appeared in V. G. Belinsky, *Selected Philosophical Works*, Moscow, 1956, with minor stylistic revisions. The essays by Dobrolyubov are reprinted, with similar revisions, from N. A. Dobrolyubov, *Selected Philosophical Essays*, Moscow, 1956. The last half of Belinsky's *Thoughts and Notes on Russian Literature* was translated by William Gard and Ralph E. Matlaw. The essays by Chernyshevsky were translated by Ralph E. Matlaw. Interpunction (. . .) does not indicate omission.

Thoughts and Notes
on Russian Literature

WHATEVER our literature may be, it has far greater significance for us than may appear: in it, and it alone, is contained
the whole of our intellectual life and all the poetry of our
life. Only in the sphere of our literature do we cease to be
Johns and Peters and become simply people dealing and
associating with people.

There is a prevailing spirit of disunity in our society: each
of our social estates possesses specific traits of its own—its
dress and its manners, and way of life and customs, and even
its language. To be convinced of this, it would suffice to
spend an evening in the chance company of a government
official, a military man, a landowner, a merchant, a commoner, a lawyer, or overseer, a clergyman, a student, a
seminarist, a professor, and an artist; seeing yourself in such
company you might think you were present at the distribution of tongues. . . . So great is the disunity reigning among
these representatives of various classes of the same society!
The spirit of disunity is hostile to society: society unites
people, caste divides them. Many believe that haughtiness,
a relic of Slavonic antiquity, destroys sociability in us. That
may be true in part, if it is true at all. Granted that the
nobleman is loath to cultivate the society of men of lower
station; but then what are men of lower station not prepared
to sacrifice in order to cultivate the society of the nobleman?
It is their passion! But the trouble is that this *rapprochement*
is always an external, formal show resembling a bowing acquaintance; a rich merchant's vanity is flattered by the acquaintance even with a poor nobleman, yet though he has
made the acquaintance of the rich nobility he still remains
true to the habits, conceptions, language, and way of life of
his own merchants' class.

This spirit of particularity is so strong with us that even the

3

new social estates that originated from the new order of things created by Peter the Great lost no time in assuming their specific features. Is it to be wondered at that the nobleman in no way resembles the merchant or the merchant the nobleman when we have sometimes almost the same distinction between the scientist and the artist? We still have scientists who have remained faithful throughout their lives to a noble resolution not to understand art and what it stands for; we still have many artists who do not suspect the vital connection that their art has with science, literature, and life. Bring *such* a scientist and *such* an artist together, and you will find that they will either keep silent or exchange noncommittal phrases, and even these will be more in the nature of work for them than conversation. At times our scientist, especially if he has dedicated himself to the exact sciences, will look down on philosophy and history and those who engage in them with an ironical smile, while poetry, literature, and journalism he simply regards as nonsense. Our so-called "man of letters" looks with contempt on mathematics that eluded him at school.

It may be argued that this is not a spirit of disunity; it is rather a spirit of quasi-education and quasi-learning! Yes, but then did not all these people receive a fairly broad if not very deep elementary education? The man of letters learned mathematics at school, and the mathematicians studied literature. Many of them can on occasion make out quite a good case to prove that the division of the sciences is merely an artificial contrivance and not a thing of intrinsic value, since all sciences comprise a single knowledge of a single subject—Being; that art, like science, is a consciousness of Being but in another form, and that literature should be a delight and luxury of the mind for all educated people alike. But when they have to apply these specious arguments to life, they immediately divide themselves into guilds that eye each other with a certain ironical smile and a sense of their own worth or with a sort of mistrust. . . . How then expect sociability among people of diverse estates, each of which has its own mode of thinking, speaking, dressing, eating, and drinking? . . .

However that may be, it would be wrong to say that we had no society whatever. Undoubtedly there exists with us a strong demand for society and a striving toward society, and that in itself is important! The reform of Peter the Great did not destroy or break down the walls that in old society had divided one class from another; but it had undermined the foundations of these walls and thrown them awry if it had not wrecked them—and now they are leaning over more and more from day to day, crumbling and being buried beneath their own debris and dust, so that to repair them would only give them added weight, which, in view of their sapped foundations, would merely accelerate their inevitable downfall. And if today the estates divided by these walls cannot overstep them as they would a smooth road, they can at any rate jump over them with ease at the spots where they have suffered most from wear and dilapidation. This was previously done slowly and imperceptibly, while now it is being done faster and more perceptibly—and the time is not far off when it will be done swiftly and thoroughly. Railroads will run their tunnels and bridges through and beneath the walls, and the development of industry and commerce will interweave the interests of people of all estates and classes and force them into the close and vital intercourse that must needs smooth down all the sharp and unnecessary distinctions.

But the beginning of this *rapprochement* among the social estates, which in fact represents the inchoation of society, does not by any means belong exclusively to our times: it merges with the beginnings of our literature. A heterogeneous society, welded into a single mass by material interests alone, would be a sorry, humanless society. However great may be the outward prosperity and outward strength of a society, one would hardly regard it as an object of envy if its commerce, industry, shipping, railroads, and generally all its material motive forces constituted the primary, principal, and direct instead of merely the auxiliary means toward education and civilization. . . . In this respect we have no cause to blame fate: social enlightenment and education flowed with us originally through the channel of a small and barely visible brook, but a brook that had sprung from a sublime and noble source— from science and literature itself. Science with us today is only beginning to take root but has not yet taken root, whereas education has taken root but not yet spread its growth. Its leaf is small and scarce, its stem neither high nor thick, but its roots have sunk so deep that no tempest, no flood, no power can tear it up: fell this young wood in one place and its roots will emit shoots in another, and you will sooner tire of felling than this vegetation tire of emitting new shoots and spreading. . . .

In speaking of the progress of society's education, we have

in mind the progress of our literature, for our education is the direct effect of our literature upon the ideas and morals of society. Our literature has created the morals of our society, has already educated several generations of widely divergent character, has paved the way for the inner *rapprochement* of the estates, has formed a species of public opinion and produced a sort of special class in society that differs from the *middle estate* in that it consists not of the merchantry and commoners alone but of people of all estates who have been drawn together through education, which, with us, centered exclusively in a love of literature.

If you wish to understand and appreciate the influence of our literature on society, glance at the representatives of its various epochs, speak with them, or make them speak among themselves. Our literature is so young, and of such recent origin, that one may still come across all its representatives in society. The first admirable Russian poem written in regular meter, Lomonosov's *Ode on the Taking of Khotin*, made its appearance in 1739, exactly 107 years ago, and Lomonosov died in 1765, some eighty years ago. There are, of course, no people today who have seen Lomonosov even in their childhood, or who, having seen him, could remember it; but there are still many people in Russia today who have learned to love poetry and literature from Lomonosov's works, and who consider him to be as great a poet as he was considered to be in his time. There is a still greater number of people today who have a lively recollection of the face and voice of Derzhavin, and consider the epoch of his full fame to have been the best time of their lives. Many old men today are still convinced in all sincerity of the excellent merits of Kheraskov's poems, and it was not so long ago that the venerable poet Dmitriev complained in print of the young generation's irreverence toward the talent of the creator of *Rossiada* and *Vladimir*. There are still many old men who are thrilled by memories of Sumarokov's tragedies and are ready, in a dispute, to recite what they consider to be the best tirades from *Dmitri the Pretender*. Others, while conceding that Sumarokov's language is really antiquated, will point out to you with special deference the tragedies and comedies of Knyazhnin as a standard of dramatic pathos and purity of language. Still more often can we meet people who, while saying nothing about Sumarokov or Knyazhnin, will speak with all the greater heat and assurance about Ozerov. As for Karamzin, both the old and elder generations belong to him body and soul, feel, think, and live by him, despite the fact that they have not only read Zhukovsky, Batyushkov, Pushkin, Griboedov, Gogol, and Lermontov, but even admired them more or less. . . . Then there are people today who smile ironically at the mention of Pushkin and speak with reverential awe and admiration of Zhukovsky, as though homage toward the latter were incompatible with homage toward the former. And how many people are there who do not understand Gogol and justify their prejudice against him by the fact that they understand Pushkin! . . .

But do not imagine that these are purely literary facts: no, if you pay closer attention to these representatives of the different epochs of our literature and different epochs of our society you will not fail to discern a more or less vital relation between their literary and their worldly conceptions and convictions. As far as their literary education is concerned, these people seem to be separated from one another by centuries, because our literature has spanned the gulf of many centuries in the space of a hundred-odd years. And that was why there was a great difference between the society that admired the cumbrous wording of turgid odes and heavy epic poems and the society that shed tears over *Liza's Pond;* between the society that avidly read *Ludmila* and *Svetlana,* was thrilled by the fantastic horrors of *The Twelve Sleeping Maidens,* or basked in romantic languor beneath the mysterious sounds of the *Aeolian Harp* and the society that forgot the *Prisoner of the Caucasus* and *The Fountain of Bakhchisardi* for *Eugene Onegin,* Fonvizin's comedies for *Wit Works Woe,* Ozerov's *Dmitri Donskoy* for *Boris Godunov* (as once Sumarokov's *Dmitri the Pretender* had been forgotten for the former), and then would seem to have cooled to former poets for Pushkin and Lermontov; all the novelists and writers of romance whom they had so recently admired were forgotten for Gogol. . . . Imagine the immeasurable gulf of time that lay between *Ivan Vyzhigin,* published in 1829, and *Dead Souls,* published in 1842. . . . This distinction in society's literary education passed into life and divided people into diversely operating, thinking, and persuaded generations whose lively disputes and controversial relations, originating as they did from principles and not from material interests, represented symptoms of a nascent and developing spiritual life in society. And that great deed is the deed of our literature! . . .

Literature was for our society a vital source even of practical moral ideas. It began with satire, and in the person of Kantemir declared implacable war on ignorance, prejudices, barratry, chicanery, pettifogging, extortion, and embezzlement, which it found in old society not as vices, but as rules of life, moral convictions. Whatever we may think of Sumarokov's gifts, his satirical attacks on corrupt bureaucrats will always earn honorable mention in the history of Russian literature. Fonvizin's comedies rendered a still greater service to society than they did to literature. The same could almost be said of Kapnist's *Slander*. The fable became so popular with us because it belongs to the satirical genre of poetry. Derzhavin himself, pre-eminently a lyrical poet, was at the same time a satirical poet, as for example in *To Felitza, The Grandee,* and other plays. Ultimately there came a time when satire in our literature passed into humor, represented by the artistic portrayal of life's reality.

Of course, it is absurd to suppose that a satire, a comedy, story, or novel could reform a vicious person; but there is no doubt that in opening society's eyes to itself, and being instrumental in awakening its self-consciousness, they cover vice with scorn and disgrace. No wonder many people cannot hear Gogol's name mentioned without a feeling of rancor, and call his *Inspector General* an "immoral" work that ought to be prohibited. Equally, no one is so simple today as to believe that a comedy or a story can make an honest man out of a bribetaker—no, you cannot straighten a twisted tree when it has grown and thickened; but bribetakers have their progeny, as do the non-bribetakers: both, while not yet having cause to regard vivid descriptions of bribery as something immoral, admire them and are, imperceptibly to themselves, enriched with impressions that do not always remain barren in their subsequent lives when they will have become actual members of society. The impressions of youth are strong, and youth believes to be the indubitable truth what has first of all appealed to its emotions, imagination, and mind. And so we see how literature influences not only education but also the moral improvement of society! Be that as it may, it is a fact beyond a shadow of doubt that the number of people who are endeavoring to realize their moral convictions in deeds to the detriment of their private interests and at the risk of their social position has been growing perceptibly with us only lately.

No less undisputed is the fact that literature with us serves as the connecting link between people who are in all other respects *inwardly* divided. The commoner Lomonosov earned important titles by virtue of his talent and learning, and grandees admit him into their circle. On the other hand, it is literature again that drew him closer to poor and socially unimportant people. The poor nobleman Derzhavin himself became a grandee through his talent, and among the men with whom literature brought him in close contact he found not only rich patrons but friends as well. Kamenev, the Kazan merchant, author of the ballad *Gromval*, arrived in Moscow on business and went to make the acquaintance of Karamzin, and through him made the acquaintance of the whole Moscow literary circle. That was *forty years* ago, when merchants got no farther than the vestibules of nobles' houses and even then on matters of business concerned with the sale of their wares or an old debt for payment of which they humbly importuned.

The first Russian magazines, whose very names are now forgotten, were published by circles of young men who had been drawn together on the basis of their common love of literature. Education levels men. And in our days it is no longer a rarity to meet a friendly circle in which you will find a titled gentleman and a commoner, a merchant and a tradesman—a circle whose members have entirely forgotten the outward distinctions that divided them, and entertain a mutual regard for one another simply as men. Here is the true beginning of educated society that literature has established! Is there anyone with a claim to the title of man who does not from the bottom of his heart wish this sociability to wax and grow by the day and the hour like the prodigy heroes of our legends!

Society, like every living thing, should be organic, that is to say, a multitude of people *internally* linked together. Pecuniary interests, trade, shares, balls, social gatherings and dances are also links, but they are external, not vital, organic links, though necessary and useful. People are internally bound together by common moral interests, similarity of views, and equality of education, combined with a mutual regard for one another's human dignity. But all our moral interests, all our spiritual life have hitherto been and will, still for a long time to come, be concentrated in literature: it is the vital spring from which all human sentiments and conceptions percolate into society.

There is *apparently* nothing easier and *actually* nothing more difficult than to write about Russian literature. That is because Russian literature is still an infant, albeit an infant

Alcides. It is much more difficult to say anything positive or
definite of children than it is of adults. In addition, our literature, like our society, presents a spectacle of diverse contradictions, opposites, extremes, and idiocrasies. This is due to
the fact that it did not originate by itself but was originally
transplanted from an alien soil. It is much easier, therefore,
to speak of our literature in extremes. Say that it is no less
rich and mature than any European literature and that we
can count our geniuses by the dozen and our talents by the
hundred; or say that we have no literature at all, that our
best writers are incidental phenomena, or simply that they
are worth nothing: in either case you will at least be understood, and your opinion will win ardent supporters.

Love of controversial extremes is one of the characteristics
of the still-unsettled Russian nature; the Russian likes to boast
beyond measure or be modest beyond measure. Hence we
have, on the one side, so many inane Europeans who speak
with rapture of the last newspaper story of a dried-up French
novelist or sing with gusto a new vaudeville tune the Pari-
sians have long forgotten, and who regard the work of genius
of a Russian poet with contemptuous indifference or offensive
suspicion; for whom Russia has no future, and everything she
has is bad and worthless; on the other side we have so many
kvass patriots who go out of their way to abominate everything European—even enlightenment, and to love everything
Russian—even cheap liquor and fisticuffs duels. Adhere to any
of these factions and it will instantly declare you to be a great
man and a genius, while the other will hate you and declare
you to be a nincompoop. At any rate, though having enemies
you will also have friends. By maintaining an unbiased and
sober view on the subject, you will incur the opprobrium of
both sides. One will burden you with its fashionable, parrot-
like scorn; the other will most likely declare you to be a
troublesome, dangerous, and suspicious character and a
renegade, and will play the literary informer against you—
before the public, of course. . . . The most unpleasant part
of this is that you will not be understood and your words
will either be construed as immoderate praise or immoderate
obloquy, and not as a faithful assessment of the fact of reality,
as it exists, with all its good and evil, its merits and defects,
with all the contradictions inherent within it.

This has a special application to our literature, which
represents so many extremes and contradictions that in saying
anything positive about it one would immediately be obliged

to make a reservation the majority of the public, mostly preferring to read than to argue, might well interpret as a negation or contradiction. Thus, for example, in speaking of the strong and salutary influence of our literature on society and, consequently, of its great importance for us, we must make a reservation lest this influence and importance be ascribed a greater value than we had intended and the inference be drawn from our words that we have not only a literature, but a rich literature at that, fully capable of standing up to comparison with any European literature. Such a conclusion would be false in every way. We have a literature, and a literature that is rich in talents and works, taking into consideration its means and its youth—but our literature exists for us alone: to foreigners, however, it does not yet represent a literature, and they are fully entitled to disregard its existence, since they are unable, through it, to study and become acquainted with us as a nation and as a society. Our literature is too young, indefinite, and colorless for foreigners to be able to regard it as a fact of our intellectual life. It was only too recently a shy though talented tyro who took pride in copying European models, and passed off copies of pictures from European life as pictures of Russian life. And this was the character of a whole epoch in our literature from Kantemir and Lomonosov to Pushkin. Then, beginning to sense its own powers, it turned from tyro to master, and instead of copying the ready-made pictures of European life, which it artlessly passed off as original pictures of Russian life, it began boldly to paint pictures of both European and Russian life. But as yet it was fully a master only in the treatment of the former, while it still aspired, and not always ineffectually, to become a master in the latter. And this was the character of a period in our literature from Pushkin to Gogol. With the appearance of Gogol our literature addressed itself exclusively to Russian life and Russian realities. It may, because of that, have become more one-sided and even monotonous, but it has on the other hand become more original, independent, and hence more genuine.

Now let us take these periods of Russian literature in connection with their importance, not to us, but to foreigners. There is no need to prove that Lomonosov and Karamzin possess great importance for *us*: but try to translate their works into any European language and you will see whether foreigners will read them, or, if they do, whether they will find them of any interest to themselves. They will say: "We

have read all this long ago at home; give us *Russian* writers."
They would say the same thing about the works of Dmitriev,
Ozerov, Batyushkov, and Zhukovsky. Of all the writers of
this period they would have been interested only in the
fabulist Krylov; but he is supremely untranslatable into any
language in the world, and he can be appreciated only by
such foreigners who know Russian and have lived a long time
in Russia. Thus, a whole period of Russian literature is
sheerly non-existent as far as Europe is concerned.

As for the second period, it may be said to exist for Europe
only to a certain degree. Were such works of Pushkin's as
Mozart and Salieri, The Covetous Knight, and *The Stone
Guest* to be worthily translated into a European language,
foreigners would be compelled to admit that they are excellent poetical works, but these plays would be practically of
no interest to them as creations of Russian poetry. The same
can be said of the best creations of Lermontov. No translation can do justice to either Pushkin or Lermontov, no matter
how excellent these translations may be. The reason is
obvious: though the works of Pushkin and Lermontov reveal
the Russian soul, the clear and positive Russian mind and
strength and depth of feeling, these qualities are more comprehensible to us Russians than to foreigners, since the Russian nationality is not yet sufficiently fashioned and developed
for the Russian poet to be able to place its sharply defined
stamp upon his works as a mode of expressing ideas common
to the whole of mankind.

The demands of Europeans in this respect are very exacting. Nor is this to be wondered at: the national spirit of
European nations is so sharply and originally expressed in
their literatures that any work, however great in artistic
merit, which does not bear the sharp imprint of nationality,
loses its chief merit in the eyes of Europeans. You will find
in Marryat, Bulwer-Lytton, or any of the lesser English
novelists the same Englishman that you will find in Shakespeare, Byron, or Walter Scott. George Sand and Paul de
Kock represent the extremes of the French spirit, and though
the former expresses all the beautiful, human, and lofty, and
the latter the narrowness and vulgarity, of French nationality,
both are obviously the exclusive products of France. A
Clauren or an August Lafontaine are as much Germans as
Goethe and Schiller. In each of these literatures the writer
expresses the good or weak sides of his native nationality, and
the national spirit lies like a customs seal both on the produc-

tions of genius and on the productions of the literary hack. The French remained supremely national when trying their hardest to imitate the Greeks and Romans. Wieland remained a German while imitating the French. The barriers of nationality are impassable for Europeans. Perhaps it is our greatest blessing that all nationalities are equally accessible to us and that our poets are able in their works so freely and easily to become Greeks and Romans and Frenchmen and Germans and Englishmen and Italians and Spaniards: but that is a blessing of the future, as an indication that our nationality will have a broad and many-sided development. At present, however, it is more a defect than a merit, not so much broadness and many-sidedness as incompleteness and indefiniteness of its own basic principle.

It would therefore be more interesting for foreigners to have good translations of those of Pushkin's and Lermontov's works in which the subject matter is drawn from Russian life. Thus, *Eugene Onegin* would be of greater interest to foreigners than *Mozart and Salieri, The Covetous Knight,* and *The Stone Guest.* And that is why the most interesting Russian poet for foreigners is Gogol. This is not a surmise, but a fact that is borne out by the remarkable success achieved in France by the translation of five of this author's stories published last year in Paris by Louis Viardot. This success is understandable: in addition to his immense artistic talent Gogol strictly adheres to the sphere of Russian *everyday* reality in his works. And that is what mostly appeals to foreigners: through the medium of the poet they want to make the acquaintance of the country that has produced him. In this respect Gogol is the most 'national of Russian poets, and he has nothing to fear from a translation, though by the very reason of his works being so national the best of translations could not avoid weakening the local color.

But we should not allow even this success to turn our heads. To a poet who would have his genius acknowledged by all and everywhere, and not only by his compatriots, nationality is the primary, but not the sole condition: in addition to being *national* he must at the same time be *universal,* that is, the nationality of his creations must be the form, body, flesh, physiognomy, and personality of the spiritual and incorporeal world of ideas common to all mankind. In other words: the national poet must possess a great *historical* significance not for his country alone—his appearance must be a thing of *world-wide historical significance.* Such poets can

appear only in nations that are called upon to play a world-
historical role in the destinies of mankind, namely, whose
national life is destined to influence the trend and progress of
all mankind. And therefore, if, on the one hand, one cannot
become a world-historical poet unless possessing great natural
genius, on the other hand, one can sometimes fall short of
becoming a world-historical poet though possessing great
genius, that is to say, to be of importance only to one's own
nation. Here the significance of the poet depends not upon
himself, upon his activity, trend, or genius, but upon the importance of the country that produced him. From this point
of view we do not possess a single poet whom we could be
entitled to rank with the first poets of Europe, even in the
event of it being obvious that he is in no way inferior to any
of them in point of talent.

Pushkin's plays: *Mozart and Salieri, The Covetous Knight,*
and *The Stone Guest* are of such excellence that they can
without the slightest exaggeration be said to be worthy of the
genius of Shakespeare himself; yet this certainly does not
mean that Pushkin is equal to Shakespeare. Let alone the
great difference of power and scope that exists between the
genius of Shakespeare and the genius of Pushkin, such an
equivalence would be too bold a hypothesis even if Pushkin
has written as much and of equal excellence as Shakespeare.
The more so today when we know that the volume and scope
of his best works are so poor in comparison with the volume
and scope of Shakespeare's works. Rather could we say there
are several works in our literature that, for *artistic merit,*
could be held up to some of the great works of European
literature; but we cannot say that we have poets whom we
could hold up against the European poets of the first magnitude. There is a deep significance in the fact that we need
acquaintance with the great poets of foreign literature and
that foreigners do not stand in need of acquaintance with ours.
The relation of our great poets to the great poets of Europe
may be expressed thus: of certain plays of Pushkin one can
say that Shakespeare would not have been ashamed to own
them as his, as Byron would not have been ashamed to own
as his certain plays of Lermontov; but we could not, without
the risk of committing an absurdity, put it the other way
round and say that Pushkin and Lermontov would not have
been ashamed to subscribe their names to some of the works
of Shakespeare and Byron. We can call our poets Shake-
speares, Byrons, Walter Scotts, Goethes, Schillers, and so on,

merely as an indication of the power or direction of their talent but not of their importance in the eyes of the educated world. He who is not called by his own name cannot be considered equal to the man by whose name he is called. Byron appeared after Goethe and Schiller, yet he remained Byron and was not called an English Goethe or an English Schiller. When the time comes for Russia to produce poets of world-wide significance, these poets will be called by their own names, and every such poet, while retaining his proper name, will become a common name and be used in the plural, because he will be *typical*.

But saying that a Russian great poet, though richly endowed by nature and equal in talent to the great European poet, cannot at present achieve importance equal to that of the latter, we mean that he can vie with him only in *form* and not in the *substance* of his poetry. The poet receives his substance from the life of his nation, consequently, the merits, depth, scope, and importance of that substance depend directly and immediately upon the historical importance of his nation's life and not upon the poet himself or his talent.

Only a hundred and thirty-six years have elapsed since Russia, by the thunder of the Battle of Poltava, proclaimed to the world her adhesion to European life and her entrance upon the field of world-historical existence—and what a brilliant path of progress and glory has she not achieved in that brief space of time! That is something fabulously great, unprecedented, never before heard of! Russia decided the fate of the contemporary world by "overthrowing into the abyss the idols that hung over kingdoms," and today, having occupied the place she has rightly earned among the first-class powers of Europe, holds with them the destinies of the world on the scales of her might. . . . But this testifies that we have not lagged behind, but have surpassed many countries in politico-historical significance, which is an important but not the sole and exclusive aspect in the life of a nation called upon to perform a great role.

Our political greatness is undoubtedly a pledge of our future great importance in other respects as well; but this alone does not testify to the achievements of such all-round development as necessarily constitutes the fullness and wholeness of life in a great nation. In the future, in addition to the victorious Russian sword, we shall lay the weight of Russian thought on the scales of European life. . . . Then shall we have poets whom we shall be entitled to rank with European poets of the first magnitude. But today let us be content with what we have, neither exaggerating nor diminishing the value of what we possess. By the standard of time our literature has achieved tremendous successes undoubtedly bearing witness to the fertility of the soil on which the Russian spirit grows. Something in our literature, if not our literature itself, is beginning to rouse interest even in foreigners. That interest is still fairly one-sided, since foreigners are able to discover in the works of Russian poets only a local color, the picturesque manners and customs of a country so sharply contrasting to their own countries. . . .

In our country there has long been maintained the custom of denouncing, first, the public for its supposed indifference toward everything native, chiefly toward national talents and national literature; and second, denouncing critics who supposedly are trying to degrade the honored authorities of Russian literature. We placed these charges alongside each other purposely: they have much in common. Let us begin with the first.

The indefatigible defenders of our literature, who modestly call themselves "patriots" and "lovers of justice," complain most of all about the decline of the book trade in Russia, about the miniscule sales of books. But facts indicate something completely different; they make as clear as two times two makes four that in Russia even quite ordinary books sell very well, to say nothing of those that are outstanding. *Three* editions of *A Hero of Our Time* were sold out in the course of *six* years. Lermontov's poems will soon need a third edition, despite the fact that they were originally all printed in journals. *Evenings on a Farm near Dikanka* by Gogol soon will have been printed four times, and there have been three editions of *The Inspector General*. The second edition (1842) of the works of Gogol sold out three thousand copies; *Dead Souls,* of which twenty-four hundred copies were printed in 1842, has long been out of print. Even the tales of Count Sollogub, read by the public in the journals, have already come out in a *second* edition; *Tarantas* will also probably soon appear in a second edition.

Enough of these facts. It is even said that in Russia an edition of the poorest book cannot help making money; that is why the booksellers print so many poor books. The only exceptions to this, apparently, are the essays of Messrs. "lovers of justice," who complain that they cannot get rid of books. But this shows only that it does not pay to hold back talent, intellect, and ideas. In bitterness and despair at the thought that the product of mind and fancy finds no market, these gentlemen have decided to place the blame for the decline of the book trade on the "thick journals" and on the new, supposedly false, school of literature founded by Gogol. These two accusations are worthy of each other. The accusers say that our literature will perish because our journals print multivolume novels, histories, and such in their entirety. They even assure us that the public itself is dissatisfied with this. Of course! It doesn't pay the public to acquire for fifty rubles a year so many works that, if published separately, would cost nearly five times as much! In view of this, how could the public not complain about the journals! Despite that, do you still want books to take their normal course? Publish them as cheaply as possible and in large numbers. The journals won't bother you.

Although books in this country have become much cheaper than they were fifteen years ago, when tiny almanacs published in a dull gray sold for ten rubles each, and poor translations of Walter Scott's novels and original Russian novels sold at twenty rubles and more per copy—despite this, books are still a frightfully expensive commodity. This is known only too well by those who consider it necessary to have the works of all well-known Russian writers in their library. Only last year an edition of Derzhavin's works came out that cost ten rubles at a time when these works ought to have long been selling twice as cheaply. The Smirdin edition of Batyushkov's works costs fifteen rubles. The first eight volumes of Zhukovsky's works can now be acquired only with difficulty for fifty rubles because that edition has been sold out for some time, and a new one still hasn't appeared. The works of Pushkin in a poor edition cost as much as sixty rubles. *Dead Souls* used to sell for ten rubles per copy; now it cannot be bought for less than thirty-five, and there is no mention of a new edition. How can the book trade flourish when the public has nothing to buy, despite all its desire to buy? It will be said that in Russia booksellers and publishers merely ruin themselves by publishing books instead of making a fortune. Yes, but are many of these booksellers good judges of the trade in which they deal? Who is to blame here? Is it really the "Thick Journals"?

Of course, one cannot help agreeing in part that our public is not quite the same as, say, the French in its love for

national talent and national literature. In Paris a new edition
of Hugo's works (in what quantity it is difficult to say) was
released at the same time that the French Academy refused
him membership; the public expressed its dissatisfaction over
this by buying out the entire edition in a few days. In Russia
such manifestations are not yet possible. Almost every educated Frenchman considers it necessary to have in his library
all the writers public opinion has accepted as classics. And
he reads and rereads them all his life. In our country—why
hide the fact?—not many inveterate men of letters consider
it necessary to own the old writers. In general we are always
more willing to buy a new book than to buy an old one. Most
persons, especially those who shout loudest about their genius
and glory, read almost nothing by the old writers. This partly
arises from the fact that our education is not yet well established, and the needs of the educated have not yet become
a habit with us.

But there is yet another, perhaps more essential, reason
that not only explains but even partly justifies this moral
phenomenon. The French read, say, Rabelais or Pascal,
writers of the sixteenth and seventeenth centuries. There is
nothing surprising in this, because these writers are still read
not only by Frenchmen but also by the Germans and the
English, in a word, by people of all educated nations. The
language of these writers, especially Rabelais, has become
old; but the *content* of their works will always possess a vital
interest because it is closely connected with the idea and
significance of an entire historical epoch. This testifies to the
fact that only *content*—not language, not style—can save a
writer from oblivion in the face of changes in the language,
customs, and ideas of society.

In this respect, talent, no matter how great, does not
constitute everything. Lomonosov was great, a genius; his
scholarly works will always have their value. But his poems
can interest us only as a historical fact of developing literature, nothing more. To read them is both boring and difficult.
One does so only as a duty, not out of desire. Derzhavin was
a positively gifted poetical genius; but his era was so little
able to provide content for his work that if he is read now it
is more for the purpose of studying the history of Russian
literature than for purely aesthetic gratification. Karamzin
lifted Russian literature from the well-worn, bumpy, and
rocky road of Germano-Latin construction, Church Slavic
diction and phrasing, and scholastic turgidity of expression

onto its real and natural path. He spoke to society in society's language and, it might be said, created both literature and public—a great and immortal service! We quite willingly admit this service and consider it not only our duty but even a pleasure to be beholden to the name of this famous man. But all this does not give content to *Poor Liza, Natalia the Boyar's Daughter, Martha the Mayor's Wife,* and so on; it does not make them interesting for our time and does not make us read and reread them. The same thing can be said for many of our writers. The objection will be raised: "Such were their times; it is not their fault that they were born in their time and not in ours." We agree, agree perfectly; but we are not blaming them; we are just removing the blame from our public. Our role is not accusatory at all, but purely explanatory. It is difficult to quarrel about tastes; but if there is one of our old writers who can be read with true satisfaction, that would be Fonvizin. His works are very similar to notes or memoirs of that era, although they are neither. Fonvisin was an unusually intelligent man. He didn't bother with the pompous, resplendent aspect of his times but considered more their internal, domestic side. Therefore his works are extremely interesting. We shall not speak of Krylov; all of us, once having learned him as children, can never forget him.

Many will take what we have said of Lomonosov, Derzhavin, and Karamzin as the *flagrant délit* of malicious degradation by criticism of our literary greats. Indeed, the evidence is plain, and there is no defense for us. But, as the proverb says, "Fear God and have no other fear!" Fortunately, the public is rapidly ceasing to think that literary greats are degraded by criticism. Now that view has fallen to the share of the so-called critics themselves; it has become the weapon of wounded pride, of forgotten reputations, fallen talents, rejected storytellers—a weapon that is completely worthy of them!

A critic who does not want to extol famous writers, or, still more, does not want to observe them, who when speaking of noted authors does not wish to repeat ready-made, stereotyped, hackneyed phrases, or to echo the opinion of others, but wants to judge according to intelligence, to the limit of his own measure of strength, to judge independently and freely and to evaluate the achievement of every writer, to show this writer's virtues and shortcomings, to point out his real place and significance in Russian literature—what is

to be done with such a critic, especially if his opinions strike
a responsive chord in the public? There is nothing left to do
but to cry out against him as loudly and often as possible that
he is degrading the literary greats, defaming Lomonosov,
Derzhavin, Karamzin, Batyushkov, Zhukovsky, and even
Pushkin! At the same time, one can hint that he is preaching
immorality and corrupting the young generation, that he is
a renegade at the very least, if not something still worse. This,
too, is called "criticism."

Can *such* criticism really still find followers among the
public? *What kind* of followers is still another question, but
that it does find them is very possible, because our reading
public is just as diverse and variegated, uncohesive as our
society. Among it are people for whom *The Inspector General*
and *Dead Souls* are crude farces, while *The Sensations of
Mrs. Kurdyukova* is a most witty work. There are people
who, as Gogol said, "love to converse about literature, praise
Bulgarin, Pushkin, and Grech, and to speak contemptuously
and caustically about A. A. Orlov." Such persons, or rather
such perusers (it would be a crime to call them readers), see
in criticism either unconditional praise or unmitigated abuse.
It is easy for them to understand that type of critic; they
would become giddy from any other, for they would be required to think; and that is only more burdensome and
difficult for them.

When a review of an author's works appears that is written
in the spirit of sincere criticism, that distinguishes unconditional from conditional merits in an author and inadequacies
of talent from inadequacies of time, the above-mentioned
perusers will not stop to read it. They will be told about him
by some critic of *their* faith, some author of all sorts of things,
who praises with all his might himself and the old writers who
are no longer dangerous to him and who rebukes out of hand
everything that is talented in the new generation. In his own
way this critic analyzes for his perusers the criticism that has
just appeared, extracts from it a line or a word from each
page, and exclaims, "Can one thus degrade our honored
authorities?" And his perusers believe him because they
understand him. He speaks to them in their language, their
concepts, their feelings, their taste—*les beaux esprits se
rencontrent*. It does not even occur to them, to these perusers,
that truth does not degrade talent, just as false opinion
cannot harm it; that only undeserved fame can degrade and,
consequently, independent judgment of literature can in no

way be harmful and is often useful. The inventor of such criticism also assures his perusers that the critic, in the presence of whose name he cannot retain his composure, praises only his friends; and the perusers believe what is printed.

How could they find out that this critic is barely acquainted with the living writers whom he admires? That is a private matter. How could they understand that he had not yet been born when Lomonosov died, could not read or write when Derzhavin died and when Zhukovsky and Karamzin were in their full glory—these men to whose merits and genius he gives full justice, but not through another's voice and not without an accounting? In order to understand, one needs the capacity for understanding. It is much easier to place confidence in the words of someone who merely repeats that, after all, the critic merely praises all his friends.

Generally, together with the surprising and rapid success in intellectual and literary education, a kind of immaturity and lack of determination is perceptible in our country. Truths that in other literatures have long since become axioms and have stopped causing quarrels and requiring proof have not yet been debated in our country and are not yet known to all. For example, you have never written a book, but have been publishing an immensely successful journal: your critics will bellow that your journal is poor *because* you haven't written a book. This "because" is quite original! Yet if the journal is good, what difference does it make whether its publisher has written a book or not? Your business is criticism, and even though you are so successful that you sharply affect others' opinions and prejudices and create enemies for yourself, don't think that your opponents will come to refute your position, to question your conclusions. No, instead, they will begin to tell you that since you have not written anything yourself, you do not have the right to criticize others, that you are young, while you are judging the works of persons already old, and so on. Such devices can put anyone in a difficult position, not because it is difficult to answer them, but precisely because it is too easy to answer them. But who has enough spirit to disprove such opinions, to declare solemnly that you do not have to be a cook in order to judge food properly, nor to be a tailor to express your opinion on the value or worthlessness of a new dress coat unerringly?—just as without being able to write poems, novels, tales, or dramas, nevertheless it is possible to be in a position to judge

the works of others sensibly and reasonably; and that if, in
the field of gastronomy, it is in its way a talent to have fine
taste, then it is all the more so in the sphere of art; and that
criticism, in its way, is art.

There are even truths that are trivial just because they are
too obvious, as for example the fact that summer is warm and
winter cold, that you can get wet in the rain and can dry out
before a fire. And yet we must at times defend similar truths
with all the force of logic and dialectics. This, however, can
only be funny or annoying, depending on the disposition
of your spirit, whereas things do occur that you don't want
to laugh about. Just recall that a work that grasps certain
features of society correctly is in Russia often considered a
libel to society or to a class or to a person. Our literature is
expected to see only virtuous heroes and melodramatic villains in real life, and not even suspect that many humorous,
strange, and ugly phenomena may exist in society. Every
person is ready whenever possible to forbid others to live
in order that he might live extensively and spaciously.

Scribblers in frieze coats, with unshaven chins, write
miserable little books at the order of petty booksellers: what
is so bad about that? Why shouldn't the scribbler gain his
crust of bread as he best can and knows? But these scribblers
ruin the public taste, deface literature, and the calling of the
literary man. Let us grant this to prevent them from harming
the public taste and the success of literature: we have
journals; we have criticism. No, that is not enough: if we
had our way, we should forbid the scribblers to write their
nonsense and the booksellers from publishing it. And from
where, from whom do such ideas come? From the journals,
from the literary men! There are some awesome forbidders
among them; except for their own works they would forbid all
writings in a body. Some would not stop even at this but
would want to prevent the sale of all other goods except their
own works, even bread and salt.

A humorous writer appeared among us whose talent had
so strong an influence on all literature that it gave it a completely new direction. He began to be discredited. They
wanted to convince the public that he was a Paul de Kock,
a painter of dirty, unwashed, and uncombed nature. He
answered no one and just went ahead. In its attitude toward
him the public divided into two camps, the more numerous
of which was decidedly opposed to him. That, however, did
not at all prevent it from buying, reading, and rereading his

works. Finally, the majority of the public also stood behind him. What could his censurers do? They began to recognize talent, even great talent, in him, although it was according to them a talent on the wrong road. But at the same time they began to let it be known and hinted directly that he was supposedly debasing everything Russian, insulting the honored class of bureaucrats, and so on. These gentlemen, however, are not at all pleading for the bureaucrats, but for themselves. They would like to silence all contemporary literature so that the public for lack of anything good would willy-nilly be forced to take up their works and would again begin to buy them. All this is printed, and the public reads it, because if nobody read it then it would not be printed. In Russia every opinion finds a place, accommodation, attention, and even followers. What is this if not immaturity and instability of public opinion?

But with all that, truth and good taste march with firm step and take the field for this disorderly battle of opinions. Though every false and empty but brilliant talent without exception enjoys success, there still is no instance of a true talent not being accepted by us and not achieving success. False authorities fall daily. Has it been long since the fame of Marlinsky, that juggler of phrases, was considered colossal? Now they no longer even speak of him, much less praise him; they don't even denounce him. Many such examples could be mentioned. This shows that both our literature and our society are still too young and immature but that there is hidden in them a great, healthy, vital strength promising a rich development in the future.

Somewhere the idea was once expressed that we have more artistic than belletristic works, more geniuses than talents. Like every new and original idea, this one aroused discussion. Actually, this idea at first glance might appear to be a strange paradox; nevertheless, it is basically justified. In order to be convinced of this, one has only to cast a cursory glance at the course of our literature from its beginning to the present time.

The belletrist is an imitator. He lives on another's idea, the idea of a genius. True, the geniuses of the first period of our literature, before Pushkin, were no more than belletrists in respect to the European writers from whom they learned to write and from whom they borrowed both form and ideas. But in our literature their role was quite different. Kantemir

imitated Horace and Boileau. Despite that, he was a completely original writer in Russian literature, a subject of
amazement for his contemporaries, who thought him a genius,
and a subject of respect for posterity, which saw in him one
of the outstanding figures of our literature.

There is no point in even speaking of Lomonosov,
Derzhavin, and Fonvizin: they were real geniuses, and the
second of them was even a real poetic genius. But Sumarokov,
Kheraskov, Petrov, Bogdanovich, and Knyazhnin were also
considered great poets in their time and even long after their
deaths. Sergei Nikolaevich Glinka, that honored and always
inspired veteran of our literature, considers them great poets
even now. And although our age views them completely
differently, it cannot but agree that even the opinion of
Sergei Nikolaevich Glinka and his age has its basis too.

The first figures of every literature, especially the imitators,
appear even to posterity in such large dimensions as no
longer exist for the same talents that arise later, during the
period of that literature's successes and development. Sumarokov's contemporaries were convinced that he far outdistanced
the fabulist La Fontaine and the tragedians Corneille and
Racine and compared him to Mr. Voltaire. Kheraskov was our
Homer, Petrov our Pindar. Zephyr gave to Bogdanovich a
feather from his wings, and Amor guided his hand when he
wrote *Dushenka*. But did these, let us say, *conditional*
geniuses engender many imitators? Did Derzhavin himself
give rise to many? It is true that in those blessed times mil-
lions of triumphal odes were written and printed. But that
was because thousands of hands wrote them, and if only one
ode came from each hand, the flow would be enormous. Yet
have many names of talented belletrists, born of the movement imparted to our literature by its first geniuses, come
down to us? Let us grant that Sumarokov, Kheraskov, and
Petrov could not possibly have had talented imitators, but
did Derzhavin have many? Dmitriev wrote a few odes and
Kapnist wrote a few more, that is all; numerically the odes
of both these poets are nothing in comparison with the quan-
titative richness of Derzhavin's odes.

In general it is natural that a belletrist can easily write a
great deal more than his model; with us the opposite has
always been the case. Makarov and Podshivalov, who wrote
very little, especially the latter, functioned independently
from Karamzin; whereas the imitators of Karamzin were

Vladimir Izmailov, Prionce Shalikov, and, to tell the truth,
we don't remember who else—they were so few and wrote so
little and spiritlessly! Zhukovsky's influence was enormous.
One can learn to translate by studying him even now, and one
will always be able to; his poems also will always remain
models. Kozlov, Mr. F. Glinka, and partly Mr. Tumansky
were echoes of Zhukovsky's muse. The genius of Pushkin
gave birth to still more imitators, whose talent cannot be
denied and who enjoyed great renown in their time. But
taken all together they wrote hardly half as much as Pushkin
did alone, although he too did not write very much—and
how quickly they outlived their talent and their fame!

Now too, many are writing. One leaves the scene; that is,
he is forgotten (with us that happens unusually quickly),
and another appears. Taken together they all produce quite
an amount (at least comparatively), but individually each
writes very little. Moreover, everyone pretends to high
artistic value, to creativity. No one wants to be simply a narrator, a storyteller, a belletrist. Almost everyone writes to
order, knowing beforehand how much each line, each word,
each comma will bring him. But at the same time everyone
writes by inspiration. Many sell still-unwritten tales, not because they write too much and receive too many orders, but
because they write too little. Some might break out one story
a year and look like Napoleon after the Battle of Austerlitz.
To succeed in writing two stories in a single year would be
equal to conquering the whole world. Therefore we have no
belletrists, and the public has nothing to read.

In any year the works that are outstanding in any way
(including those that are only tolerable) can be counted on
one's fingers. Things are different in France. There they
write in spells, and every belletrist who is known at all
annually fills up whole volumes, almost tens of volumes,
never concerning himself with what the public will take him
for, a genius or simply a talent. There the belletrist writes
more than the poet-artist. George Sand wrote very much,
more than is written here by many people over many years.
But the stack of George Sand's works in comparison with
those of Eugène Sue or Alexandre Dumas is like a lake
compared to the sea, or the sea to an ocean. This is as it
should be; creation does not submit to will, and the artist
needs time to think over his conception and carry out the
thought conceived in his mind. In the real, the true, meaning

of the word, we had and have only three belletrists: these
are Messrs. Bulgarin, Polevoy, and Kukol'nik. Their indefatigability is amazing.

Of all the types of poetry in this country, we recognize
drama, especially comedy, as being weaker than the others.
But at least the so-called classical tragedy had its period of
development and success in Russia. The tragedies of
Sumarokov gave sustenance to our growing theater, and
not only delighted contemporaries, but *The False Dmitry*
was played in provincial theaters as late as the early twenties
of this century. For their time, the tragedies and comedies
of Knyazhnin had an undeniable value; it can be said
generally if such an intelligent and deft imitator as
Knyazhnin was for his time should now appear, our age
would gain much. Ozerov was still greater. From all this it
is apparent that our classical tragedy developed in the course
of three complete generations. Romanticism appeared and romantic dramas were played—bloody, horrifying, effective, and
finally even native dramas that were incoherent and empty.
Now they too are written only for benefit performances, and
at that more and more rarely. There is hope that they will
soon cease altogether. And a good thing, too! It is better to
have nothing at all than a great deal of nonsense, whatever
its quality!

But in the drama, too, indeed more than elsewhere, the
proposition that we have more geniuses than talents (although they are few enough) is borne out. Pushkin, in his
Boris Godunov, gave us a genuine and genial model for
national drama. But perhaps because he was too truthful and
too much a genius, it remained without any influence on our
dramatic literature. At any rate, not a single dramatic work
that has a vestige of talent reflects the influence of *Boris
Godunov.* It will be said: "That is because no drama with a
vestige of talent has appeared in our country." True! But
why then did there appear and do there still appear narrative
poems with signs of talent, sometimes even remarkable
talent, thereby indicating how strong and fruitful the influence of Pushkin and Lermontov on our literature has been?
The best dramatic work in the national spirit after *Boris
Godunov* belongs, again, to Pushkin: *Rusalka.* His dramatic
poems, *Scene from Faust, Mozart and Salieri, The Covetous
Knight,* and *The Stone Guest,* also did not call forth any
experiments in Russian literature that were at all fortunate.

Nevertheless, all Pushkin's dramatic works are great artistic creations.

Such, too, is the fate of our comedy: it either offers something remarkable or offers something that is less than nothing. There is practically nothing to be said for Russian comedies before Fonvizin. They were either translations or reworkings (in this field the labors of Knyazhnin deserve respect), but as original Russian comedies they were a strange anomaly. *The Brigadier* and *The Hobbledehoy*, not being artistic creations in the strict sense of the word, were nevertheless creations of genius. By their nature they can be called reliable and accurate satires in the form of comedy. These were imitated, but the imitations were unnatural and awkward. Their belated influence, incidentally, was felt in Osnovianenko's comedy *Elections of the Nobility*, a work that has its inadequacies yet is not without merit.

Between *The Brigadier* and *The Hobbledehoy*, Ablesimov somehow casually blurted out a charming national vaudeville sketch. This was an accident, though a wonderful one. It properly remained without consequence for literature. Kapnist's *Slander* is more remarkable for its aims than for its fulfillment. Now one must go directly to Griboedov's *Woe from Wit*, because the multitude of comedies in prose and verse written during the interval from Fonvizin to Griboedov are not worth mentioning—*Woe from Wit*, this semiartistic, semisatirical comedy, this eminent pattern of mind, wit, talent, genius, of angry, bitter inspiration—*Woe from Wit* remains up to now the sole work in our literature in whose genre not a single talent has decided to test his strength.

From Griboedov's comedy we must move directly to *The Inspector General*. Besides this highly artistic comedy filled with the most profound humor and startling truth, Gogol also wrote a small comedy, *Marriage*, and a few scenes that, by their size, cannot be called comedies, standing in relation to a comedy as a tale does to a novel. All these scenes bear the sharp imprint of the talent of the author of *The Inspector General*, and, like it, remain in our literature to this time as isolated monuments in the midst of a wide sandy steppe where not a tree, not a blade of grass is visible. There were, it is true, two or three attempts that were not completely unsuccessful, but these were too indecisive.

One-sidedness in one's view of things always leads to false conclusions, even though the view is not without profundity

and insight. The capacity to have convictions, one of the
most wonderful capacities of human nature, leads to fanaticism in the presence of one-sidedness. Literary fanaticism is
just as deaf and blind as any other, especially when it exists
in the name of theory. German aesthetic theories were so well
received in the receptive soil of our recent education that
they found for themselves followers who were so zealous and
fanatical that they would be looked upon as marvels of
theoretical frenzy, even in Germany, especially now. For
incorrigible fanatics of this type, French literature and
French art are veritable stumbling blocks. Since such fanatics
do not understand French literature, and persist in confessing
so, they take a great deal of trouble not to recognize its
existence. That, however, is not surprising. During the
restoration some historians insisted that Napoleon was only
a regimental commander under Louis XVIII!

As a matter of fact, from a purely theoretical point of view,
without resorting to actual historical observation, not much
good can be found in French literature when one is en-
raptured with German literature. German aesthetics emerged
from the scholar's study, and German poetry emerged from
German aesthetics. To be convinced of this, one has only
to recall how the genius Schiller wrote. In *Wallenstein* not
only was everything thought out by him beforehand; it was
also proved and justified. Everything emerged from theory,
and the author took *eight* years to write this drama. Schiller
wanted to write an epic poem on the life of Frederick the
Great, but he did not want to understake the task until he had
philosophically developed a theory of the epic poem for
modern times. All these phenomena, somewhat strange if not
abnormal, and quite harmful to the genius of Schiller, as well
as to other German poets, arose directly from the German
social environment—peaceful, contemplative, based on family
and study.

On the other hand, all French literature arose from French
social and historical life, and is closely tied up with it.
Therefore, French cannot be judged according to ready-made
theories without falling into one-sidedness and reaching
false conclusions. The tragedies of Corneille, it is true, are
very awkward in their classical form; and theoreticians have
every right to attack this Chinese form, to which the majestic
and powerful genius of Corneille yields as a result of the
forcible influence of Richelieu, who wanted to be the prime
minister of literature also. But the theoreticians would have

been cruelly mistaken if behind the awkward classical form of Corneille's tragedies they had glimpsed the awesome internal strength of their pathos. The French of our time say that Mirabeau is indebted to Corneille for the greatest inspiration of his speeches. After this, what wonder that the French quickly forget their romantic tragedies à la Shakespeare, and continue, as they always will, to read old Corneille. Every one of their famous writers was directly connected with the era in which he lived, and has the right to a place in the history of France as well as in the history of French literature.

In Russia all ideas about creation have a somewhat different meaning from those in German literature: they must share their authority and strength with ideas about society and its historical course. We have people who succeeded in understanding that *The Inspector General* is a deeply creative and artistic work and that not one comedy of Molière can bear aesthetic criticism. They are right in that respect, but they are not right in the conclusion they draw from that fact. Actually, not one comedy by Molière can bear aesthetic criticism because they were all *made* rather than *created*. Often they wander off into farce, or at least tolerate farce within themselves (like, for example, the false mufti, dervishes, and Turks in *Le Bourgeois gentilhomme*). The mainsprings of their actions are always artificial and monotonous, the characters abstract; the satire emerges too sharply from forms of poetical invention, and so on. But with all that, Molière had an enormous influence on contemporary society and raised French theater high, a thing that could not be done with mere talent, but required genius. In order to judge his comedies, one must not read them but see them on the stage—and, at that, certainly on the French stage—because their scenic value is greater than their dramatic. The French do not have a right to be proud about this or that specific comedy by Molière, but have a complete right to be proud of his comedies, or better to say the theatre of Molière, because Molière gave them an entire theatre. The same may also be said of Scribe. Not one of his dramas nor one vaudeville sketch can be pointed to as a work of art that will always have its value. But it can be stated affirmatively that the theatre of Scribe will always have its value, and now it is priceless; so important is it to the members of contemporary society, of all classes, educated and uneducated, who flock to the theater to see themselves on the stage.

We have a few highly artistic comedies that, by their num-

ber, cannot make up a constant repertoire for the theatre.
With all their merit, they would become deadly dull to everyone if the theatre presented nothing but them, because one
and the same thing without change is always boring.

Let us suppose that the French have not a single artistic
comedy. Despite that, there is a theatre that exists for everyone, and in which society is both instructed and entertained
aesthetically.

Whose is the advantage?

Let the reader decide; we are not concerned.

What distinguishes genius from talent? The question is
very important, the more so since it is always solved very
cleverly. We shall not burden ourselves but shall attempt to
explain it simply. That both genius and talent are given by
nature, that both one and the other, so to speak, are properties
of the very organism of man, as light and heat are the properties of flame, there is no point even in stating, since it is a
subject concerning which everyone has long been in agreement. The question lies in distinguishing between genius and
talent, and the other way round.

Who has not chanced to meet a multitude of people who
like to read, to follow literature, and who want to judge it,
but who dare to judge a new book only after they have
managed to read a discussion of it by a journal that enjoys
their absolute confidence, and who feel themselves in a most
difficult situation if a review or criticism of a book that is
making a big splash doesn't appear in the journal for a long
time? Who has not chanced to meet people who are ready
to judge anything but who immediately renounce their
opinion and agree wholeheartedly with the opinion of their
critic as soon as someone takes sharp exception to them?

There are people without opinions, without the capacity
for forming an opinion, people who can be firm only through
another's opinion, and for whom authority is a requirement
of the first order. It must be noted that people of this type
have a very strongly developed instinct for feeling another's
strength, and always recognize it. Incidentally, these people
might be quite intelligent: they recognize proofs; they have
the ability to judge. But this capacity of theirs lacks independence, and needs support from authority. The mass consists primarily of such people, and it is always and everywhere
controlled by people with more or less independent opinions.
This is the reason why the mass does not long fancy the false

and ugly, but always sooner or later recognizes the worth of
the true and beautiful. Others act for it, and it merely obeys.
Without this moral discipline terrible anarchy would reign in
people's concepts, instead of unity.

Talent, *as the ability to make, to produce,* concerns more
and more a form of creation; and, from this point of view,
talent is an internal strength that can exist in man independent of his mind, his heart, and other intellectual and
moral sides of human nature. But content is necessary for
form. Therefore, this is the particular place where the independent activity of man's spiritual forces gains all its meaning.

If there are people who lack the ability to have their own
opinion on things, and who accept another's opinion completely as something they no longer need to think about, then
there are others who, while constantly living on another's
opinion, have the ability to make it their own, to develop it,
to extract new corollaries from it, to discover other ideas
through it. This ability so deceives people of this type that
they are very sincerely convinced of their own ability to
think. They are almost correct about this; with their lively
and receptive natures, they themselves do not know and do
not understand who transmitted a certain idea to them
because everything from without adheres to them almost
unconsciously, instinctively. They have only to speak with
an intelligent person or to read a good book, and immediately
a whole series of new ideas that they cannot help accepting
as their own rises within them. These people, controlled by
others, have in their turn a great influence on the mass. You
often meet them in this world. There is an especially great
number of them in the capitals. Generally, the more enlightened and educated a society is, the more such people
there are in it.

Finally, there are people (very few of them) who really
possess the capacity for the creative independent function of
their capacities. They look upon everything in a sort of
special, original way; in everything they specifically see what
no one else sees without them and what everyone sees after
them and is amazed that he did not see it before. These are
completely uncomplicated people, not clever at all. They see
everything simply, but their simple understanding at first
seems complicated to everyone and sometimes seems unin-
telligent or clumsy. But later it seems so simple that not a
single fool fails to wonder why this did not occur to *him—*

why, it is so simple! When Columbus was preparing to discover America, everyone looked at him as if he were a mad
dreamer; but when he did discover America, almost no one
wanted to recognize merit in this accomplishment, because a
discovered America seemed to everyone so simple to discover!

In speaking of these three groups of people, we wanted to
speak of *the mass*, of *talent*, and of *genius*. . . .

These days talent is no rarity in anything, especially in
literature. Mere child's play! It is often even confused with
genius, and not wisely. A great talent of sorts is needed to
distinguish genius from talent in the first place. This reminds
us of a passage from a tale by a famous French author of our
day, wherein he writes about the hero's literary work as
follows:

He recognized that everything begun by him, after the first
ten lines or three or four verses, became so similar to the
writers he was reading, that he blushed at seeing himself
capable only of imitating. He showed me a few verses and
phrases, beneath which Lamartine, Victor Hugo, Paul Courier,
Charles Nodier, Balzac, and even Béranger could have placed
their names. But all these experiments, which could have
been called fragments of fragments, in the works of those
writers would have served to adorn their individual ideas. But
Horace lacked just this individuality. If he wanted to express
some kind of idea, you would immediately see (and he himself immediately saw) obvious plagiarism; this idea was not
his. It belonged to those writers; *it belonged to everyone but
not to him.*

Here is the eternal story of talent! Of course, it does not
always occur exactly the way it was presented in the words
of the author we cited, but that is always its essence. No
matter how great a talent is, he cannot set the seal of his
personality on his works, and therefore cannot be original
and unique. No matter how great his ability to adopt the
ideas of others, he will not long conceal that his inspiration
does not gush like a flowing stream from the inner recesses
of his nature, but is only "the aggravation of a captive idea."
But, on the other hand, no matter how narrow or limited the
sphere of talent, if his works contain the sharp imprint of
personality that makes works so individual that it is impossible to imitate them, then it is no longer a talent, but a
genius. Among such poets of genius in our literature belongs
the fabulist Krylov.

A Survey of Russian

Literature in 1847: Part Two

*The Significance of the Novel and the Story Today—
Remarkable Novels and Stories of Last Year, and a
Characteristic of Contemporary Russian Authors of
Belles-Lettres: Iskander, Goncharov, Turgenev, Dal',
Grigorovich, Druzhinin—Mr. Dostoevsky's New Work
—"The Mistress"—Mrs. T. Ch.'s "Travel Notes"—
Mr. Nebolsin's Stories of the Siberian Gold Fields—
Mr. Botkin's Spanish Letters—Remarkable Scientific
Articles of Last Year—Remarkable Critical Articles—
Mr. Sheviryev—A. Smirdin's Complete Edition of
Russian Authors*

THE NOVEL and the story now stand in the lead of all other
genres of poetry. They now constitute the whole of our belles-
lettres, so that, compared with them, any other work appears
to be exceptional and accidental. The reasons for this lie in
the very essence of the novel and the story as genres of poetry.
In them, in finer and more convenient fashion than in any
other genre of poetry, fiction mingles with reality and artistic
invention with simple, if only it be faithful, copying from nature. The novel and the story, even when they depict the most
ordinary and hackneyed prose of everyday life, can be representative of the ultima thule of art, of the highest creative
endeavor; on the other hand, in reflecting only the choice
and sublime moments of life they may contain no poetry at
all, no art. . . . This is the widest and most universal genre
of poetry; in it talent feels itself to be infinitely free. It unites
in itself all the other genres of poetry—the lyrical, as an emo-
tional effusion of the author in connection with the event
he describes, and the dramatic, as the most vivid and salient
device for making the characters speak their thoughts. Di-

gressions, disquisitions, and didactics that are intolerable in
other branches of poetry have their legitimate place in the
novel and the story. The novel and the story enable the writer
to give full scope to the predominant peculiarities of his talents, character, tastes, tendency, and so on. That is why so
many novelists and story writers have appeared of late.

For the same reason the range of the novel and the story
has been extended: besides the "tale" that has already been in
existence a long time as a lower and lighter form of the narrative, full recognition has recently been granted to the so-
called "physiologies," character sketches of various aspects of
social life, and finally memoirs eschewing all fiction and valued only inasmuch as they render a faithful and precise picture of actual events—memoirs that, if skillfully written, also
pertain to the domain of the novel, forming, as it were, the
concluding link in the chain we have just discussed. What is
there in common between the inventions of the imagination
and the strictly historical presentation of actual events? Why,
artistic exposition, of course! It is not for nothing that historians are called artists. Might it not seem that art, as such,
has no place in the case of a writer who is tied down to
sources and facts, and whose only concern is to present these
facts as faithfully as he can? But that is just the point—a faithful presentation of facts is impossible with the aid of erudition
alone; imagination too is required. The historical facts contained in sources are no more than stones and bricks; only an
artist can build up a beautiful edifice out of these materials.

In our first article we asserted that without creative talent
it is just as impossible faithfully to copy nature as it is to
create fiction that resembles nature. The proximity of art to
life, of fiction to reality, has in our day particularly manifested itself in the historical novel. From here it is only a step
to a true conception of memoirs in which character studies
and personal sketches play such an important part. If these
sketches are lively and interesting, it means they are not
copies, not imitations, which are always bloodless and expres-
sionless, but an artistic portrayal of persons and events. It is
thus that we set a value on the portraits of artists like Van
Dyck, Titian, and Velázquez, caring not to know who their
sitters were: they are valued as pictures, as works of art.
Such is the power of art: a face that in itself is in no way
remarkable receives through art a universal significance, of
equal interest for all, and a person who in his lifetime attracted no attention is gazed upon by the centuries through

the grace of the artist whose brush has given this person new life!

The same applies to memoirs, and narratives and all kinds of copies from nature. Here the degree of a work's merits depends on the degree of the writer's talent. In a book you may admire a man you would not like to meet anywhere, whom perhaps you have always known as an inane and boring creature. Belated aesthetes aver that "poetry should not be a pictorial art, because in the latter the faithful representation of an object seen at a given moment is all-important." But if poetry undertakes to portray persons, characters, and events, in a word, pictures of life, it goes without saying that in doing so it takes upon itself the same duty as pictorial art, which is to be faithful to the reality it purports to reproduce. And this fidelity is the primary demand presented to poetry, its primary task.

The poetical talent of an author may be judged in the first place by the extent to which he meets this demand, solves this task. If he is no pictorial artist, it is patent that neither is he a poet, that he has no talent. It is another matter that poetry must not be *only* pictorial art: that stands to reason. The pictures drawn by the poet should contain thought; the impressions they produce should appeal to the reader's mind, should give a certain direction to his view on certain aspects of life. For this purpose the novel and the story, together with works similar to them, are the most convenient genre of poetry. It is mainly to its lot that the task has fallen of representing social pictures, of the poetical analysis of social life.

Last year, 1847, was particularly rich in outstanding novels, stories and other narratives. Of these works, the first place, measured in terms of their tremendous success with the public, is beyond doubt held by two novels, *Who Is To Blame?* and *An Ordinary Story;* therefore we shall begin our review of last year's belles-lettres with these books.

Mr. Iskander [Herzen] has long been known to the public as the author of various articles, noteworthy as the products of remarkable intellect, talent, wit, originality of views and originality of expression. As a novelist, however, he is a new talent who has won the special interest of the Russian public only since last year. True, the *Notes of the Fatherland* published two of his essays in the art of storytelling: *Notes of a Young Man* (1840) and *More from Notes of a Young Man* (1841), which, judging by the faithfulness and vivacity of

these light studies, bore the earmarks of a future gifted
novelist. Mr. Goncharov, the author of *An Ordinary Story*, is
a newcomer in our literature, but one who has already gained
therein a most prominent place for himself. Whether it is due
to the fact that both these novels, *Who Is To Blame?* and *An
Ordinary Story*, appeared almost at the same time and shared
the glory of unprecedented success, they are generally mentioned together, and even compared, as though they were
phenomena of the same kind. One magazine, which recently
proclaimed Iskander's novel to be a work of supreme artistic
merit, expressed dissatisfaction with Mr. Goncharov's novel
on the grounds that it did not find in the latter the merits of
the former. We, too, intend to examine these novels together,
but not in order to show their similarity, of which, being
works utterly dissimilar in essence, there is not the slightest
trace, but in order to use their very oppositeness as a means
of tracing their respective peculiarities and showing their
merits and faults.

To regard the author of *Who Is To Blame?* as an uncom-
mon artist signifies an utter failure to understand his talent.
True, he possesses to a remarkable degree the ability of
rendering a faithful picture of reality; his sketches are definite
and clear-cut, his pictures are vivid and immediately catch
the eye. But these very qualities prove that his forte lies not
in creativeness or artistic treatment, but in thought, profoundly cogitated, fully conscious, and developed thought.
It is in the power of mind that the main strength of his talent
lies; the artistic manner of faithfully portraying phenomena
of actual life is a secondary, an auxiliary, force of his talent.
Deprive him of the former, and the latter will prove incapable of original activity.

A talent of this kind is not something special, exceptional,
or fortuitous. No, such talents are just as natural as talents
that are purely artistic. Their activities form a special sphere
of art, in which imagination stands in the background and
mind in the foreground. Little notice is taken of this distinction, whence great confusion ensues in the theory of art. There
is an inclination to regard art as a sort of intellectual China,
cleanly walled off by precise boundaries from everything that
is not art in the strict sense of the word. Such borderlines,
however, exist more conjecturally than in actual fact; at any
rate, one cannot point them out as one could a country's borders on the map. Art, in proportion as it approaches one or another of its borders, gradually loses something of its essence,

and assumes something of the essence of that with which it borders, so that instead of a line of demarcation there appears a region that brings both sides together.

The artist-poet is more of a pictorial artist than people think. A sense of form—in this his whole nature lies. An eternal competition with nature in the ability to create—such is his greatest delight. To grasp a given subject in all its truth and to infuse into it, as it were, the breath of life—in this lies his strength, his triumph, satisfaction, and pride. But poetry is superior to pictorial art, its borders are wider than those of any other art; and therefore the poet cannot, of course, confine himself to pictorial art alone—which is something we have already discussed. Whatever other excellent qualities his work may possess, qualities that evoke admiration and amazement, his main power lies nevertheless in his poetical pictorial art. He possesses the ability rapidly to comprehend all forms of life, to penetrate any character, any individuality, and for this he needs neither experience nor study; a single hint or swift glance sometimes suffices. Give him two or three facts, and his imagination reconstructs a complete, separate, self-contained world, with all its conditions and relations, with the color and shades peculiar to it. Thus Cuvier through science achieved the art of mentally reconstructing the entire organism of an animal from a single fossilized bone belonging to that animal. But that was the operation of genius, developed and aided by science; the poet, however, pre-eminently depends upon his senses, his poetical instinct.

Another category of poets that we have begun to speak of and that includes the author of the novel *Who Is To Blame?* is able to render faithfully only those aspects of life that for some reason or other have particularly impressed themselves on their minds and are especially familiar to them. They do not understand the delight of faithfully portraying a fact of reality for the mere sake of faithfully portraying it. They lack both the desire and patience for what, in their opinion, is a useless task. It is not the subject they prize, but its underlying drift, and with them inspiration flares up only in order that, by faithfully presenting a subject they may render its meaning obvious and tangible to the sight of all. It follows then that with them a definite and clearly realized aim comes before all else and that poetry is only a means to the achievement of this aim. Hence the world of life accessible to their talent is determined by their cherished thought, by their view of life; this is a magic circle from which they cannot emerge

with impunity, that is to say, without suddenly losing the ability to depict reality with poetical fidelity. Deprive them of this
thought that inspires them, make them give up their view of
things, and their talent is gone; whereas the talent of the
artist-poet always remains with him as long as life, *such as it
may be,* moves on around him.

What is the cherished idea of Iskander that serves as the
source of his inspiration and, in his faithful depiction of the
facts of social life, sometimes raises him almost to the height
of art? It is the idea of human dignity debased by prejudices
and ignorance, debased by the injustice of man to his fellow
men, or by his own voluntary distortion of himself. The hero
of all Iskander's novels and stories, however many he may
write, will always be one and the same—man as a general and
generic concept, man in all the fullness of this word, in all the
sanctity of its meaning. Iskander is pre-eminently a poet of
humanity. That is why his novel abounds in characters, most
of them portrayed in masterly fashion, but there is no hero, no
heroine.

In the first part, after winning our interest in the Negrov
couple, he presents Krutsifersky as the hero of the novel and
Lyubonka as the heroine. The hero of the episode written to
link both parts together is Beltov, but Beltov's mother and his
Swiss tutor interest the reader perhaps more than does he
himself. In the second part the heroes are Beltov and
Krutsiferskaya, and it is only here that the underlying idea
of the novel, at first so puzzling in the title *Who Is To Blame?*
fully unfolds itself. We must confess, however, that this idea
least of all interests us in the novel, just as Beltov, the hero,
is in our opinion the least convincing personage of the whole
novel. When Krutsifersky became Lyubonka's fiancé, Dr.
Krupov said to him, "That girl is no match for you, say what
you like—those eyes, that complexion, the tremor that sometimes passes over her face—*she's a tiger cub* that is not yet
conscious of its strength; and you, what are you? You are the
bride; you, brother, are like a German woman; you will be
the wife—and that won't do." These words contain the plot
of the novel, which, according to the author's intention,
should have begun with the wedding instead of ending
with it.

After acquainting us with Beltov, the author conducts us
into the peaceful abode of the young couple who for four
years had already been enjoying the halcyon bliss of matri-
mony; however, recollecting the gloomy prediction of the

oracle in the person of the skeptical doctor the reader expects
the author to show him in this very scene of the Krutsiferskys'
matrimonial bliss the embryo and precursor of future troubles.
Indeed, Krutsifersky did not marry; he was married. His wife
was far too superior to him, and, consequently, far too un-
suited to him. It is natural that he was quite happy with her,
but it is not natural that she should be serenely happy, should
not have disturbing dreams, and perturbed thoughts in her
waking hours. She could respect and even love her husband
for his childlike purity and nobility, for his having, moreover,
saved her from the hell of her parental home; but could such
a love satisfy such a woman, gratify the requirements and
strivings of her nature, which were all the more tormenting
for being indefinite and unconscious? Her acquaintance with
Beltov, which soon grew into love, could only open her eyes
to her condition, arouse in her the realization that she could
not be happy with a man like Krutsifersky. This the author
did not do.

The idea was a splendid one, full of a profoundly tragical
significance. It was this idea that attracted most readers and
prevented them from seeing that the whole story of the tragic
love of Beltov and Krutsiferskaya had been told cleverly, very
cleverly, even adroitly, but in no way artistically. It is a
masterly narrative, but without a trace of live poetical
imagery. It was the idea that helped and saved the author: his
mind helped him to understand correctly the position of his
heroes, but he depicted this position only as a clever man
with a good understanding of the matter might have done,
but not as a poet. Thus sometimes a gifted actor, who has
taken upon himself a role that is beyond his abilities and
talent, will nevertheless avoid spoiling it, but will perform
it cleverly and adroitly instead of acting it. The idea of the
role is not lost, and the tragical sense of the play makes up
for the shortcomings in the performance of the leading role,
and it is not immediately that the audience realizes that it
has only been carried away, but not satisfied.

This, by the way, is proved by the fact that, in the second
part of the novel, Beltov's character is arbitrarily changed by
the author. In the beginning, he was a man thirsting for useful activity and finding it nowhere, because of the wrong
education the noble dreamer from Geneva had given him.
Beltov knew a good deal and had a general conception of
everything, but he was completely ignorant of the social
milieu that was the only one in which he could make himself

useful. All this is both said and shown by the author in masterly fashion. We think that the author might also have hinted at the nature of his hero, which was most unpractical and badly spoiled by wealth no less than by education. He who is born rich must be endowed by nature with a special propensity for some kind of activity if he is not to lead an idle life and be bored by inactivity. This propensity is not at all to be seen in Beltov's nature. His nature was extremely rich and versatile, but in this richness and versatility there was nothing that had deep roots. He was endowed with intellect, but an intellect that was contemplative and theoretical, and not so much probed into things as glided over them. He was able to understand much, almost everything, but this very universality of sympathy and understanding prevents people like him from concentrating on one object and bending all their will to it. Such men have a constant urge for activity, endeavoring to find their path, but, of course, they do not find it.

Thus Beltov was doomed to languish in a craving for activity that was never satisfied, in a dejection born of inactivity. The author has given a masterly description of all his unsuccessful attempts to work in the civil service and later to become first a doctor, then an actor. If it cannot be said that he has fully depicted and explained this character, he has nevertheless given us a well-drawn, intelligible, and natural picture of the man. In the last part of the novel, however, Beltov suddenly appears before us as a sort of superior nature, a genius, to whom life does not furnish a worthy career. This is quite a different man from the one whose acquaintance we had already made; this is no longer Beltov but something in the nature of Pechorin. Needless to say, the former Beltov was much better, like any man who plays his own role. The resemblance to Pechorin is decidedly not in his favor. We cannot understand why the author had to leave his own path and follow another! . . . Can it be that he wished in this way to raise Beltov to the level of Krutsiferskaya? A vain desire, because she would have found him as interesting in his former aspect, and even then he would have dwarfed poor Krutsifersky, beside whom he was a veritable giant. He was a grown-up, a man in his majority, at least in mind and in his views on life; whereas Krutsifersky, with his noble dreams in lieu of a real understanding of people and life, would even beside the former Beltov have seemed a child whose development had been retarded by some illness.

Krutsiferskaya, for her part, is of far more interest in the first part of the novel than in the last. It cannot be said that her character there was sharply drawn, but then her position in Negrov's house was sharply drawn. There she is a convincing figure, despite her silence and absence of any activity. The reader senses her although he hardly hears a single word from her. In describing her position the author has displayed an unusual mastery. It is only in passages from her diary that he makes her speak. We are, however, not entirely satisfied with this confession. Apart from the fact that the device of acquainting the reader with the heroines of novels through their diaries is out-of-date, worn threadbare and false, Lyubonka's diary entries smack somewhat of the spurious; at all events not everybody will believe that they were written by a woman. . . . Evidently here, too, the author has strayed beyond the limits of his talent. We shall say the same of the brief snatches of Krutsiferskaya given at the end of the novel. In both cases the author merely skillfully disposed of a task he could not cope with. In general, Lyubonka, when she marries Krutsifersky, ceases to be a character, a personage, and becomes a masterly, cleverly developed idea. She and Beltov are the only two persons the author has not properly coped with. But even in them one cannot but admire the author's adroitness and art in sustaining the interest till the end, and in amazing and moving most readers, where any other writer with his talent, but without his intelligence and correct view of things, would only have been ridiculous.

And so it is not in the picture of the tragic love of Beltov and Krutsiferskaya that the merits of Iskander's novel should be sought. We have seen that this is not at all a picture, but a masterly written document. Strictly speaking, *Who Is To Blame?* is not really a novel, but a series of biographies, written in masterly fashion and cleverly linked together externally into one whole through the medium of that idea which the author failed to develop poetically. But these biographies also contain an internal link, although the latter has nothing to do with the tragic love of Beltov and Krutsiferskaya. It is the idea that lay deep at their roots, breathed life and soul into each feature, each word of the story, that gave it the convincingness and interest that have the same irresistible appeal both to readers that sympathize and readers that do not sympathize with the author, to the educated and the uneducated alike. This idea manifests itself with the author as a sentiment, a passion; in brief his novel shows it to form

the pathos of his life as well as of his novel. Whatever he
speaks of, into whatever digressions he is drawn, he never
forgets it, continually returns to it, and it seems involuntarily
to speak for itself. This idea has become welded with his
talent; herein lies his strength; if he cooled toward it, rejected
it, he would instantly lose his talent.

What is this idea? It is suffering, pain at the sight of un-
recognized human dignity, spurned with malice aforethought,
and still more without it; it is what the Germans call
Humanität. Those to whom the idea contained in this word
may seem unintelligible will find its best interpretation in the
works of Iskander. Of the word itself we shall say that the
Germans formed it from the Latin word *humanus*, which
means belonging to man. Here it is opposed to the word
"beast." When a man treats his fellow men, his brothers in
nature, as befits a human being he acts humanly; otherwise
he acts as befits a beast. Humanity is love of mankind, but a
love that is cultivated by the consciousness and by education.

A man who adopts a poor orphan not for personal gain or
boastfulness, but out of a desire to do good, one who brings
up such an orphan as though he were his own son, yet at the
same time makes the latter feel that he is his benefactor,
that he spends money on him, and so on—such a person, of
course, deserves to be called kind, moral, and philanthropic,
but certainly not humane. He has a good deal of sentiment
and love, but they have not been developed by his consciousness and lie under a coarse crust. His crude mind does not
even suspect that there are fine and tender fibers in the
human heart that must be delicately handled to avoid making a person unhappy despite all external evidences of happiness, or to avoid debasing and brutalizing a person who,
with more humane treatment, might become worthy of
respect.

How many such benefactors are there in the world who
torture and often ruin the lives of those upon whom their
benefactions are showered, doing so without evil design,
sometimes feeling the warmest love for their protégés, wishing them well in all humility—and then are ingenuously surprised that instead of devotion and respect they are rewarded
with coldness, indifference, and ingratitude, even with hatred
and animosity, or that their protégés turn out to be scoundrels after having received a most moral upbringing! How
many mothers and fathers are there who really love their children in their own way, but consider it their sacred duty to

drum in their ears that they are obliged to their parents for
their lives and clothing and education! These wretched people do not even suspect that they are depriving themselves
of their children, and replacing them with foundlings and
orphans whom they have adopted out of charity. They calmly
doze on the moral rule that children must love their parents,
and later, in their old age, they repeat with a sigh the well-
worn truism that nothing but ingratitude can be expected
from children. Even this fearful experience does not remove
the thick crust of ice from their benumbed minds or make
them realize at last that the human heart obeys its own laws,
and will not and cannot accept any others, that love from a
sense of duty or obligation is a feeling contrary to human
nature, supernatural, fantastic, and incredible, that love is
given only for love, that love cannot be demanded as though
it were something we are entitled to, but must be won and
deserved, no matter who the giver is, whether he be higher
than us, or lower, whether it goes from father to son or from
son to father. Now take children; it often happens that a
child regards its mother with indifference, although the
mother suckles it, and this same child will set up a wail if,
on awakening, it does not see nearby its nurse, whom it is
accustomed to seeing at its side at all times. A child, you
see, that complete and perfect expression of nature, gives its
love to those that prove their love for it in actual deed, to
those that for its sake deny themselves all pleasures and, as it
were, have fettered themselves with a chain of iron to its
pitiful and weak existence.

The sentiment of humanity in no way runs counter to respect for high estate and rank, but it is in direct contradiction
with contempt for anybody but scoundrels and villains. It
willingly acknowledges social superiority, but regards it more
from within than from without. Humanity does not oblige one
to heap upon a person of lower estate and coarse manners and
habits courtesies that he is unaccustomed to; on the contrary,
it forbids this, since such treatment would make that person
feel embarrassed and suspect mockery or evil design. A humane person will treat his inferior and uncultivated fellow
man with that degree of politeness that will not strike the
latter as queer or extravagant; but the human person will
not allow the other to debase his human dignity before him,
will not allow him to humble himself, will not call him
"Vanka" or "Vanyukha" or other similar diminutives reminiscent of the names dogs are called by, will not pull the other

familiarly by the beard in token of his amiable predisposition, while the other with an obsequious smirk says fawningly: "It's very kind of Your Honor! . . ." The sentiment of humanity is outraged when men do not respect in others their human dignity, and is still more outraged and wounded when a man does not respect his own dignity.

It is this feeling of humanity that constitutes, so to say, the soul of Iskander's works. He is its proponent, its advocate. The characters he brings onto the stage are not ill-natured people—most of them are even good people, who torment and persecute themselves and others more often with good intentions rather than bad, more from ignorance than from malice. Even those of his personages whose feelings and odious acts repel us are shown by the author more as victims of their own ignorance and the environment in which they live than of their ill-nature. He describes crimes that are not challenged by existing laws and are qualified by most people as rational and moral behavior. He has few villains; in the three stories so far published it is only in the *Thieving Magpie* that a villain is depicted, but the kind of villain whom even today many would be prepared to consider a most virtuous and moral person.

Iskander's chief weapon, one that he wields with such amazing mastery, is irony frequently becoming sarcasm, but more often expressed with a light grace and most good-natured humor. Remember the kindhearted postmaster, who on two occasions very nearly killed Beltova, first with grief and then with joy, and who so good-naturedly rubbed his hands in anticipation of the surprise he was about to spring, that "there is not in the world a heart so cruel as could reproach him for this joke, and would not invite him to take a snack." Yet, even in this trait, in no way reprehensible, but only amusing, the author remains true to his cherished idea. Everything in the novel *Who Is To Blame?* that pertains to this idea is distinguished by its fidelity to actual life and a skill of exposition that is above all praise. It is here, and not in the love of Beltov and Krutsiferskaya, that the novel's brilliance and the triumph of the author's talent lie.

We have said above that this novel is a series of biographies linked together by a single idea, but infinitely varied, profoundly truthful, and rich in philosophical significance. Here the author is fully in his element. What is there better in that very part of the novel dealing with the tragic love of Beltov and Krutsiferskaya than the biography of the most worthy Karp Kondratich, his lively spouse, and their poor daughter Varvara Karpovna, called Vava for short—a biography included in the book as a mere episide? When are Krutsifersky and Lyubonka interesting in the novel? When they live in the Negrov house and suffer from their surroundings. Such situations lend themselves to the author's talent, and he displays unusual mastery in depicting them. When is Beltov himself of interest? When we read the history of his perverted and improper education, and then the history of his abortive attempts to find his way in life. This too is within the scope of the author's talent.

The author is pre-eminently a philosopher and a little of a poet besides, and he has availed himself of this to expound his concepts of life in the form of parables. This is best proved by his splendid story, *From the Work of Dr. Krupov "On Mental Ailments in General and Their Epidemic Development in Particular."* Here the author has not, by a single trait or word, overstepped the bounds of his talent, and hence his talent here is more clearly in evidence than in his other works. His idea is the same, but here it has assumed exclusively a tone of irony, for some, very gay and amusing, and for others, sad and painful; and only in the depiction of the squint-eyed Lyovka, a figure that would do honor to any artist, does the author speak seriously. In conception and execution this is positively the best work that appeared last year, although it did not make any particular impression on the public. However, the public is right in this case: in the novel *Who Is To Blame?* and certain works by other writers it found more intimate and hence more necessary and useful truths for itself, and the latter work has the same spirit and substance as the former.

In general, to reproach the author for being one-sided would mean not understanding him at all. He can represent faithfully only the world that comes within the range of his cherished idea; his splendid sketches are based on an innate power of observation and on the study of certain aspects of actual life. A receptive and impressionable nature, the author has preserved in his memory many images that had struck his imagination as far back as in his childhood. It is not difficult to understand that the characters he draws are not the sheer creatures of imagination, but rather skillfully finished, and sometimes even completely remodeled, materials taken wholly from reality. Have we not already said that the author is more of a philosopher and only a little of a poet? . . .

In this respect the author of *An Ordinary Story* presents
a complete contrast to him. He is a poet, an artist, and nothing more. He has neither love nor enmity for the persons he
has created; they neither cheer nor anger him, and he gives
no moral lessons either to them or to the reader; he seems
to think: "As ye sow, so shall ye reap; I wash my hands of
you." Of all present-day writers he, and he alone, approaches
the ideal of pure art, while all the others have moved an immeasurable distance away from it—and therefore thrive. All
present-day writers possess something else besides talent, and
it is this something that is more important than talent itself,
that constitutes its srengh; Mr. Goncharov has nothing besides
talent; more than anybody else today he is a poet-artist. His
talent is not of the first magnitude, but it is a strong and
notable one.

A feature of his talent is an extraordinary skill in depicting
feminine characters. He never repeats himself, not one of his
women reminds us of another, and all of them are superlative
as portraits. What is there in common between the rough
and ill-tempered Agraphena who, in her way, is capable of
tender feelings, and the woman of society with her dreams
and bad nerves. Each of these is, in its way, a splendid work
of art. The mother of the young Aduyev and the mother of
Nadenka are both old women, both very kindhearted and devoted to their children, and both of them do harm to their
children; both are, furthermore, stupid and vulgar. At the
same time, these two personages are absolutely different; one
of them is a provincial lady of a bygone age, who reads nothing and understands nothing besides the petty cares of her
household, in a word a kindhearted granddaughter of the ill-
tempered Madam Prostakova; the other is a lady of the capital who reads French books and understands nothing besides
the petty cares of her household—in a word a kindhearted
great-granddaughter of the ill-tempered Madam Prostakova.

In representing such insipid and vulgar personages, devoid
of any independence and originality of character, talent is
sometimes at its best, because it is all the more difficult to
endow these characters with any individuality. What is there
in common between the vivacious, scatterbrained, wayward,
and somewhat artful Nadenka and Liza, outwardly calm but
consumed by an inner fire? The aunt of the hero of the novel
is an incidental character, cursorily drawn, but what a splendid feminine type! How wonderful she is in the concluding
scene of the first part of the novel! We shall not dwell on the

mastery with which the masculine characters have been drawn; we could not but mention feminine characters, because until now even our first-class talents have rarely been able to cope with them; with our writers woman has been either a cloyingly sentimental creature or a seminarist in a skirt, full of sentences from books. The women of Mr. Goncharov are living creatures, true to actual life. This is a novelty in our literature.

Let us now turn to the two chief masculine personages of the novel, the young Aduyev and his uncle Pyotr Ivanich: in speaking of the former at least a few words must be said about the latter, who by sheer force of contrast succeeds in bringing out the hero of the novel in still greater relief. It is said that the type of young Aduyev is out-of-date, that such characters no longer exist in Russia. No, such characters have not disappeared and will never disappear, because they are produced not always by circumstances but sometimes by nature itself. Their forerunner in Russia was Vladimir Lensky, himself directly descended from Goethe's Werther. It was Pushkin who first noticed that such natures exist in our society, and pointed them out. They will undergo changes in the course of time but their essence will always be the same. . . .

Young Aduyev, on arriving in St. Petersburg, dreams of the joy with which he will embrace his adored uncle and his uncle's delight at seeing him. He puts up at a tavern and is afraid that his uncle will be angry with him for not having come direct to his house. The cold reception given him by his uncle destroys his provincial dreams. So far young Aduyev is more of a provincial than a romanticist. He was even disagreeably shocked when his uncle called Zayezhalov a fool, and used the same epithet for the village aunt, with her yellow flower, both of whom had sent him most stupid letters. Provincials are often highly ridiculous in their attitude toward their relations and acquaintances. Life in small towns is monotonous, shallow, and petty, everybody knows one another and, if they are not at daggers drawn, are sure to be on terms of the most tender friendship; there are almost no intermediate relations.

So a young man sets out from his little town to seek his fortune in the capital; he is the object of general interest, all see him off, wish him good luck and ask him not to forget them. He has now grown elderly in the capital; his native town is now a dim memory; under the influence of new impressions,

new acquaintances, relations, and interests, he has long ago
forgotten both the names and faces of the people he knew so
intimately in childhood; he recollects only his closest kith and
kin, and he pictures them just as they were when he left them,
but they too have changed since then. From their letters he
sees that he has nothing in common with them. When he re-
plies to them, he tries to fit in with their mood and ideas;
it is not surprising that he writes to them more and more
rarely, and finally stops writing altogether. The thought of a
relative or acquaintance coming to the capital scares him in
the same way as the inhabitants of a border town are scared
in wartime by the thought that the enemy may march their
way.

In the capital, love at a distance is not understood; people
here think that love, friendship, attachment, and acquaintance
are sustained by personal relationships, and are cooled and
destroyed by parting and absence. In the provinces, people
think the opposite; owing to the monotony of life, an inclination toward love and friendship is surprisingly developed
there. People there are glad of anybody, and it is held to be a
most sacred duty to interfere with one another and give people no peace. If relatives and friends cease bothering you,
you consider yourself the most unfortunate, the most offended
person in the world. When a provincial living in a small town
is suddenly visited by a horde of relatives who turn his little
house into a barrel packed with sardines, he makes a show of
being overcome with joy; his face wreathed in smiles, he
dashes about, fusses the whole time, and feeds the whole
crowd while inwardly he heartily curses them. Yet if these
same people did not put up at his house next time he would
never forgive them. Such is the patriarchal logic of the provinces! And it is with this kind of logic that the provincial
sometimes comes to the capital on business with all his family.

He has a relative in the capital who left his home town some
twenty years before and has long forgotten all his relations
and friends. Our provincial flies to him with open arms, with
dear children who have to be fixed up at schools, and with his
adored spouse, who has come to admire the fashionable shops
of the capital. Oh's and Ah's, shouts, screams, and squeaks fill
the air. "Now, we have come straight to you; we wouldn't
think of putting up at a tavern!" The city kinsman turns pale,
and he does not know what to do, what to say; he resembles
an inhabitant of a town captured by the enemy, into whose
house a band of looting soldiers has broken. In the meantime

he has been listening to a lengthy account of how much he is loved, how much he is remembered, how much talked about and depended on, and how all are confident that he will assuredly help to place Kostya, Petya, Fedya, and Mitya in the cadet corps, and Mashenka, Sashenka, Lyubochka, and Tanechka in the ladies' institute. The city kinsman sees that his ruin or his salvation is the question of a minute; he nerves himself, and explains to the invading foe in tones of frigid civility that he cannot possibly put them up, that his apartment is too small for his own family, that children are enrolled at corps and institutes by examination and in accordance with the regulations, that no patronage will help if vacancies are not available, or if the children are below or above the reception age, or fail to pass the examinations, especially the patronage of such an unimportant man as he is, and one who, moreover, is employed in quite a different department, and is not acquainted with any of the educational officers. The disappointed provincials retire in a fury, upbraiding the selfishness and depravity of dwellers in the capital, and regarding their relative as a monster.

Yet the latter may be a most estimable person, whose only fault was that he did not wish to turn his apartment into a disgusting gipsy camp, deprive himself of privacy in his own home, of any possibility of devoting himself to his official affairs in the quiet of his study, receiving at his home of an evening people of his acquaintance or men who were officially useful or necessary to him, and thus discommode himself, and undergo privations for the sake of utter strangers with whom he would not wish to keep up even an ordinary acquaintance.

Yet these provincials, too, are, in their own way, kindhearted and not at all stupid people; their only fault is that in setting out for the capital, they had expected to find there, besides its hugeness, splendor and fashionable shops, their own little town, with the same customs, habits, and concepts. In their own way, they love luxury and splendor and, if they have the means, they are prepared, albeit without any taste, to adorn their drawing rooms and reception rooms in every possible way; they have no idea of private studies and do not know what they are meant for; their bedrooms and nurseries are always the dirtiest rooms in the house; they think nothing of cramping or discommoding themselves; the idea of comfort does not exist for them; they are accustomed to overcrowding, and love it, following the popular adage—

the more, the merrier. They are at home to everyone, and are ready, in the words of Pyotr Ivanich, to muster a supper even in the dead of night. This trait, it is remarked by the nephew, is a virtue of the Russians, a statement with which Pyotr Ivanich emphatically disagrees.

"What kind of virtue is this?" he says. "People there welcome any rascal out of sheer boredom; come, make yourself at home, eat your fill, only amuse us in some way, help us to kill time, let us have a good look at you—after all it is something new—and we shall not grudge you the food—it doesn't cost us much anyway. . . . A disgusting virtue!"

Pyotr Ivanich expressed himself rather bluntly but not entirely with injustice. Indeed, provincial heartiness and hospitality are mainly based on inactivity, idleness, boredom, and habit. They measure the prestige of dwellers in the capital not by the place they hold, the connections they have, or the influence they enjoy, but by their rank; and our provincials fondly believe that if a man holds the rank of councilor of state, he is sure to be an omnipotent personage, a single word from whom will suffice to settle a lawsuit in your favor that has been dragging on for fifty years, or have your children enrolled at a particular school, or you yourself provided with an advantageous post, rank, and decoration. If you refuse any request of theirs, even though you were eager to fulfill it but powerless to do so, they will say that you are the most immoral person in the world, that you have grown conceited, are giving yourself airs, despise provincials. For with them the prime virtue is never to flaunt their superiority, never to refuse acquaintance with anybody, to be at the service of all and sundry. True, nowhere is there such showing off and posing, such respect for rank, seniority, or titles, but there this vice, dangerous to peace and harmony, is mitigated by a virtuous readiness to make one's self small in the presence of a person who stands even one rank higher, and at the same time not to lower one's dignity in the presence of another who is one rank lower. Indeed, this virtue flourishes in the capital as well, although in forms more subtle. In the provinces, however, all this is done with truly Arcadian naïveté.

"My dear fellow," says a rich landowner or important official to a poor landowner or official, "what's the matter, have you quite forgotten me, or am I in your bad books, or do I feed my guests badly? I've always got a plate at my table for you, you silly ass!" And the poor fellow feels abashed, mutters apologies, while he stands in respectful posture before his patron; his eyes, however, shine with pleasure; he knows that where there is anger there can also be kindness, and in the scolding of one man there may be more love than in the soft words of another. "Well, never mind, God will forgive you! Dinner is served, so let's have a bite."

Both are pleased, one because he has punctiliously observed the laws of patriarchal hospitality and has shown kindness to a poor fellow; the other because he has been well received and kindly treated by a person of such importance. And this poor fellow will always prefer the society of the aristocrats of this provincial backwoods and even the society of his inferiors to that of his complete equals, since he has a sense of his own dignity only when he humbles himself before those above him, and struts before those beneath him. This cannot be applied to all provincials, of course; there are everywhere people of education, wit, and dignity, but they are everywhere in the minority, and we speak of the majority.

The direct influence of a man's environment is so strong that the best of provincials are not without provincial prejudices, and lose themselves on first arriving in the capital. Everything is so queer, so different from things at home. There life is simple, free and easy; people call on each other at any time and enter unannounced. A neighbor calls on another; there is nobody in the entrance hall unless it be an unshaved lackey or a ragged urchin asleep on a dirty bench; he sleeps for nothing better to do, although the filth and stink all around could provide him with work for two days. And so our guest enters the reception room and finds it empty, walks into the drawing room and finds that empty too; goes into the bedroom where he is greeted with a little feminine shriek—mumbles his apologies in an agreeable flutter of confusion and hastily retreats into the drawing room, where somebody runs out to him, expresses delight at his coming, and both laugh at the amusing adventure. While here in the capital, everything is shut, there are bells everywhere, the inevitable "Whom should I announce, sir?" is sure to be asked, followed by the reply that the master is either not at home or is indisposed, regrets that he is engaged; and if the guest is received, he is met with politeness, of course, but such a frigid and indifferent politeness: no heartiness, no invitation to lunch or dinner.

But let us turn to the hero of *An Ordinary Story*. He possesses a sense of delicacy and decorum; although he was sure of a hearty welcome from his uncle, a sort of intuition made

him put up at an inn. Were he in the habit of pondering on
things that most concerned him, he would have stopped to
think of the intuition that made him go to the inn and not
straight to his uncle's house, and he would very soon have
realized that there was no reason to expect from his uncle any
other kind of reception except one of kindly indifference, that
he had no claims on the amenities of his home. Unfortunately,
however, he was in the habit of thinking only on matters of
love, friendship, and other lofty and remote things, and therefore he appeared at his uncle's house a provincial from head
to foot. The latter's words, full of wit and common sense, explained nothing to him, and only produced upon him a painful and sad impression, made him suffer romantically. He was
thrice a romanticist—by nature, by education, and by circumstances; any one of these causes would be enough to throw
a steady man off his balance, and make him commit all sorts
of follies. Some find that with his material tokens of im-
material relations and his other extremely childish vagaries,
our hero is an improbable type, especially in our days. We
concede—there may be a particle of truth in this observation,
but that is not the point; the full portrayal of young Aduyev's
character should be sought not here, but in his love adventures. Here he is himself; here he is representative of a
numerous class of people who are as like him as two peas,
and really exist in this world. We shall say a few words about
this old but still interesting breed to which our romantic
little creature belongs.

This is a breed of people whom nature has plentifully endowed with a nervous sensitivity that frequently verges on
morbid susceptibility. They reveal at an early age a fine per-
spicacity of vague sensations and emotions, which they love
to observe and analyze, and call it enjoying an inner life.
They are therefore great dreamers, and love either solitude or
a select circle of friends with whom they can discuss their
sensations, feelings, and ideas, although they are as poor in
ideas as they are rich in sensations and emotions. In general,
nature has bestowed upon them rich gifts of the soul, but
these are of a purely passive kind. Some of these people have
wide understanding, but not one of them is capable of doing
or producing anything. He is a bit of a musician, a bit of a
painter, a bit of a poet, if need be even a bit of a critic and
littérateur, but all these talents are such that he cannot
acquire fame or reputation through them, but earns only a
moderate livelihood.

Of all the mental faculties, imagination and vision are most strongly developed with them—not the vision by which means the poet creates, but the vision that makes a person prefer the enjoyment of dreams of the blessings of life to the enjoyment of the actual blessings of life. This they call living the life sublime, one that is beyond the reach of the vulgar crowd, soaring on high while the despised crowd crawls in the dust. By nature they are kindhearted, genial, and capable of generous impulses, but since in them imagination dominates over reason and the heart, they soon achieve a conscious contempt for "vulgar common sense, a quality which in their opinion pertains to people that are material, coarse, and paltry, for whom nothing lofty and beautiful exists"; their heart, continually violated in its instincts and strivings by their will, under the domination of their imagination soon becomes scant in love, and these people, themselves unaware of it, develop into horrible egoists and despots, fondly believing that they are the most loving and selfless of men.

Since they surprised everybody in childhood by their precocity, and exerted, as much through their merits as through their shortcomings, a strong influence on their fellows, many of whom stood higher than they did, it is natural that they should have been praised from their early years and conceived a high estimation of their own persons. Nature withal had provided them with a greater measure of vanity than is essential for the equipoise of human life, and it is not to be wondered at that easy and ill-merited successes swell their vanity to extraordinary proportions. This vanity is always so effectively covered up that they honestly do not suspect it in themselves, and sincerely take it to be the strivings of genius toward fame, toward everything that is great, lofty, and beautiful.

They are frequently obsessed by three cherished ideas—fame, friendship, and love. All the rest does not exist for them; it is, in their opinion, the attribute of the contemptible crowd. All species of glory are equally seductive to them, and at first they hesitate long before choosing the path that will lead them to fame. It does not enter their mind that one who considers himself equally proficient in all fields of fame is proficient in none, that the greatest of men learned that they were geniuses only after they had performed something really great and worthy of genius, and they learned this not from their own selves but from the enthusiastic plaudits of the crowd. And so they are enamored of military glory, and they would fain be

Napoleons, but only on condition that they receive, to begin
with, command of a small army, say a hundred thousand
strong, so that they may be able to launch on a brilliant
career of victories immediately. Or they may be attracted
toward civic glory, stipulating that the rank of minister be
immediately conferred upon them so that they may be able
to reform the state immediately. (They always have ready in
their heads splendid projects for all kinds of reforms, which
can be committed to paper without delay.) But since men's
envy has rendered it impossible for such geniuses to rise
like meteors, and requires that every one should start his
career from the beginning and not from the end, that genius
should prove its worth in deed and not merely in words, our
geniuses are perforce constrained very soon to seek other paths
of glory. Sometimes they seize upon science, but not for long;
it is dull and dry stuff that calls for study and hard work, and
provides food neither for the heart nor for the imagination.
There remains art, but which branch should they choose?
No genius can master architecture, sculpture, painting, or
music without arduous and long labor, and what is worse
and most offensive to the romanticist, labor whose initial
stages are purely material and mechanical.

There remains poetry, and they attack it full tilt, to crown
themselves in dreams with a flaming halo of poetic glory,
without yet having done a single stroke of work. Their chief
delusion consists in the absurd conviction that poetry requires
merely talent and inspiration, that he who has been born a
poet does not need to learn or know anything; he who really
possesses great talent will, by the force of that selfsame talent,
be very soon obliged to realize the absurdity of this idea, and
will begin to study everything, to scrutinize and listen to
everything with keen attention. No! Their principal and fatal
error consists in their having irrevocably convinced themselves of their poetical calling; that unfortunate idea has
grown upon them, so that were they to be disappointed in it
they would lose all faith in themselves and in life, and become palsied old men in the heyday of their lives.

And so our romanticist begins to write poetry, in which
he speaks of things that have long ago been spoken of by
poets, great and small, and by men who were not poets at all.
He sings of sufferings he has not known, and speaks of vague
hopes that merely show that he does not know himself what
he wants. He stretches out to men his arms full of brotherly

love, and would press all mankind to his bosom, or bitterly complains that the crowd has coldly spurned his love. The poor fellow does not realize that there is nothing easier than flaring up with a fierce love of humanity in the quiet of one's study; at least it is far easier than spending one sleepless night at the bedside of a very sick person. The romanticists usually set up an extremely high value on feelings, thinking that only they have been endowed with the capacity for deep feelings, that others do not possess them since they do not publish the fact. Feeling is, of course, an important aspect of human nature, but people do not always act in life in accordance with their capacity for profound and powerful feeling. There are such that become more impervious to sentiment in actual life, the more they feel; such a person will be reduced to tears by verses, music, or a vivid presentation of human distress in a novel or a story, but will pass by with indifference actual sufferings that he witnesses with his own eyes. Some landowner's steward, perhaps a German by origin, will read to his Minchen with tears in his eyes Schiller's rapturous epistle to Laura and, on finishing the last verse, will proceed with no less relish to flog peasants for having dared timorously to hint to their gracious master that they were not entirely pleased with the paternal solicitude of his steward for their weal, a solicitude from which he grows fat while they grow thin.

Our romanticist's verses are smooth and polished, and even do not lack a certain poetical finish; although they have ample rhetorical padding, they do here and there reveal sentiment, sometimes even a spark of idea (an echo of someone else's); in a word, one can discern something in the nature of talent. His verses are published in the magazines and evoke praise from many; if they appear at a transitional period of our literature, they may even acquire a considerable reputation. But transitional periods in literature are particularly fatal to such poets. Their fame, acquired in a short time by *something*, disappears in a very short time simply from *nothing*; at first, people stop praising their verses, then stop reading them, and finally printing them. Young Aduyev, however, did not succeed for an instant in enjoying even spurious fame; he was prevented from so doing both by the time in which he brought out his poems and by his clever and outspoken uncle. His misfortunes lay not in the fact that he was untalented, but in his possessing a semi-talent instead of talent;

and this in poetry is worse than lack of talent, because it inspires false hopes. Remember how he was affected by disappointment in his poetical calling. . . .

Friendship, too, demands a heavy price from these romanticists. To be genuine, sentiment must above all be natural and simple. Friendship sometimes develops from similarity, and sometimes from oppositeness of natures. It is, however, an involuntary sentiment, because it is free; it is governed by the heart, and not by the mind or the will. A friend cannot be sought as one might seek a contractor to perform a certain piece of work; a friend cannot be chosen; friendship is contracted accidentally and unnoticeably, and is cemented by habit and circumstances. Real friends do not label the feeling that binds them together, do not prate about it without end, demand nothing of each other in the name of friendship, but do whatever they can for each other. There have been instances of one friend not being able to survive the death of another and dying soon afterward; another, from being a merry person, falls into an incurable melancholy after losing a friend, whilst a third will grieve and mourn for a time, and soon find solace, but if he preserves the memory of the departed, it will always be for him a remembrance both sad and comforting—he was a true friend of the departed, though he not only did not die of his bereavement, did not go mad or fall into melancholy, but found the strength to be happy enough in life without his friend.

The degree and character of friendship depend upon the personalities of the friends; the chief thing is that their relations should not in any way be strained, forced, or rapturous, there should be nothing resembling obligation or duty; there are some people who are prepared to go to any lengths for a friend so as to be able to say to themselves or to others, "That's the sort of friend I am," or "Such is the friendship I am capable of!" This is the kind of friendship that romanticists adore. They form friendships on a pre-established plan, where the substance, duties, and rights of friendship are exactly specified; the only thing they do not do is to conclude a contract with their friends. They need friendship to amaze the world with and show it how in friendship great natures differ from ordinary people, from the crowd. They feel drawn to friendship not so much by a need for sympathy, which is so strong in youth, as by a need for the companionship of a person whom they could ceaselessly talk to about their own precious selves. To use their own high-flown style, a friend to

them is a precious vessel into which one can pour his most
sacred and cherished sentiments, thoughts, hopes, dreams, and
the like; whereas in actual fact, a friend for them is simply a
dustbin into which the dross of their vanity can be thrown.
Such people do not know what friendship is because it soon
transpires that their friends are ingrates, recreants, and
monsters, and they wax wrathful against people who could
not and did not want to understand and appreciate them. . . .

Love costs them still dearer, because this feeling itself is
stronger and more poignant than others. Love is usually divided into many species and kinds, but these divisions are for
the most part absurd, because they have been contrived by
people who are more capable of dreaming or discoursing
about love than actually loving. First of all, they divide love
into material or sensual, and platonic or ideal, and despise the
former and admire the latter. There are indeed people so
coarse that they can give themselves up only to the animal delights of love, without bothering even about beauty or youth;
but even this love, however coarse it may be, is to be preferred to the platonic, because it is the more natural; the
latter is suited only to the guardians of Oriental harems. . . .

Man is neither a brute nor an angel; he must love neither
carnally nor platonically, but humanly. However much love
may be idealized, it is obvious that nature has endowed people with this wonderful feeling as much for their own happiness as for the multiplication and maintenance of the human
race. There are as many kinds of love as there are people on
earth, because each person loves in accordance with his
temperament, character, concepts, and so on. Every kind of
love is genuine and beautiful in its way, if only it has its
seat in the heart and not in the head. Romanticists, however,
are particularly prone to the love of the head. First, they
draw up the plan of their love, and then search for a woman
worthy of sharing it, failing which they put up with a temporary expedient; it costs them nothing to bring themselves
to love, since it is their head that does it all and not their
heart. They need love not for the sake of happiness or delight, but for the sake of vindicating in practice their lofty
theory of love. Such people love by the book, and are afraid
to depart from a single paragraph of their program. Their
main concern is to appear great in love and to resemble
ordinary people in nothing.

Nevertheless, in young Aduyev's love for Nadenka there
was so much sincere and genuine feeling; his romanticism

was silenced for a time by nature, but not overcome. He might have enjoyed long happiness, but was happy only for a fleeting moment, and had only himself to blame. Nadenka was cleverer than Aduyev, and, what is more, simpler and more natural. A spoiled and capricious child, she loved him with her heart and not with her head, without theories and without claims to genius; she saw in love only its brighter and gayer side, and so seemed to make a happy game of it: she was playful, coquettish, and constantly teased Aduyev with her caprices. But his love was "grievous and heavy," gasping for breath, and all in a lather, like a horse dragging a load uphill. Being a romanticist he was also a pedant, and in his eyes lightness and levity were an outrage to the sacred and sublime feeling of love. He wished in love to be a theatrical hero. In his talks with Nadenka, he very soon exhausted the theme of his feelings and had to repeat what had already been said before, whereas Nadenka wanted to occupy not only her heart but her mind as well, because she was impulsive and impressionable and longed for everything new; what was customary and monotonous soon palled. But for this Aduyev was the most inadequate person in the world, because his mind was virtually wrapped in profound sleep: considering himself a great philosopher, he did not think, but dreamed, and went about with his head in a cloud.

Such being his attitude toward the object of his love, any rival was a source of danger to him; this rival might be worse than Aduyev, but so long as he did not resemble him there was even the danger of Nadenka discovering in him the charm of novelty. And suddenly a count appears upon the scene, a brilliant man of the world. Aduyev, intending to conduct himself like a hero toward this man, for that very reason behaved like a stupid, ill-bred boy and thus ruined all his chances. His uncle explained to him, albeit too late and to no purpose, that he had only himself to blame for what had happened. How pitiful is this wretched martyr to his own perversive and narrow nature in his last talk with Nadenka and then in the conversation with his uncle! His sufferings are unbearable. He cannot but agree with what his uncle says, but at the same time he cannot see the affair in its true light. How can he stoop to so-called wiles, he who loved in order to amaze himself and the world by the immensity of his passion, albeit the world had not thought either of him or of his love! According to his theory, fate should have sent him a heroine as great as he was himself, instead of which it had sent him a frivolous minx, a heartless coquette! Nadenka, who but recently had been above all women in his eyes, suddenly fell lower than any of them! All this would have been very funny, had it not been so sad. False reasons cause no less exquisite sufferings than genuine reasons do. And so Aduyev gradually passed from some somber despair to a cold dejection and, true romanticist that he was, began to flaunt his "picturesque gloom."

A year lapsed, and he now despised Nadenka, asserting that there had been no heroism or self-sacrifice in her love. When his aunt asked him what sort of love he would demand of a woman, he replied, "I would demand first place in her heart; the woman I love should not notice or see any other men beside me; they must all seem unbearable to her. I alone stand higher, am handsomer (here he drew himself up to his full height), better, and nobler than all others. Every moment lived without me should seem to her a moment lost; in my eyes and in my conversation she must find happiness, and know no other; for me she must give up everything— despised advantages and interests, throw off the despotic yoke of mother or husband, fly with me if necessary to the ends of the earth, put up with all privations, and finally despise death itself. That is what I call love!"

How this balderdash reminds one of the words which an Oriental despot addresses to his chief eunuch: "If any of my odalisques utters a man's name in her sleep, and that name is not mine, tie her up in a sack and throw her into the sea!" The poor dreamer is confident that his words express a passion that only demigods are capable of, and not ordinary mortals. In actual fact he has merely expressed unbridled vanity, a most disgusting egoism. What he needs is not a woman to love, but a slave to torture with impunity at the caprices of his egoism and vanity. Before demanding such a love from a woman, he should ask himself whether he was able to return it. His feeling assured him that he was capable, but in this neither feeling nor mind can be trusted, only experience. But for the romanticist feeling is the only infallible authority in the solution of all problems of life. Even had he been capable of such a love, it should have been a reason for him to fear love and flee it, because this love is not human, but savage, a mutual tormenting of each other.

Love requires freedom; while they belong to each other from time to time, those who love wish to belong to themselves at times. Aduyev demanded an eternal love, without understanding that the more living and passionate love is, and the closer it approaches to the ideal of love sung by the poets, the shorter-lived it is, the sooner it cools and passes into indifference, and sometimes into aversion. On the contrary, the calmer and quieter love is, that is to say, the more prosaic it is, the longer-lived it is; habit cements love so that it lasts a lifetime. Poetical and passionate love is the flower of our life, of your youth; it is experienced by few and only once in a lifetime, although some may afterward love again, and several times, but never in the same way, because, as the German poet said, the May of life blossoms but once. It was not for nothing that Shakespeare made Romeo and Juliet die at the end of his tragedy; in this way they remain in the reader's mind as heroes of love, its apotheosis; had he let them live, they would have appeared to us in the role of happy man and wife who, sitting together, might yawn, and even quarrel at times, which is not at all poetical.

Then fate sent our hero just the kind of woman he desired, that is, such as he was himself, spoiled, and with heart and brains turned inside out. At first, he trod on enchanted ground, forgot everything else in the world, spent his time with this woman from early morning till late at night. What did this bliss consist in? In talking of his love. And this passionate young man, sitting alone with a beautiful young woman who loved him and whom he loved, neither blushed nor paled nor languished with burning desires, it sufficed him to talk about their mutual love! . . . This, by the way, is understandable. A strong penchant for idealism and romanticism is nearly always a sign of lack of temperament; such people are sexless, like the Cryptogamia of the vegetable kingdom, mushrooms, for example. We understand the palpitant, timid adoration of a woman, which does not contain a single audacious desire; but that is not platonic love—it is the first fresh moment of virginal love—it is not the absence of passion, but passion that is still fearful of its own manifestation. One's first love begins with this, but to stop at this stage would be as ridiculous and silly as to wish to remain a child all one's life and ride a hobbyhorse.

Love has its own laws of development, its ages, like flowers or human life. It has its luxuriant spring, its sultry summer, and finally its autumn, which for some is warm, bright, and fruitful, for others cold, bleak, and barren. But our hero did not wish to know the laws of the heart, of nature, of reality; he invented for them his own laws, and proudly regarded

the real world as a figment, and the figment created by his
imagination as the world of reality. In defiance of practica-
bility, he stubbornly wished to remain all his life at the first
stage of love. However, these effusions of the soul with
Tafayeva very soon began to tire him, and he decided to
mend matters by a proposal of marriage. If so, he should have
hurried; but he thought only that he had made up his mind;
what he wanted was merely a subject for new dreams.

Meanwhile he was becoming thoroughly sick of Tafayeva's
cloying love; he began to tyrannize her in the most rough
and repellent manner, because he no longer loved her. He
had begun to realize before this that freedom in love was not
at all a bad thing, that it was pleasant to visit a beloved
woman, but also pleasant to be able to take a walk along
the Nevsky Prospect, to dine with one's friends and acquaintances when one feels like it, to spend an evening with
them—that in the final analysis, one can be in love and not
give up one's pursuits. After most barbarously tormenting the
poor woman for an unfortunate situation, for which he was
much more to blame than she, he ends by telling himself that
he does not love her and that it is time to bring his affair with
her to an end.

Thus his stupid ideal of love was shattered under the impact of experience. He perceived his own inefficacy in the
face of a love of which he had dreamed all his life. He saw
clearly that he was no hero, but a very ordinary person,
worse than those he had despised, that he was ambitious
without worth, exacting without the right to be, presumptuous
without the aptitude, proud and puffed up without merit, an
ingrate and an egoist. The discovery stunned him like a
thunderbolt, but did not induce him to make his peace with
life and take the right road. He fell into a dead apathy, and
decided to avenge himself upon nature and mankind for his
nonentity by associating with the brute Kostyakov and
indulging in empty dissipation without feeling any desire
for it.

His last love affair was despicable; he intended to ruin a
poor passionate girl out of sheer ennui, without even the
excuse of sensual lust as a possible justification, although
this is but a poor excuse, especially when there is a more
direct and honest path to this. The girl's father taught him
a lesson that was a terrible blow to his pride; he promised
to give him a thrashing. Our hero, in despair, wanted to throw
himself into the Neva, but could not muster the courage to

do so. A concert to which his aunt dragged him stirred his former dreams, and brought about a frank talk with his aunt and uncle. Here he accused the latter of being responsible for all his misfortunes. The uncle had indeed, in his way, been mistaken in a number of things, but he had been true to himself, had not lied or pretended, had sincerely said what he had thought and felt; if his words had done more harm than good to his nephew, it was the fault of the narrow, morbid, and tainted nature of our hero. He was one of those people who sometimes see the truth, but either do not reach it when they make a dash for it, or jump over it, so that they are only near it but never in it. On leaving St. Petersburg for the country, he got even with him by aid of phrases and verses, quoting Pushkin's poem: "The barbarian artist wielding his lazy brush. . . ." These gentlemen are never without their monologues and verses, the babblers! . . .

He arrived in the country a living corpse. His moral life was completely paralyzed; his very appearance had changed so much that his mother hardly recognized him. He treated her respectfully but coldly, and confided nothing to her. Finally he realized that they had nothing in common between them, that if he tried to explain why his hair had grown so thin, she would understand it just as Yevsei and Agraphena would. His mother's kindness and compliance soon became irksome to him. His surroundings, which had witnessed the years of his childhood, revived his former dreams, and he began to lament their irretrievable loss, asserting that happiness lay only in illusions and phantoms. This is the common conviction of all spineless, futile, and deficient natures. Experience would seem to have adequately taught him that all his misfortunes were due to his giving himself up to illusions and dreams, to imagining that he possessed a great poetical talent when he possessed none at all, that he had been created for a kind of heroic and self-sacrificing friendship and stupendous love, when there was nothing in him that was heroic or self-sacrificing. He was an ordinary man, but not in any way vulgar. He was kindhearted, loving, intelligent, and not without education; all his misfortunes arose from his desire to play the part of an extraordinary man, though he was merely an ordinary man. Who of us in his youth has not dreamed, harbored illusions, and chased mirages, and who has not been disappointed in them? Who has escaped paying for these disappointments with heartburnings, anguish, and apathy, and who has not later laughed heartily at all these things?

Healthy natures, however, only gain from this practical logic of life and experience; they develop and mature morally. It is the romanticists that perish from it. . . .

We were somehow oddly affected when we first read the letter that our hero wrote to his uncle and aunt after his mother's death, a letter full of spiritual calm and common sense. But we explained it to ourselves as a desire on the author's part to send his hero back to St. Petersburg to complete his quixotic career by the perpetration of fresh follies. This letter concludes the second part of the novel, and the epilogue begins four years after our hero's return to St. Petersburg.

Pyotr Ivanich now appears upon the scene. This personage has been introduced into the novel not for its own sake, but for the sake of better showing up the hero by sheer force of contrast. This has given the whole novel a somewhat didactic coloring, for which many, not without reason, have reproached the author. The latter has nevertheless been able in this case as well to show himself a person of unusual talent. Pyotr Ivanich is not an abstract idea but a living person, a figure depicted in full stature with a bold, sweeping, and true brush. As a man he is judged by some too good, by others too bad, and in both cases he is judged erroneously. Some would see in him a sort of ideal, a model to be imitated; these people are of the positive and sensible kind. Others would see in him almost a monster; such people are dreamers.

Pyotr Ivanich is a very good man in his way; he is clever, very clever, because he perfectly understands feelings and passions which he himself does not possess, and despises; though in no way poetical, he understands poetry a thousand times better than his nephew, who contrived from Pushkin's best works to imbibe ideas and a frame of mind such as he could only have obtained from the works of phrasemongers and rhetoricians. Pyotr Ivanich is selfish, by nature cold and incapable of generous impulses, but at the same time he is not only without malice, but decidedly good-natured. He is honest, upright, not a hypocrite or a pretender; he is dependable, and will not promise what he cannot or will not do; what he promises, he is sure to fulfill. In a word, he is an honorable man in the full sense of the word—would there were more like him!

He drew up for himself a list of unalterable rules of life, in conformity with his nature and common sense. He did not pride himself upon them or boast of them, but he held them

to be infallibly true. Indeed, the mantle of his practical
philosophy was made of a strong and durable material that
could well protect him from life's inclemencies. What was his
amazement and horror when, on reaching the age of gray
hairs and lumbago, he suddenly noticed a rent in his mantle,
true only one rent, but what a big one! He made no special
effort to secure domestic bliss but was sure that he had established it on a firm foundation, only to discover suddenly that
his poor wife was the victim of his wisdom, that he had
ruined her life, suffocated her in a cold and stifling atmosphere.

What a lesson for sober-minded men, the representative of
common sense! Human beings evidently need a little of
something more besides common sense! It is evidently on the
borders of extremes that fate most frequently lies in wait for
us. Passions too are evidently essential for human nature to be
complete, and it is not always possible with impunity to im-
pose upon another the happiness that can satisfy only us, for
a person can be happy only according to his own nature.
Pyotr Ivanich had cleverly and subtly calculated that he had
to possess himself of his wife's concepts, convictions, and
inclinations, without letting her notice it, and lead her upon
the road of life in a way that would make her believe that
she was traveling of her own accord. However, he made one
serious blunder in his calculations. For all his cleverness, he
did not realize that for this purpose he should have chosen a
wife utterly impervious to passion and the need for love and
sympathy, a cold, good-natured, insensible woman, preferably
an empty person, and even a little stupid. His vanity, however, would not have allowed him to marry such a woman, so
that it would have been better had he not married at all.

The character of Pyotr Ivanich is sustained from beginning
to end with amazing faithfulness, but the hero himself in the
epilogue is unrecognizable. This is an entirely false and
unnatural character. Such a change might have been con-
ceivable had he been an ordinary babbler and phrasemonger
who repeats the words of others without understanding them,
and assumes feelings, ecstasies, and sufferings that he has
never felt. But young Aduyev had the ill luck to be frequently
oversincere in his aberrations and absurdities. His romanticism lay in his nature; such romanticists never become sober-
minded people.

The author would have done better to abandon his hero to
his rustic seclusion, leading a life of apathy and idleness, than

to give him a profitable post in the civil service in St. Petersburg and make him marry a rich dowry. Still better and more natural would it have been to turn him into a mystic, a fanatic, or sectarian, but the best and most natural thing to do would have been to make him, for example, a Slavophile. Here Aduyev would have remained true to his own nature, would have continued his old mode of life, believing that he had made tremendous strides forward, whilst in actual fact he would have only planted the banners of his old dreams on new soil. He who had formerly dreamed of glory, friendship and love would now have dreamed of nations and tribes, of how fate had endowed the Slavs with love, and the Teutons with enmity, of how in the legendary days of Gostomysl the Slavs had enjoyed a higher civilization that served as a model for the whole world, of how modern Russia was rapidly approaching that stage of civilization, and how only the blind and bigoted could not see this, when all those who had eyes and sober imagination had clearly perceived it a long time ago. Our hero would then have been a quite modern romanticist, and it would not have entered anybody's head that men of that stamp no longer exist.

The denouement invented by the author spoils the impression produced by this splendid work, because it is false and unnatural. In the epilogue it is only Pyotr Ivanich and Lizaveta Alexandrovna that are well depicted to the very end; as for the hero of the novel, one might do better not to read the epilogue at all. . . . How could such a powerful talent fall into such strange error? Was he perhaps unable to cope with his subject? That cannot be said! The author was carried away by a desire to test his strength in a field that was not his—the field of conscious thought—and he ceased to be a poet. It is here that the difference between his talent and that of Iskander most clearly unfolds itself; even in the sphere of a reality that was foreign to his talent, Iskander was able to extricate himself from the situation by the power of mind; the author of *An Ordinary Story* lapsed badly because he relinquished for a moment the guidance of immediate talent.

With Iskander thought always goes first, and he knows in advance what and why he is writing; he presents realities with amazing fidelity with the sole purpose of having his say on them, pronouncing his judgment. Mr. Goncharov draws his figures, characters, and scenes primarily to satisfy his own requirements and to enjoy his pictorial ability; he must leave it to his readers to pass opinions, pronounce judgment, and

draw the moral. Iskander's pictures are conspicuous not so
much for fidelity of depiction and delicacy of brush as for a
profound knowledge of the realities which he describes;
they are conspicuous more for their actual than their poetical
veracity, entertaining not so much by their poetical style as
by a style replete with intelligence, thought, humor, and wit,
always remarkably original and novel. The principal force of
Mr. Goncharov's talent is always in the elegance and delicacy
of his brush, the faithfulness of his drawing skill; he unexpectedly relapses into poetry even when depicting trivial
and extraneous details, as for instance in the poetical description of the young Aduyev's works burning in the fireplace.
In Iskander's talent, poetry is a secondary agent, and thought
the primary; in Mr. Goncharov's talent, poetry is the primary,
principal, and sole agent. . . .

In spite of the weak, or rather spoiled, epilogue, Mr. Goncharov's novel remains one of the remarkable works of Russian literature. Among its particular merits is its pure, correct, smooth, free, and flowing language. In this respect, Mr.
Goncharov's narrative is not a printed book, but a living im-
provisation. Some have complained that the dialogues between
uncle and nephew are too long and tiresome. For us these
conversations belong to the best part of the book. They contain nothing that is abstract or irrelevant; they are not debates,
but lively, passionate, and dramatic arguments, in which each
of the participants reveals himself as a person and a character, defends, as it were, his moral existence. True, in this
kind of dialogue, especially in view of the novel's slightly
didactic tone, any talent might easily have stumbled. All the
more is it to the credit of Mr. Goncharov that he so happily
solved a difficult problem, and remained a poet where he
might so easily have dropped into the tone of a moralist.

We next have to deal with Mr. Turgenev's *A Hunter's
Sketches*. There is much in common between Mr. Turgenev's
talent and that of Lugansky (Mr. Dal'). Both of them are
most at home in physiological sketches of various aspects of
Russian life and Russian people. Mr. Turgenev began his
literary career by writing lyrical poetry; among his shorter
verses are three or four noteworthy plays, as for instance *The
Old Landowner, A Ballad, Fedya,* and *A Man Like Many
Others*. However, he came off well with these plays because
they either do not contain anything lyrical or their principal
feature is not lyricism but hints at Russian life. Mr. Turgenev's
lyrical verses proper reveal a complete absence of inde-

pendent lyrical talent. He has written several poems. When *Parasha,* the first of them, appeared, it was noted by the public for its facile verse, its gay irony, and faithful Russian landscapes, but chiefly for its felicitous physiological sketches depicting in detail the life and manners of the landowners. The poem, however, failed to achieve a lasting success, because when he penned it the author was concerned not with writing a physiological sketch but a poem of the kind for which he possessed no independent talent. Hence its best features shone forth in sort of casual, haphazard flashes. Next he wrote a poem, *A Conversation.* Its verses are powerful and resonant and contain much feeling, thought, and intellect; since, however, this thought is borrowed and not his own, the poem, though it might even please at a first reading, evokes no desire for a second reading. Mr. Turgenev's third poem, *Andrei,* contains much that is good, for it has many faithful sketches of Russian life, but as a whole the poem was a failure, because it is a story of love, the portrayal of which does not lie within the scope of the author's talent. The heroine's letter to the hero is long and prolix, and it contains more sentimentality than pathos. Generally speaking, these efforts of Mr. Turgenev reveal talent, but a talent that is sort of irresolute and indefinite.

He also tried his hand at the narrative; his *Andrei Kolossov* contains many splendid sketches of characters and Russian life, but as a story, this work as a whole was so queer, inconsequential, and clumsy that very few people noticed the good points it really contained. It was then obvious that Mr. Turgenev was seeking a path of his own and had not yet found it, for this is not a thing that anybody can always easily or quickly find. Finally Mr. Turgenev wrote a story in verse, *The Landowner,* not a poem, but a physiological sketch of the life of the landowning class, a joke if you will, but a joke that somehow turned out to be much superior than any of the author's poems. Its racy epigrammatical verse, its gay irony, the faithfulness of its pictures, and at the same time an integrity sustained throughout the work—all tend to prove that Mr. Turgenev has discovered the real genre of his talent, has found his own element, and that there are no reasons why he should give up verses entirely. At the same time there appeared his story in prose, *Three Portraits,* which reveals that Mr. Turgenev had found his real road in prose as well. Finally his story *Khor and Kalinich* appeared in the first issue of the *Contemporary* of last year. The success of

this short story, which had been published in the "Miscellany"
column, was unexpected for the author, and induced him to
continue his hunter's sketches. Here his talent was fully
displayed.

Evidently he does not possess a talent for pure creative
genius; he cannot create characters and place them in such
mutual relationships in which they form themselves of their
own accord into novels or stories. He can depict scenes of
reality that he has observed or studied; he can, if you wish,
create, but only out of material that is ready at hand, provided
by actual life. This is not simply copying from real life; the
latter does not provide the author with ideas but, as it were,
suggests them to him, puts him in their way. He reworks the
ready-made substance according to his ideal and gives us a
scene, more alive, more eloquent and full of meaning than the
actual incident that prompted him to write the scene; this
sort of thing requires a certain measure of poetical talent.
True, his entire ability sometimes consists only in faithfully
describing a familiar person or an event of which he was a
witness, since in actual life there are sometimes phenomena
which, when faithfully put on paper, have all the features of
artistic fiction. This, too, requires talent, and talents of this
kind have their degrees. In both cases Mr. Turgenev possesses
a highly remarkable talent. The chief characteristic feature of
his talent lies in the fact that he would hardly be able faithfully to portray a character whose likeness he had not met in
actual life. He must always keep his feet on the soil of reality.
For that kind of art he has been endowed by nature with
ample means: the gift of observation, the ability swiftly and
faithfully to grasp and appreciate any phenomenon, instinctively to divine its causes and effects, and thus through
surmise and reflection to complement the store of information
that he needs, when mere inquiries explain little.

It is no wonder that the short piece *Khor and Kalinich* met
with such success. In it the author approached the people
from an angle from which no one had ever approached them
before. Khor, with his practical sense and practical nature,
his crude but strong and clear mind, his profound contempt
for womenfolk and his deep-rooted aversion to cleanliness
and neatness, is a type of Russian peasant who has been able
to create for himself a position of significance under extremely adverse circumstances. Kalinich, however, is a fresher
and fuller type of the Russian peasant; he is a poetical nature
in common folk. With what sympathy and kindliness the

author describes his heroes, and how he succeeds in making the readers love them with all their hearts! In all, seven sportsman's stories were published last year in the *Contemporary*. In them the author acquaints his readers with various aspects of provincial life, with people of diverse rank and condition. Not all his stories are of equal merit; some are better, others are worse, but there is not one that is not in some way interesting, entertaining, and instructive. So far, *Khor and Kalinich* remains the finest of all these sportsman's tales; next comes *The Steward* and then *The Freeholder Ovsyanikov* and *The Counting-House*. One can only wish that Mr. Turgenev will write at least entire volumes of such stories.

Although Turgenev's story *Pyotr Petrovich Karataev,* which appeared in the second issue of the *Contemporary* for last year, does not belong to his hunting tales, this work is just as masterly a physiological sketch of the purely Russian character, and with a Moscow flavor at that. In this story, the author's talent is as fully expressed as in the finest of his hunting tales.

We cannot but mention Mr. Turgenev's extraordinary skill in describing scenes of Russian nature. He loves nature not as a dilettante but as an artist, and therefore he never tries to present it only in its poetical aspects, but takes it exactly as it appears to him. His pictures are always true, and you never fail to recognize our Russian landscapes in them.

Mr. Grigorovich has devoted his talent exclusively to depicting the life of the lower classes of the people. His talent too has much that is analogous with that of Mr. Dal'. He too keeps to actual life, which he knows well and has thoroughly studied, but his two latest essays, *The Village* and especially *Anton Goremyka,* are much more than physiological sketches. *Anton Goremyka* is more than a story; it is a novel in which everything is true to a basic idea, everything refers to it, and the plot and denouement proceed naturally from the very essence of the matter. Although outwardly the whole story revolves on the subject of a peasant losing his miserable horse, and although Anton is a common peasant, not at all of the smart or shrewd kind, he is a tragical figure in the full sense of the word. The story is a moving one, after the reading of which sad and weighty thoughts involuntarily crowd into one's mind. We sincerely hope that Mr. Grigorovich will continue to follow this road, from which so much may be expected of his talent. . . .

70   V. G. BELINSKY

Let him not be daunted by the obloquy of detractors; these gentlemen are useful and necessary for the exact determination of talent's measure; the larger the pack of them that follows on the heels of success, the greater that success is. . . .

The last issue of the *Contemporary* for last year published *Polinka Saks,* a story by Mr. Druzhinin, a complete newcomer to Russian literature. Much in this story smacks of immaturity of thought and exaggeration, and Saks is a somewhat ideal personality, but despite this, the story contains so much truth, so much warmth of soul and a faithful intelligent understanding of reality, so much originality that it immediately attracted general attention. Especially well sustained is the character of the heroine; apparently the author has a keen understanding of Russian women. Mr. Druzhinin's second story, which appeared this year, confirms the impression created by his first story—that the author possesses an independent talent—and leads us to expect much of him in the future.

Among the most outstanding stories published last year was *Pavel Alexeyevich Igrivy* by Mr. Dal'. (Published in *Notes of the Fatherland.*) As characters, as types, Karl Ivanich Gonobobel and Captain Shilokhvastov are among the finest sketches from the pen of the author. All the personages in the story have been splendidly depicted, especially Lyubonka's adorable parents, but the young Gonobobel and his friend Shilokhvastov are creations of genius. These are types that are fairly familiar to many in real life, but art has made use of them for the first time and turned them over to the world for its pleasant acquaintance. This story pleases not by its details and particularities alone, like all Mr. Dal's stories; it remains a story *almost* throughout. We say *almost* because an event that forms the tragedy of the hero of the story produces upon the reader the impression of something unexpected and incomprehensible. A woman is deeply loved by a man who does so much for her; she too seems to love him deeply. Her rake of a husband dies, and the hero hastens abroad to join her, full of fond hopes, only to find her married to another. The author, in fact, did not wish to give his story a coloring that would make the reader find such a denouement natural. Igrivy is absurdly shy and reserved, which is why he allowed two scoundrels to snatch from him the woman he loved. While she was suffering in her married life, he bore himself toward her in a most delicate and noble-

hearted manner, but in no way like a lover. Hence her awed
and frightened feeling for him soon developed into gratitude,
respect, amazement, and finally into veneration. She regarded
him as a friend, a brother, a father, the personification of
virtue, and for that reason did not regard him as a lover.
After this, the denouement is comprehensible, just as is the
fact that Igrivy became for the rest of his life a sort of insane
clown.

Adventures from the Sea of Life by Mr. Veltman dragged
on throughout *The Readers' Library* of last year, ending with
the second issue of this journal for the present year. Since this
novel began, we think, in 1846, we have already had occasion
to speak of it. We shall therefore repeat that in this work romance is mingled with fairy tale, the fabulous with the probable, the credible with the incredible. Thus, for instance,
Dmitritsky, the hero of the novel, availing himself of the
documents and clothes of a gullible young merchant, who
very conveniently bears a striking resemblance to him,
presents himself at the house of his victim's father in the
capacity of the latter's son. He plays his part so skillfully that
neither the father, the mother, nor anybody in the household
suspected that the impostor was not the real son. The impostor
marries a wealthy bride, and, on learning on the night of his
wedding that the real son had put in an appearance, makes
away with a huge sheaf of bank notes received as his wife's
dowry, and on the very next day begins to play in the
Moscow *beau monde* the part of a wealthy Hungarian mag-
nate. Rather farfetched!

However, though he places his personages in the most
incredible situations, the author describes their adventures in
a very entertaining fashion. Wherever the author does not
draw the long bow his talent appears in a very favorable light.
Thus, for instance, the adventures of the real son, who wishes,
but cannot bring himself, to fall at the feet of his "daddy,"
fearing lest that fond parent might make short work of him,
are full of truth and a profound knowledge of life, and hold
the reader's interest. There are many such splendid episodes
in Mr. Veltman's novel. He is most in his element when he
depicts the ways and manners of the merchants, burghers,
and the common people. His pictures of the life of high
society are his weakest point. Thus, for instance, Charov, a
young man of the fashionable world, plays an important part
in the novel, but his only affinity with high life consists in
the fact that he addresses all his friends and acquaintances

as "you beastly rotter!" Despite all the oddities and, we
might say, absurdities of Mr. Veltman's novel, it is a highly
outstanding work.

We shall now mention several works of less importance.
The *Notes of the Fatherland* published *Sboyev,* a story by
Mr. Nestroyev. The inner domestic life of a Moscow civil
servant is herein described with great art, the character of
Anna Ivanovna, the poor wife of Ivan Kirillovich, being
delineated with a special originality and delicacy. The accidental breaking of a big mirror fills the reader with involuntary horror—so masterfully has the author succeeded in
conveying a hint of what the poor family could expect from
its worthy head. . . . But this is only the background of the
story, which revolves around the love of Sboyev for Olga,
the daughter of a titular councilor, and in general around the
original characters of these two persons. It is, however, just
this principal aspect of the story that is its least convincing
feature. The personalities of the hero and heroine are somehow unnatural, not that such people do not exist in life, but
simply because the author of the story has not been able to
do them justice. This is not to be wondered at. In the beginning of the story the author himself says that he was inspired
by the work of another author; borrowed thoughts are rarely
a success. At the conclusion a second story is promised, which
is to be a sequel to the first; such promises too are rarely a
success. . . .

The *Contemporary* published another story by the same
author, *Without a Dawn.* The idea of the story is a splendid
one and held out for the work greater hopes of success than
it actually achieved. The reason, it seems to us, lies in the fact
that the secondary figures of the story have been depicted
more or less convincingly (the character of the heroine's husband is even a masterly piece of work), whereas the heroine's
character is a colorless affair. This woman is a limp and negative creature, helpless in face of the circumstances that op-
press her. Could she evoke any sympathy from the reader?
Can she be compared with Polinka Saks? Her upbringing had
made the latter a child, but experience of life awoke her
spiritual forces and made a woman out of her. Dying, she
wrote to a woman friend, "It is in vain that your brother
sleeps at my feet and watches my eyes to anticipate any
wish of mine. I cannot love him, I cannot understand him,
he is not a man but a child. I am too old for his love. But *he*
is a person, a man in the full sense of the word; *his* soul is a

great and calm one. . . . I love him and will never cease to love him."

We have yet to mention *Notes of a Man by Sto-Odin, Kiryusha,* a story by an anonymous author, and *The Jew* by Mr. Turgenev, to conclude our critical summary of everything that was in any way remarkable in the way of novels, narratives, and stories of last year's publication. We must, however, say a few more words about *The Landlady,* a remarkable story by Mr. Dostoevsky, but remarkable in a sense different from that we have hitherto used. Had it appeared over any other name we would not have said a word about it. The hero of the story is a certain Ordynov, a man deeply immersed in scientific pursuits, the exact nature of which the author does not specify, although the reader's curiosity on this score is a legitimate one. Science leaves its imprint not only on the opinions of a man but on his behavior too. Remember Dr. Krupov. However, there is nothing in Ordynov's speech or behavior that would show that he was engaged in any kind of science; what they do suggest is that he has gone in a good deal for occultism, necromancy, in a word *charomutiye.* . . . But this is not science; it is stuff and nonsense; nevertheless it has left its impress on Ordynov; that is to say, it has made him resemble a man mentally deranged, a lunatic.

Somewhere or other, Ordynov meets the beautiful wife of a merchant; we do not remember whether the author mentions the color of her teeth, but these are probably an exception, being pearl-white, for the sake of greater poetry in the narrative. She was walking arm in arm with an elderly and bearded man in the attire of a merchant. This man's eyes hold so much electricity, galvanism, and magnetism that he might have commanded a good price from any physiologist to supply the latter at times if not with his eyes, at least with their lightning-charged crackling glances for scientific observations and experiments. Our hero immediately fell in love with the merchant's lady. Despite the magnetic glances and the venomous sneers of the fantastic merchant he not only discovers their address but contrives to foist himself upon them as their lodger, and occupies a separate room. Curious scenes follow; the lady talks drivel, of which we cannot make out a single word, while Ordynov listens to her and constantly falls into fainting fits. The merchant with his fiery glances and sardonic smile frequently intervenes. What they said to each other to make them gesticulate so wildly, grimace, swoon and

recover we positively do not know because we have not understood a single word in all these long and pathetic monologues. Not merely the idea but the very sense of this perhaps highly interesting story will remain a secret to our
understanding until the author publishes the necessary com-
mentaries and explanations to this strange riddle of his
fantastic imagination.

What can this be, abuse or paucity of a talent that wishes
to rise higher than it is able to, and is therefore afraid to
follow the usual road and seeks a way that is unusual? We do
not know. It merely strikes us that the author wished to try
to reconcile Marlinsky and Hoffmann, adding to this mixture
a little humor in the latest fashion, and thickly covering all
this with the varnish of a Russian folk style. No wonder the
result is a monstrosity reminiscent of the fantastic stories of
Tit Kosmokratov, which amused the public in the twenties of
the present century. Throughout the whole of this story there
is not a single simple or living word or expression: everything
is farfetched, exaggerated, stilted, spurious and false. What
sentences we meet here: Ordynov is *scourged* by some
strangely sweet and stubborn feeling; he passes by the *cunning* workshop of a coffinmaker; he calls his beloved his turtle-
dove and asks from what skies she has flown into his heaven.
But no more! If we were tempted to quote all the bizarre sentences from this story, we would never end. What in the name
of wonder is this? It is mighty strange, a most incomprehensible thing! . . .

Of the books pertaining to belles-lettres that appeared last
year in separate editions, only *Travel Notes* by T.Ch. is
worthy of note. This is a small, beautifully printed book
published in Odessa. The author is a woman; that is obvious
in everything, particularly in the point of view. There is much
warmth of heart, much feeling and life; life, however, not
always understood, or understood in a too feminine way, but
life that has not been whitewashed or painted, not exaggerated or distorted; the narrative grips the interest, and the
language is splendid. Such are the merits of two stories by
Madam T.Ch.

Of particular interest is the first story, *Three Variations on
an Old Theme*. A grown-up girl falls in love with a mere boy.
She loses sight of him and marries a good and honorable man,
for whom she does not feel any particular affection. She later
meets the boy Lelya, now grown up and become Alexis. A
curious kind of relationship springs up, which is resolved by

a passionate kiss on both sides, a heart-to-heart talk, and Alexis' departure on the firm insistence of the heroine, in whom love has not conquered a sense of duty. She then accompanies her sick husband to a foreign spa. Here she receives a letter from a woman friend in which she learns that Alexis loves her passionately. The letter evokes a profound emotion. Once, while rereading the letter and dreaming of Alexis, she suddenly hears a strange noise in the next room, where her sick husband is lying. She runs into the room to find him almost in a swoon, the result of a bad attack of consumption. When he comes to himself, he begins to speak of the approach of death, thanks her for her care and consideration, and expresses satisfaction at leaving her well provided for; he advises her to marry, since she is young, good-looking, and there have been no children. As is usual with exalted women, she turns down the latter suggestion with horror. Then her conscience begins to worry her. How can it be otherwise? Her dying husband has thanked her for her love and care, and she thinks of another, loves another. The poor woman is on the point of telling her secret to her dying husband, but fortunately the swoon she falls into prevents this unnecessary and absurd confession, which could only have poisoned the last minutes of a good and noble man. Such is the logic of an exalted woman! . . .

The husband dies. She is thirty-five, when she again meets Alexei Petrovich; he is married, and lives for ambition. Our heroine is hardly able to control her emotions when she sees him, but he treats her with a frigid courtesy. Here she loses all faith in those monsters called men, and sheds bitter tears. How could he have forgotten all! Yes, but what did he have to remember? A kiss? The story of a love that ended in nothing, was nipped in the bud, one of those affairs many men encounter more than once in their lives? A man has many interests in life, and that is why his memory retains only such affairs as are more serious than a mere kiss. Not so in the case of a woman: she lives wholly for love; the more she is obliged to conceal her emotions, the deeper they are. Women are particularly prone to love affairs that end in nothing serious, that call for no risk, no sacrifice; they may betray their husbands in their hearts, and remain formally faithful to their vows, satisfy their need of love and strictly observe the obligations society imposes upon them.

The heroine of the second story is a *governess,* one of those women in whom imagination prevails over the heart, one that must be attacked from the head; that is to say, who must first of all be astonished, amazed, whose curiosity must be aroused by ugliness if not comeliness, by stupidity if not wit, by oddity if not merit, by vice if not virtue. She is courted by a man of ill-favored appearance who does not love her in the least, and is passionately loved by a noble and handsome man. She knows the worth of both, but is drawn to the former, as a moth is attracted by a flame. The story is well narrated, but the heroine has evidently failed to arouse any particular sympathy, which is why the first story has found greater favor than the second. Both, however, display a talent that promises fair if it develops.

Of foreign novels of outstanding merit published in the *Contemporary* and the *Notes of the Fatherland,* we would mention the translation of *Lucrezia Floriani* (already dealt with in our magazine) and also the continued translation of *Dombey and Son.* We shall deal with this superb novel, which has surpassed all Dickens's former works, when it appears in full in the Russian translation.

Memoirs or reminiscences of the past also belong to the category of literature. The *Contemporary* has published two interesting articles of this genre, *From an Artist's Notes* by X, and *Ivan Philippovich Vernet, Swiss-born Russian Writer* by Mr. L. We would also mention a splendid article by Mr. Nebolsin, interesting both in content and style, entitled *Stories of the Siberian Gold Fields,* which has been spread over so many issues of the *Notes of the Fatherland,* in its "Miscellany" Section.

Mr. Botkin's *Letters About Spain* (in the *Contemporary*) was an unexpectedly pleasant novelty in Russian literature. With us Spain is terra incognita. Political news merely confuses anyone who wishes to get an idea of conditions in that country. The chief merit of the author of *Letters About Spain* consists in his having witnessed everything with his own eyes, without being influenced by ready-made judgments about Spain scattered in books, magazines, and newspapers; you feel from his letters that he first examined, listened, questioned, and studied, before he formed an opinion of the country. That is why his views are new and original, and everything in them assures the reader that they are correct, that he is reading not about some fantastic country, but one that really exists. The merits of Mr. Botkin's letters are still more enhanced by their attractive style. His *Letters from*

Avenue Marigny were met by some readers almost with displeasure, although, in the main, this work found only approval. And indeed, the author unwittingly fell into error in his judgment on the state of present-day France as a consequence of his too narrow understanding of the meaning of the word *bourgeoisie.* By this word he understands only the rich capitalists, and has excluded from the term the most numerous, and therefore the most important, mass of this class. Despite this, the *Letters from Avenue Marigny* contain so much that is alive, entertaining, interesting, clever and true, that one cannot help reading them with pleasure, though one might not always agree with the author.

Among this group of articles of mixed content, but belonging more in form to the category of literature, we would include *New Variations on Old Themes* by Iskander (in the *Contemporary*); *Stories* by Mr. Ferry (*ibid.*); *The Peregrinations of the Portuguese Fernão Mendes Pinto, Described by Himself and Published in 1614,* translated by Mr. Butkov from the Old Portuguese, and Mignet's *Antonio Pérez and Philippe II* (in the *Notes of the Fatherland*).

Last year, our magazines were particularly rich in noteworthy scientific articles. We shall here name the chief among these. The *Notes of the Fatherland* published: *Proletarians and Pauperism in England and France* (three articles); *A Physico-Astronomical Review of the Solar System* by D. M. Perevoshchikov; *The United States of America* (three articles); *The Discoveries of Hencke and Leverrier* by D. M. Perevoshchikov; *The Causes of Fluctuations in Grain Prices* by A. P. Zablotsky. The *Contemporary* published: *A View on the Juridical Life of Ancient Russia* by K. D. Kavelin; *A Research into the Eleusinian Mysteries* by Count S. S. Uvarov; *Daniil Romanovich, King of Galich* by S. M. Solovyov; *The Importance of Physiology and Discoveries in This Field* by Littré; *A Popular Essay on How the New Planet Neptune Was Discovered* by A. Savich; *Constantinople in the Fourth Century; On the Possibility of Definitive Measures of Confidence in the Result of the Sciences of Observation and Particularly Statistics* by Academician Bunyakovsky; *The State Economy Under Peter the Great* (two articles) by Afanasyev; *Malthus and His Opponents* by V. Milyutin; *Alexander von Humboldt and His Cosmos* (two articles) by N. Frolov; *Ireland* by N. Satin. The *Readers' Library* published, in serials lasting more than half a year, a very curious

article entitled *The Travels and Discoveries of Lieutenant
Zagoskin in Russian America,* which has now appeared in a
separate edition under another title.

Mr. Kavelin's article *A View on the Juridical Life of
Ancient Russia* and the article by Mr. Zablotsky *The Causes
of Fluctuations in Grain Prices in Russia* are indubitably
among the most remarkable in our scientific literature of last
year. Also highly remarkable in their way are the articles by
Mr. Poroshin published in the *St. Petersburg Chronicle.*

We do not enumerate here works of different kinds that appeared as separate books last year, since most of them have
already been analyzed in the critical and bibliographical sections of the *Contemporary,* and the others have been named
in the *Bibliographical News* that appeared as supplements to
the seventh and eighth issues of the *Contemporary* for last
year. . . .

Of the critical articles published last year, the following
are noteworthy: *Historico-Critical Excerpts* by Mr. Pogodin;
*M. Pogodin's Researches, Remarks and Lectures on Russian
History; Lectures in the Imperial Society of History and Russian Antiquities of the University of Moscow; European
Religious Sects in Russia* by Mr. Grigoryev; *The Works of
Fonvizin* published by Smirdin (in the *Notes of the Fatherland).* The two latter articles, apart from their intrinsic and
extrinsic merits, are of particular interest as coming from an
author who has until now written nothing. Mr. Dudishkin's
articles display a knowledge of his field. He makes good use
of the historical study of development as a means of interpret-
ing the literary works of a given period. The chief defects of
first efforts in this field are usually prolixity and verbosity;
such articles sometimes say nothing about the book they deal
with, but say very much, sometimes very well, but always
out of place, about things that have nothing whatever to do
with the book under review. Mr. Dudishkin has been able to
avoid these defects; he has obviously set about his business
with the subject matter fully arranged in his head, has full
command of his mind, does not allow it to run away with him
in one direction or another, keeps it constanty focused on the
subject, and hence begins at the beginning and finishes at the
end, speaks in moderation, and therefore fully acquaints the
reader with the subject he is writing on.

We cannot speak of all the critical articles published in the
Contemporary of last year; we are prevented from so doing
in view of the close association that exists between the maga-

zine and certain persons who wrote these articles. We shall
therefore merely confine ourselves to mentioning the following
articles: *The Last Novels of George Sand* by Mr. Kroneberg;
Historical Literature in France and Germany in 1847 by Mr.
Granovsky; *An Essay on National Wealth or the Principles of
Political Economy,* the work of Mr. Butovsky (three articles
by Mr. Milyutin); Mr. Kavelin's article on S. Solovyov's
*History of the Relations Between the Princes of the House
of Rurik.* We shall observe here that the *Contemporary* published full reports on all outstanding works on Russian history.
At the same time, the *Contemporary* must acknowledge that,
for reason beyond the control of the editorial board, it did
not in other respects fully meet the expectations of the public
in the field of criticism. It hopes, however, to give this section
greater fullness and development this year.

Russian criticism now stands on a firmer foundation. It is
to be met with not only in magazines but also among the
public, as the consequence of an ever-growing cultivation of
taste and education. This should exert an extremely favorable
influence on the development of criticism itself. It is a matter
that falls under the judgment of public opinion, and is no
longer a bookish occupation dissociated from life. It is no
longer possible for anyone to be a critic who takes it into his
head to be one, and not every opinion is accepted because it
appears in print. Party bias can no longer kill a good book or
ensure a favorable reception for a bad one. Convictions are
frequently set forth today in critical writing, and people who
have none try at least to feign them. The struggle of opinions
as expressed in criticism is evidence of the fact that Russian
literature is rapidly moving toward its maturity, but has not
yet attained it. Of course, there are people everywhere whom
nature itself seems to have appointed to provoke others, to
find fault with everything, to censure everybody and instigate
endless quarrels, commotion, and abuse. Besides a natural
inclination, which nothing can conquer, they are provoked
to this both by irritated vanity and petty private interests that
have nothing to do with literature. Such people are everywhere an inevitable evil, which may even have its useful side:
these people undertake voluntarily the role in society the
Spartans forced the helots to perform for their children. . . .
But it is strange and deplorable that these people's tone is
continually adopted by men who would seem to have nothing
in common with them, men who would seem to be activated
by some deeply cherished convictions, and finally by men

whose position in society, years, and repute should oblige
them to give an example in literature of good taste and respect
for decency. Here are some fresh examples.

The first issue of the *Son of the Fatherland* for last year
published a review of Mr. Sheviryev's lectures. In this article
it was stated and proved that Mr. Sheviryev's work was "a
splendid castle built out of clouds; a charming utopia turned
toward the past." This refers more to the theoretical side of
the lectures; on the factual side the review sees merely a
compilation. The author of the review has concealed his name,
but has not concealed his erudition and familiarity with
Byzantine and Bulgarian sources. His article, therefore, so
powerfully affected Mr. Sheviryev that it was only a year
later that he could bring himself to reply. The stronger the
attack on Mr. Sheviryev, the greater the dignity to be expected
from him in his defense. Did Mr. Sheviryev act in this way?
In the first place, he expressed his displeasure at the fact that
the critic of the *Son of the Fatherland* withheld his name, as
though it were a matter of names and not of science, ideas,
and convictions. It was probably under the influence of his
dissatisfaction with this annoying anonymity that Mr. Sheviryev suddenly fell upon Mr. Nadezhdin. He ironically calls
the latter "this erudite gentleman," "this most learned
philologist," and mocks his opinions on Slavic dialects, little
suspecting that his Attic salt tastes for all the world like Slav
groats.

It is proper and fitting to refute the opinions of others if
they seem unjust to you, but this should be done, first, in a
relevant manner, and second, with respect for decency. It
would not be a bad thing for Mr. Sheviryev to remember that
he is a scientist, that he has a standing of at least twenty years
in Russian letters, and that all this obliges him to set a good
and not a bad example to our young littérateurs. Neither
would it do harm for Mr. Sheviryev to remember that Mr.
Nadezhdin was once his colleague at the university, a professor like himself. But Mr. Sheviryev completely lacks the
literary serenity that is the strength of men who have been
developed by science and experience of life; on the contrary
he shows himself in literature to be restless and turbulent, and
is therefore continually falling into extremes and blunders
peculiar to young men who have plunged into literary activities straight from the school desk.

Another instance: In speaking of a former collaborator of
the *Notes of the Fatherland* now employed on the *Con-*

temporary, Mr. Sheviryev permitted himself to remark of him
that he had "betrayed the banners of the *Notes of the Fatherland*"! Is not this statement a consequence of the turbulent
and irritable condition we have already mentioned? Does
Mr. Sheviryev really believe his own words? No, he simply
wished to sting his opponent, forgetting that this is done by
the weapon of truth, and not through fabrications. The person
he refers to acted in a very natural way: he found it more
convenient and better for himself to publish his articles in
another magazine, which he was fully entitled to do, since he
does not consider himself attached to any particular magazine.

Among similar sallies of this gentleman is the idea, continually repeated by many others, that Gogol, in renouncing
his former works, has placed us in a predicament, so that we
do not know what to do. More than a year has passed since
this book appeared, and we have already spoken several
times about Gogol's works in the same spirit as we did before
this book came out. In general, we have always praised
Gogol's works and not Gogol himself, praised them for their
own sake and not for the sake of the author. His former works
still remain for us what they were before, and we are not
concerned with what Gogol thinks of his former works.

Mr. Sheviryev's most unpleasant sally has been directed
against Iskander. Mr. Sheviryev's extremely nervous attitude
toward this author has made him adopt a tone that is anything but literary. He has copied out of the novel *Who Is To
Blame?* all the phrases and words he chooses to regard as a
distortion of the Russian language. Some of these words and
phrases may indeed be censurable, but the greater part prove
only Mr. Sheviryev's dislike of Iskander. We do not understand how Mr. Sheviryev finds the time to engage in such
trivialities worthy only of the industry of a well-known
quondam professor of eloquence and prosodic cunnings! What
if it occurred to somebody to copy from Mr. Sheviryev's
articles entire periods like the following: "that which today
to some Russian soul that comprehends not the real sense of
ancient Russian life seems exclusively Byzantine and a sort of
mystical and theoretical philosophizing, and 'even a trivial
contemplation,' *that which* contains in itself the simplest and
highest truths, *then that means nothing else than that that*
Russian soul has broken the union with the basic foundations
of the life of Russian people and has retired into its abstract
individuality from the close confines of which it sees its own

illusions and not real affairs." A period of this kind we do not regard as a distortion of the Russian language, but rather as a distortion of Mr. Sheviryev's language, and of course we must be more exacting in this respect to Iskander, who is a writer of influence. Nevertheless, to find fault with such trifles means to display more dislike for one's opponents than love of the Russian language and literature, means threatening one's opponent from afar with a hatpin when it is impossible to reach him with a spear.

Last year the attention of critics was chiefly occupied with Gogol's *Correspondence with Friends.* It may be said that the memory of this book is today sustained only by the articles that deal with it. The best article against it has come from the pen of N. F. Pavlov. In his letters to Gogol, he has assumed the latter's standpoint in order to prove his unfaithfulness to his own principles. A fine wit and dialectical skill combined with a supreme elegance of style make N. F. Pavlov's letters a model that holds a special place in our literature. It would be a pity if no more than three letters appear.

Mr. Smirdin, our well-known bookseller, has, with his publications of Russian authors, prepared a good deal of work and trouble for Russian critics, and promises still more. He has already published Lomonosov, Derzhavin, Fonvizin, Ozerov, Kantemir, Khemnitzer, Muravyov, Knyazhnin and Lermontov. One newspaper has reported the impending publication of works by Bogdanovich, Davidov, Karamzin, and Izmailov. Assurances have been given by the same source that these are to be followed by Karamzin's *History of the Russian State,* the works of Empress Catherine II, the works of Sumarokov, Kheraskov, Tredyakovsky, Kostrov, Prince Dolgoruky, Kapnist, Nakhimov, and Narezhny, and that, furthermore, steps have been taken to acquire the copyrights of Zhukovsky, Batyushkov, Dmitriev, Gnedich, Khmelnitsky, Shakhovskoy and Baratyinsky. Ample work for the critics! Let each voice his opinion without worrying that others do not think the way he does. One must be tolerant of the opinions of others. It is impossible to make all people think in the same way. By all means, refute opinions that are not in accordance with your own, but do not persecute them with violence simply because you do not like them. Do not endeavor, outside the literary approach, to show them in an unfavorable light. This does not pay. By wishing to gain more space for your opinions, you may perhaps in this way remove the ground from under their feet.

Letter to N. V. Gogol

You ARE only partly right in regarding my article as that of an *angered* man: that epithet is too mild and inadequate to express the state to which I was reduced on reading your book. But you are entirely wrong in ascribing that state to your indeed none too flattering references to the admirers of your talent. No, there was a more important reason for this. One could endure an outraged sense of self-esteem, and I should have had sense enough to let the matter pass in silence were that the whole gist of the matter; but one cannot endure an outraged sense of truth and human dignity; one cannot keep silent when lies and immorality are preached as truth and virtue under the guise of religion and the protection of the knout.

Yes, I loved you with all the passion with which a man, bound by ties of blood to his native country, can love its hope, its honor, its glory, one of its great leaders on the path toward consciousness, development, and progress. And you had sound reason for losing your equanimity at least momentarily when you forfeited that love. I say that not because I believe my love to be an adequate reward for a great talent, but because I do not represent a single person in this respect but a multitude of men, most of whom neither you nor I have ever set eyes on, and who, in their turn, have never set eyes on you. I find myself at a loss to give you an adequate idea of the indignation your book has aroused in all noble hearts, and of the wild shouts of joy that were set up on its appearance by all your enemies—both the non-literary—the Chichikovs, the Nozdrevs, and the mayors—and by the literary, whose names are well known to you. You see yourself that even those people who are of one mind with your book have disowned it. Even if it had been written as a result of deep and sincere conviction, it could not

have created any impression on the public other than the
one it did. And it is nobody's fault but your own if everyone
(except the few who must be seen and known in order not
to derive pleasure from their approval) received it as an
ingenious but all too unceremonious artifice for achieving a
sheerly earthly aim by celestial means.

Nor is that in any way surprising; what is surprising is
that you find it surprising. I believe that is so because your
profound knowledge of Russia is only that of an artist, but
not of a thinker, whose role you have so ineffectually tried
to play in your fantastic book. Not that you are not a thinker,
but that you have been accustomed for so many years to look
at Russia from your *beautiful far-away;* and who does not
know that there is nothing easier than seeing things from
a distance the way we want to see them; for in that *beautiful
far-away* you live a life that is entirely alien to it; you live
in and within yourself or within a circle of the same mentality as your own that is powerless to resist your influence
on it.

Therefore you failed to realize that Russia sees her salvation not in mysticism or asceticism or pietism, but in the successes of civilization, enlightenment, and humanity. What she
needs is not sermons (she has heard enough of them!) or
prayers (she has repeated them too often!), but the awakening in the people of a sense of their human dignity lost for
so many centuries amid dirt and refuse; she needs rights and
laws conforming not to the preaching of the church but to
common sense and justice, and their strictest possible observance. Instead of which she presents the dire spectacle of a
country where men traffic in men, without even having the
excuse so insidiously exploited by the American plantation
owners who claim that the Negro is not a man; a country
where people call themselves not by names but by nicknames
such as Vanka, Vaska, Steshka, Palashka; a country where
there are not only no guarantees for individuality, honor and
property, but even no police order, and where there is nothing but vast corporations of official thieves and robbers of
various descriptions. The most vital national problems in
Russia today are the abolition of serfdom and corporal punishment and the strictest possible observance of at least those
laws that already exist. This is even realized by the government itself (which is well aware of how the landowners treat
their peasants and how many of the former are annually done
away with by the latter), as is proved by its timid and

abortive half-measures for the relief of the white Negroes
and the comical substitution of the single-lash knout by a
cat-o'-three tails.

Such are the problems that prey on the mind of Russia in
her apathetic slumber! And at such a time a great writer,
whose astonishingly artistic and deeply truthful works have
so powerfully contributed toward Russia's awareness of herself, enabling her as they did to take a look at herself as
though in a mirror—publishes a book in which he teaches the
barbarian landowner to make still greater profits out of the
peasants and to abuse them still more in the name of Christ
and Church. . . . And would you expect me not to become
indignant? . . . Why, if you had made an attempt on my
life I could not have hated you more than I do for these
disgraceful lines. . . . And after this, you expect people to
believe the sincerity of your book's intent! No! Had you
really been inspired by the truth of Christ and not by the
teaching of the devil you would certainly have written something entirely different in your new book. You would have
told the landowner that since his peasants are his brethren
in Christ, and since a brother cannot be a slave to his brother,
he should either give them their freedom or, at least, allow
them to enjoy the fruits of their own labor to their greatest
possible benefit, realizing, as he does, in the depths of his
own conscience, the false relationship in which he stands
toward them.

And the expression *"Oh, you unwashed snout, you!"* From
what Nozdrev and Sobakevich did you overhear it, in order
to present it to the world as a great discovery for the edifica-
tion and benefit of the peasants, whose only reason for not
washing is that they have let themselves be persuaded by
their masters that they are not human beings? And your
conception of the national Russian system of trial and punishment, whose ideal you have found in the foolish saying that
both the guilty and innocent should be flogged alike? That,
indeed, is often the case with us, though more often than
not it is the man who is in the right who takes the punishment, unless he can ransom himself, and for such occasions
another proverb says: *Guiltlessly guilty!* And such a book
is supposed to have been the result of an arduous inner
process, a lofty spiritual enlightenment! Impossible! Either
you are ill—and you must hasten to take a cure, or . . . I am
afraid to put my thought into words! . . .

Proponent of the knout, apostle of ignorance, champion of

obscurantism and Stygian darkness, panegyrist of Tartar morals—what are you about! Look beneath your feet—you are
standing on the brink of an abyss! . . . That you base such
teaching on the Orthodox Church I can understand: it has
always served as the prop of the knout and the servant of
despotism; but why have you mixed Christ up in it? What
have you found in common between Him and any church,
least of all the Orthodox Church? He was the first to bring
to people the teaching of freedom, equality, and brotherhood and to set the seal of truth to that teaching by martyr-
dom. And this teaching was men's *salvation* only until it became organized in the Church and took the principle of
Orthodoxy for its foundation. The Church, on the other hand,
was a hierarchy, consequently a champion of inequality, a
flatterer of authority, an enemy and persecutor of brotherhood
among men—and so it has remained to this day. But the
meaning of Christ's message has been revealed by the philosophical movement of the preceding century. And that is
why a man like Voltaire who stamped out the fires of fanaticism and ignorance in Europe by ridicule, is, of course, more
the son of Christ, flesh of his flesh and bone of his bone,
than all your priests, bishops, metropolitans, and patriarchs
—Eastern or Western. Do you really mean to say you do not
know that! Now it is not even a novelty to a schoolboy. . . .
Hence, can it be that you, the author of *Inspector General*
and *Dead Souls,* have in all sincerity, from the bottom of
your heart, sung a hymn to the nefarious Russian clergy
whom you rank immeasurably higher than the Catholic
clergy? Let us assume that you do not know that the latter
had once been something, while the former had never been
anything but a servant and slave of the secular powers; but
do you really mean to say you do not know that our clergy
is held in universal contempt by Russian society and the
Russian people? About whom do the Russian people tell
dirty stories? Of the priest, the priest's wife, the priest's
daughter, and the priest's farm hand. Does not the priest in
Russia represent the embodiment of gluttony, avarice, ser-
vility, and shamelessness for all Russians? Do you mean to
say that you do not know all this? Strange! According to you
the Russian people is the most religious in the world. That
is a lie! The basis of religiousness is pietism, reverence, fear
of God. Whereas the Russian man utters the name of the
Lord while scratching himself somewhere. He says of the

icon: *If it isn't good for praying it's good for covering the pots.*

Take a closer look and you will see that it is by nature a profoundly atheistic people. It still retains a good deal of superstition, but not a trace of religiousness. Superstition passes with the advances of civilization, but religiousness often keeps company with them too; we have a living example of this in France, where even today there are many sincere Catholics among enlightened and educated men, and where many people who have rejected Christianity still cling stubbornly to some sort of god. The Russian people is different; mystic exaltation is not in its nature; it has too much common sense, a too lucid and positive mind, and therein, perhaps, lies the vastness of its historic destinies in the future. Religiousness has not even taken root among the clergy in it, since a few isolated and exceptional personalities distinguished for such cold ascetic contemplation prove nothing. But the majority of our clergy has always been distinguished for their fat bellies, scholastic pedantry, and savage ignorance. It is a shame to accuse it of religious intolerance and fanaticism; instead it could be praised for exemplary indifference in matters of faith. Religiosity among us appeared only in the schismatic sects who formed such a contrast in spirit to the mass of the people and who were numerically so insignificant in comparison with it.

I shall not expatiate on your panegyric to the affectionate relations existing between the Russian people and its lords and masters. I shall say point-blank that panegyric has met sympathy nowhere and has lowered you even in the eyes of people who in other respects are very close to you in their views. As far as I am concerned, I leave it to your conscience to admire the divine beauty of the autocracy (it is both safe and profitable), but continue to admire it judiciously from your *beautiful far-away:* at close quarters it is not so attractive, and not so safe. . . . I would remark but this: when a European, especially a Catholic, is seized with religious ardor he becomes a denouncer of iniquitous authority, similar to the Hebrew prophets who denounced the iniquities of the great ones of the earth. We do quite the contrary: no sooner is a person (even a reputable person) afflicted with the malady that is known to psychiatrists as *religiosa mania* than he begins to burn more incense to the earthly god than to the heavenly one, and so overshoots the mark in doing so that the former would fain reward him for his slavish zeal did he not perceive that he would thereby be compromising himself in society's eyes. . . . What a rogue our fellow the Russian is! . . .

Another thing I remember you saying in your book, claiming it to be a great and incontrovertible truth, is that literacy is not merely useless but positively harmful to the common people. What can I say to this? May your Byzantine God forgive you that Byzantine thought, unless, in committing it to paper, you knew not what you were saying. . . . But perhaps you will say: "Assuming that I have erred and that all my ideas are false, but why should I be denied the right to err and why should people doubt the sincerity of my errors?" Because, I would say in reply, such a tendency has long ceased to be a novelty in Russia. Not so very long ago it was drained to the lees by Burachok and his fraternity. Of course, your book shows a good deal more intellect and talent (though neither of these elements is very richly represented) than their works; but then they have developed your common doctrine with greater energy and greater consistence; they have boldly reached its ultimate conclusions, have rendered all to the Byzantine God and left nothing for Satan; whereas you, wanting to light a taper to each of them, have fallen into contradiction, upholding, for example, Pushkin, literature, and the theater, all of which, in your opinion, if you were only conscientious enough to be consistent, can in no way serve the salvation of the soul but can do a lot toward its damnation. . . .

Whose head could have digested the idea of Gogol's identity with Burachok? You have placed yourself too high in the regard of the Russian public for it to be able to believe you sincere in such convictions. What seems natural in fools cannot seem so in a man of genius. Some people have been inclined to regard your book as the result of mental derangement verging on sheer madness. But they soon rejected such a supposition, for clearly that book was not written in a single day or week or month, but very likely in one, two, or three years; it shows coherence; through its careless exposition one glimpses premeditation, and the hymn to the powers that be nicely arranges the earthly affairs of the devout author. That is why a rumor has been current in St. Petersburg to the effect that you have written this book with the aim of securing a position as tutor to the son of the heir apparent. Before that, your letter to Uvarov became known in

St. Petersburg, wherein you say that you are grieved to find that your works about Russia are misinterpreted; then you evince dissatisfaction with your previous works and declare that you will be pleased with your own works only when the Tsar is pleased with them. Now judge for yourself. Is it to be wondered at that your book has lowered you in the eyes of the public both as a writer and still more as a man? . . .

As far as I can see, you do not properly understand the Russian public. Its character is determined by the condition of Russian society in which fresh forces are seething and struggling for expression; but weighed down by heavy oppression, and finding no outlet, they induce merely dejection, weariness, and apathy. Only literature, despite the Tartar censorship, shows signs of life and progressive movement. That is why the title of writer is held in such esteem among us; that is why literary success is easy among us even for a writer of little talent. The title of poet and writer has long since eclipsed the tinsel of epaulettes and gaudy uniforms. And that especially explains why every so-called liberal tendency, however poor in talent, is rewarded by universal notice, and why the popularity of great talents that sincerely or insincerely give themselves to the service of orthodoxy, autocracy, and nationality declines so quickly. A striking example is Pushkin who had merely to write two of three verses in a loyal strain and don the *kammerjunker's* livery to forfeit popular affection immediately! And you are greatly mistaken if you believe in all earnest that your book has come to grief not because of its bad trend, but because of the harsh truths alleged to have been expressed by you about all and sundry. Assuming you could think that of the writing fraternity, but then how do you account for the public? Did you tell it less bitter home truths less harshly and with less truth and talent in *Inspector General* and *Dead Souls?* Indeed, the old school was worked up to a furious pitch of anger against you, but *Inspector General* and *Dead Souls* were not affected by it, whereas your latest book has been an utter and disgraceful' failure. And here the public is right, for it looks upon Russian writers as its only leaders, defenders, and saviors against Russian autocracy, orthodoxy, and nationality, and therefore, while always prepared to forgive a writer a bad book, will never forgive him a pernicious book. This shows how much fresh and healthy intuition, albeit still in embryo, is latent in our society, and this likewise proves that it has a future. If you love Russia, rejoice with me at the failure of your book! . . .

I would tell you, not without a certain feeling of self-satisfaction, that I believe I know the Russian public a little. Your book alarmed me by the possibility of its exercising a bad influence on the government and the censorship, but not on the public. When it was rumored in St. Petersburg that the government intended to publish your book in many thousands of copies and to sell it at an extremely low price, my friends grew despondent; but I told them then and there that the book, despite everything, would have no success and that it would soon be forgotten. In fact it is now better remembered for the articles that have been written about it than for the book itself. Yes, the Russian has a deep, though still undeveloped, instinct for truth.

Your conversion may conceivably have been sincere, but your idea of bringing it to the notice of the public was a most unhappy one. The days of naïve piety have long since passed, even in our society. It already understands that it makes no difference where one prays and that the only people who seek Christ and Jerusalem are those who have never carried Him in their breasts or who have lost Him. He who is capable of suffering at the sight of other people's sufferings and who is pained at the sight of other people's oppression bears Christ within his bosom and has no need to make a pilgrimage to Jerusalem. The humility you preach is, first of all, not novel, and, second, it savors on the one hand of prodigious pride, and on the other of the most shameful degradation of one's human dignity. The idea of becoming a sort of abstract perfection, of rising above everyone else in humility, is the fruit of either pride or imbecility, and in either case leads inevitably to hypocrisy, sanctimoniousness, and incomprehensibility. Moreover, in your book you have taken the liberty of expressing yourself with gross cynicism not only of other people (that would be merely impolite) but of yourself—and that is vile, for if a man who strikes his neighbor on the cheek evokes indignation, the sight of a man striking himself on the cheek evokes contempt. No, you are not illuminated; you are simply beclouded; you have failed to grasp either the spirit or the form of Christianity of our time. Your book breathes not the true Christian teaching but the morbid fear of death, of the devil and of hell!

And what language, what phrases! "Every man hath now

become trash and a rag"—do you really believe that in saying *hath* instead of *has* you are expressing yourself biblically? How eminently true it is that when a man gives himself wholly up to lies, intelligence and talent desert him. If this book did not bear your name, who would have thought that this turgid and squalid bombast was the work of the author of *Inspector General* and *Dead Souls?*

So far as I myself am concerned, I repeat: You are mistaken in taking my article to be an expression of vexation at your comment on me as one of your critics. Were this the only thing to make me angry I would have reacted with annoyance to it alone and would have dealt with all the rest with unruffled impartiality. But it is true that your criticism of your admirers is doubly bad. I understand the necessity of sometimes having to rap a silly man whose praises and ecstasies make the object of his worship look ridiculous, but even this is a painful necessity, since, humanly speaking, it is somehow awkward to reward even false affection with enmity. But you had in view men who, though not brilliantly clever, are not quite fools. These people, in their admiration of your works, have probably uttered more ejaculations than talked sense about them; still, their enthusiastic attitude toward you springs from such a pure and noble source that you ought not to have betrayed them completely to your common enemies and accused them, into the bargain, of wanting to misinterpret your works. You did that, of course, while carried away by the main idea of your book and through indiscretion, while Vyazemsky, that prince in aristocracy and helot in literature, developed your idea and printed a denunciation against your admirers (and consequently mostly against me). He probably did this to show his gratitude to you for having exalted him, the poetaster, to the rank of great poet, if I remember rightly for his "pithless, dragging verse." That is all very bad. That you were merely biding your time in order to give the admirers of your talent their due as well (after having given it with proud humility to your enemies)—I was not aware; I could not, and, I must confess, did not want to know it. It was your book that lay before me and not your intentions: I read and reread it a hundred times, but I found nothing in it that was not there, and what was there deeply offended and incensed my soul.

Were I to give free rein to my feelings this letter would probably grow into a voluminous notebook. I never thought of writing you on this subject, though I longed to do so and though you gave all and sundry printed permission to write you without ceremony with an eye to the truth alone. Were I in Russia I would not be able to do it, for the local "Shpekins" open other people's letters not merely for their own pleasure but as a matter of official duty, for the sake of informing. This summer incipient consumption has driven me abroad, and Nekrasov has forwarded me your letter to Salzbrunn, which I am leaving today with Annenkov for Paris via Frankfort-on-Main. The unexpected receipt of your letter has enabled me to unburden my soul of what has accumulated there against you on account of your book. I cannot express myself by halves, I cannot prevaricate; it is not in my nature. Let you or time itself prove to me that I am mistaken in my conclusions. I shall be the first to rejoice in it, but I shall not repent what I have told you. This is not a question of your or my personality; it concerns a matter that is of greater importance than myself or even you; it is a matter that concerns the truth, Russian society, Russia. And this is my last concluding word: If you have had the misfortune of disowning with proud humility your truly great works, you should now disown with sincere humility your last book, and atone for the dire sin of its publication by new creations that would be reminiscent of your old ones.

Salzbrunn
July 15, 1847

N. G. CHERNYSHEVSKY

L. N. Tolstoy's Childhood
and Boyhood *and* Military Tales

"THE distinguishing features of Count Tolstoy's talent are an extraordinary power of observation, delicate analysis of psychological processes, precision and poetry in depicting nature, and elegant simplicity." Such is the opinion of everyone who follows literature. Criticism has repeated this evaluation suggested by the common consensus, and in doing so was completely faithful to the truth of the matter.

While it is true that criticism noted the traits that do distinguish Count Tolstoy's talent, can it really limit itself to this judgment without discussing the particular way in which these qualities are expressed in the works of the author of *Childhood, Boyhood, Notes of a Billiard Marker, The Snowstorm, Two Hussars,* and *Military Tales*? Observation, delicacy of psychological analysis, poetry in the depiction of nature, simplicity and elegance may be found as well in Pushkin and Lermontov and in Mr. Turgenev. It would be just to define the talent of each of these writers solely by those epithets, but it would be inadequate to differentiate them from one another; and to say the same thing about Count Tolstoy is not yet to catch the distinguishing features of his talent nor to show how that splendid talent differs from many other equally splendid talents. It must be characterized more accurately.

One cannot say that the attempts to do so have been very successful. In part the difficulty lies in the fact that Count Tolstoy's talent is developing rapidly and that practically every new work discloses new traits in him. Naturally, anything one might have said about Gogol after *Mirgorod* would be inadequate after *The Government Inspector,* and opinions expressed about Mr. Turgenev as the author of *Andrey Kolosov* and *Khor and Kalinich* would have to be changed and amplified in many respects when his *Notes of a Hunter* appeared, just as these opinions would appear inadequate when he wrote new stories distinguished by different merits. Yet an earlier opinion of a developing talent must be true and justified at the time it appears, even if it necessarily turns out to be inadequate every time he takes a further step ahead. We are certain that what we are about to write now will require considerable amplification as soon as *Youth* appears. Count Tolstoy's talent will disclose new qualities to us, just as he disclosed aspects in his *Sevastopol Sketches* that he had no occasion to disclose in *Childhood* and *Boyhood*, just as later, in *Notes of a Billiard Marker* and *Two Hussars*, he took a further step forward. But in any case that talent is already sufficiently brilliant so that each period of its development is worth noting with the greatest care. Let us examine the special traits he has already had occasion to disclose in the works known to the readers of this journal.

In some talents the power of observation is marked by something cold and dispassionate. The most remarkable representative of that special trait in our literature was Pushkin. In Russian literature it is difficult to find a more precise and lively picture of the customs and habits of a great landowner in the old days than the one at the beginning of his tale *Dubrovsky*. But it is difficult to decide what Pushkin himself thought about the traits he depicted. It seems that he would be ready to reply to such a question that "there are various ways of looking at it. What business is it of mine whether that life arouses sympathy or antipathy in you? I myself cannot decide whether it merits amazement or dissatisfaction." That kind of observation requires simply sharpness of eye and a good memory.

You won't find such indifference in our modern writers; their feelings are aroused to a greater extent; their mind is more precise in its judgments. They do not fill their fantasy with every image found on their path with equal eagerness. They look particularly carefully at those traits that belong to the sphere of life that interests them most. Thus, for example, Mr. Turgenev is attracted primarily by phenomena that are related, whether positively or negatively, to what is called the poetry of life and to the question of humaneness. Count Tolstoy's attention is primarily turned to examining how certain feelings and thoughts develop out of others. He is interested in observing how a feeling that rises immediately out of a given situation or impression turns into another feeling when it is subjected to the influence of memory and the power of

association that the imagination has, then again returns to its
point of departure and voyages again and again, continually
changing, along the whole chain of memory; how a thought,
begotten by a first sensation, leads to other thoughts, is carried further and further, blends reverie with real feelings,
dreams about the future with reflections about the present.
Psychological analysis may take different directions: one poet
is primarily concerned with describing characters; another
with the influence of social relations and the experiences of
life on characters; a third with the connection between feelings and actions; a fourth with the analysis of passion; Count
Tolstoy is primarily interested in the psychic process itself,
its forms, its laws, or, to express it in terms of a definition,
in the dialectic of the soul.

Among our other remarkable poets, that aspect of psychological analysis is most developed in Lermontov. Yet for him
it always plays somehow too much of a secondary role, it
appears rarely, and at that almost completely subordinated to
the analysis of feelings. It appears most clearly and most
memorably in those pages everyone remembers when Pechorin
thinks about his relations to Princess Mary, when he notes
that she has fallen in love with him completely, that she has
given up flirting with Grushnitsky for a serious passion:

I frequently ask myself why I so obstinately seek the love
of a young lady whom I do not want to seduce and whom I
will never marry, and so on. Why am I going to all that
trouble? Out of envy for Grushnitsky? The poor fellow! He
doesn't merit it at all. Or is this the consequence of that
despicable but uncontrollable feeling which makes us destroy
the sweet delusions of someone near to us in order to have the
petty satisfaction of telling him, when he asks in despair what
he should believe in:
"My friend, the same thing happened to me, yet you see
that I can lunch and dine and sleep most peacefully and, I
hope, that I shall be able to die without cries and tears, and
so on."

Here Lermontov catches the psychic process of the origin
of thought more clearly than anyplace else; nevertheless it
does not bear the slightest similarity to those depictions of
the course of feelings and thoughts in a man's head that
Count Tolstoy so likes. It is not at all the same things as
those half-dreamy, half-meditative conjunctions of concepts
and feelings which grow, move, change before our eyes as

we read Count Tolstoy—it doesn't bear the slightest similarity
to his depiction of pictures and scenes of expectations and
fears that go on in the minds of his characters. Pechorin's
meditations are observed from an entirely different point of
view than are those various moments of psychic life in the
characters Count Tolstoy depicts. Let us take as an example
that description of what a man feels during the minute preceding a blow that is expected to be mortal, and then at the
moment of the final convulsion of nerves from that blow:

Praskukhin, who was walking together with Mikhaylov, had
just left Kalugin and was beginning to revive a little as he approached a less dangerous spot, when he saw a flash gleaming
brightly behind him and heard the shout of the sentry,
"Mortar!" and the words of one of the soldiers walking behind, "It will fly straight to the bastion!" Mikhaylov looked
back. The bright point of the bomb, it seemed, had just
stopped in his zenith in a position where it was impossible to
determine its direction. But this lasted only a moment: faster
and faster, nearer and nearer, so that the sparks of the fuse
could be seen and the fatal whistling could be heard, the
bomb was coming down into the battalion.

"Lie down!" cried somebody's voice.

Mikhaylov and Praskukhin lay down on the ground. Praskukhin closed his eyes and heard only the bomb's thud against
the hard earth nearby. A second passed—it seemed an hour—
and the bomb did not explode. Praskukhin was frightened:
Had he been cowardly for nothing? Maybe the bomb had
fallen far away, and he merely imagined that the fuse was
hissing near him. He opened his eyes, and saw with pleasure
that Mikhaylov lay motionless on the ground near his very
feet. Just then his eyes for a moment met the burning fuse of
the bomb spinning around within a yard away from him.

Cold terror, which excluded all other thoughts and feelings, seized his whole being. He covered his face with his
hands.

Another second passed, a second during which a whole
world of feeling, thoughts, hopes, and memories flashed
through his imagination.

"Whom will it kill, me or Mikhaylov? or both of us together? And if me, where will it be? If it's in the head, then
everything is finished; but if it's in the leg, they will amputate
it, and I will insist on their giving me chloroform, and I may
still live. And, maybe, it will kill only Mikhaylov: then I will
tell how we walked together, and how I was bespattered by
blood when he was killed. No, it is nearer to me—I will be the
man!"

Here he remembered the twelve rubles he owed Mikhaylov,

and he remembered another debt in St. Petersburg, which he should have paid long ago; the gypsy melody he had sung the night before passed through his mind. The woman he had loved appeared before his imagination in a cap with lilac ribbons; he recalled an insult he had not yet avenged—though inseparably from these and from a thousand other recollections, the feeling of the present, the expectation of death, did not leave him for an instant. "Still it may not burst," he thought, and, with desperate determination, wished to open his eyes. But at this moment, even while his lids were closed, his eyes were startled by a red fire, something struck his chest with a terrible crash; he ran, tripped over his saber, which was dangling between his legs, and fell on his side.

"Thank God! I am only wounded," was his first thought, and he wanted to touch his breast with his hands; but his arms felt fettered, and a vise gripped his head. Soldiers flashed past his eyes, and unconsciously he counted them: "One, two, three soldiers; and the one with his overcoat rolled under him is an officer," he thought. Then lightning flashed in his eyes, and he wondered what they were firing, a mortar or a cannon. Then they fired again; and there were more soldiers: five, six, seven soldiers passed by. He was suddenly horrified at the thought that they might crush him. He wanted to cry out that he was wounded; but his mouth was so parched that his tongue cleaved to the palate, and terrible thirst tormented him. He felt how wet it was near his breast; this sensation of wetness reminded him of water, and he wanted to drink even that which caused that moisture. "I must have torn the flesh as I fell," he thought, and, beginning more and more to succumb to the fear that the soldiers who continued flashing past him would crush him, he collected all his strength and wanted to shout, "Take me!" But instead he groaned so terribly that he was himself horrified at the sound he made. Then some red flames leaped in his eyes, and he thought that the soldiers were putting rocks on him; the flames leaped about ever less frequently, and the rocks pressed him more and more. He made an effort to push aside the rocks, and he no longer saw, or heard, or thought, or felt. He had been instantly killed by a splinter that struck his chest.

This depiction of an interior monologue must without exaggeration be called amazing. You will not find psychological scenes noted from that point of view in any other writer. And in our opinion the aspect of Count Tolstoy's talent that makes it possible for him to catch these psychological monologues contains the special, individual force of his talent. We do not want to suggest that Count Tolstoy will always present us such pictures. That depends entirely upon the circumstances he describes and, in the final analysis, simply upon his will. At one time he wrote *The Snowstorm,* which consists entirely of a series of similar interior scenes; he wrote next the *Notes of a Billiard Marker,* where not a single scene like that exists because the concept of the story did not require it. Speaking figuratively, he can fiddle more than one tune; he may play it or not, but the very fact that he can play it gives his talent a particular quality that may constantly be seen in everything. Thus a singer whose range includes unusually high notes may not use them if his role does not call for them; yet no matter what note he sings, even one equally accessible to all voices, each note of his will have a completely special sonority that derives from his capacity for taking the high note, and the connoisseur will recognize the extent of his range in every note he sings.

The special trait in Count Tolstoy's talent that we have been discussing is so original that it must be examined with great care, and only then shall we be able to understand all its significance for the artistic merit of his works. Psychological analysis is practically the most essential quality necessary for powerful creative talent. Yet ordinarily it has a descriptive character—if one may so express it—it takes a certain stable feeling and breaks it down into its component parts, presents us an anatomical table, if one may so express it. We note another direction in the works of great poets in addition to that aspect of it—a direction that acts upon the reader or viewer very strikingly—and that is the apprehending of the dramatic transitions of one feeling into another, of one thought into another. Yet ordinarily only the two extreme terms of this chain are presented to us, only the beginning and the end of the psychic process, and that is because most poets whose talent contains the dramatic element are primarily concerned with the results, with the manifestations of inner life, with the conflict between people, with action and not with the secret process through the mediation of which a thought or a feeling is worked out; even monologues, which apparently would serve to express that process more than any other form, most frequently express the conflict of feelings, and the noise of that conflict distracts our attention from the laws and the transitions responsible for the associations of notions—we are occupied by their contrast rather than by the forms of their origin.

Monologues almost invariably differ from dialogues only externally even if they contain more than simple anatomizing

of a stable feeling: Hamlet seems to be divided into two and
to argue with himself in his famous meditations; his monologues really belong to the same sort of scene as that between
Faust and Mephistopheles or the Marquis Posa's arguments
with Don Carlos. The particularity of Count Tolstoy's talent
consists in that he does not limit himself to depicting the
results of the psychic process. The process itself interests him,
and Count Tolstoy masterfully depicts the evanescent manifestations of that inner life that replace each other extremely
rapidly and with an inexhaustible variety. There are painters
who are noted for their art of capturing the flickering reflection of a ray on the quickly rolling waves, the shimmer of
light on rustling leaves, its cast on the changeable outlines
of clouds. They are mostly said to be able to capture the
life of nature. Count Tolstoy does something similar in respect
to the mysterious movements of psychic life. It seems to us
that therein lies the completely original aspect of his talent.
Of all famous Russian writers, he is the only master in that
field.

Naturally, that ability, like any other ability, must be in-
born. But it would be inadequate to limit oneself to this over-
generalized explanation. Talent develops only through independent moral activity, and in that activity, whose extraordinary energy attests to the peculiarity of Count Tolstoy's
talent that we have mentioned, must be seen the bases of the
force acquired by his talent. We talk about self-analysis, about
the tendency toward indefatigable observation of one's self.
We can study the laws of human activity, the play of passions, the connection of events, the influence of circumstances
and relationships by studying others. But all knowledge obtained by that means will lack depth and precision if we
fail to study the most precious laws of psychic life, the
operation of which is disclosed to us only in our own consciousness. Whoever has failed to study man in himself will
never arrive at a profound knowledge of people. That peculiarity of Tolstoy's talent that we discussed above proves that
he has studied the secrets of the human spirit in himself very
carefully; that knowledge is valuable not only because it
enabled him to write the scenes of inner movements of human
thought to which we called the reader's attention, but also,
and perhaps even more so, because it gave him a firm basis
for the study of human life in general, for seeing through
characters and the springs of action, the conflict of passions
and impressions. We shall make no mistake in saying that

self-observation must have sharpened his observation greatly
in general and taught him to look at people with a penetrat-
ing eye.

That quality is precious in a talent, and it is perhaps the
most substantial of all claims to fame a truly remarkable
writer has. Knowledge of the human heart, the ability to
unfold its secrets to us—that, after all, is the most important
thing in the make-up of every one of those authors whose
works we read and reread with amazement. And, to return
to Count Tolstoy, his profound knowledge of the human
heart gives great value to anything he might write and
whatever spirit he might write it in, without fail. No doubt
he will write much that will strike every reader with other
qualities and more effective ones—profundity of idea, striking conception, powerful depiction of characters, clear descriptions of life. And in those of his works already known
to the public these qualities always heighten the interest,
but to the true connoisseur it will always be clear—as it is
clear now—that knowledge of the human heart is the basic
strength of his talent. A writer may attract readers through
more brilliant qualities, but his talent becomes truly powerful
and substantial only if he possesses that quality.

There is still another aspect of Count Tolstoy's talent that
with its extremely remarkably freshness imbues his works with
a completely special merit, and that is the purity of his moral
feeling. We are no preachers of Puritanism; on the contrary,
we fear it: The purest Puritanism is harmful if for no other
reason than that it makes the heart harsh and hard. The most
sincere and righteous moralist is harmful in that he trails
behind himself a dozen hypocrites who use his name for a
blind. On the other hand we are not so obtuse that we fail
to see the pure light of a high moral idea in all the remarkable literary works of our age.

Social morality has never yet attained so high a level as
in our noble time, noble and splendid despite all the rem-
nants of ancient dirt, because it harnesses all its powers to
cleanse itself from inherited sins. And the literature of our
time is the noble manifestation of the purest moral feeling
in each of its remarkable works, without exception. We do
not want to imply thereby that this feeling is stronger in
Count Tolstoy than in the works of any other of our remarkable writers. In that respect they are all equally high and
noble, but that feeling has a particular shade of meaning in
his work. In others it is purified by suffering, rejection, en-

lightened by conscious conviction, appears only as the fruit of long trials, tormenting battles, and perhaps a whole series of falls. Count Tolstoy is different: moral feeling for him is not re-established only through reflection and experience in life; it has never wavered; it has been maintained in all its youthful immediacy and freshness. We shall not compare this shade of meaning and another one from the humanitarian point of view; we shall not say which is higher in its absolute meaning—that's a subject for a philosophical or social tract and not for a review—we are talking here only about the relationship of moral feeling to the merits of an artistic work, and we must admit that in such a case the immediate freshness of moral feeling that seems to have been kept in all its purity since the chaste days of youth gives poetry a special touching and graceful fascination. In our estimation much of the splendor of Count Tolstoy's stories depends upon this quality. We shall not prove that *Childhood* and *Boyhood* could only have been written with that extreme vividness, with that tender gracefulness, that give real life to these tales only through that immediate freshness of heart. So far as *Childhood* and *Boyhood* are concerned, it is obvious to everyone that these works could not even have been conceived, much less written, without that purity of moral feeling. Take another example, *Notes of a Billiard Marker*. Only a talent that had maintained its pristine purity could have conceived and written so strikingly and truthfully, could have created with noble intentions the story of man's fall.

The beneficial influence exerted by that aspect of his talent is not limited to those stories or episodes where it noticeably appears in the foreground; rather, it constantly serves as a vivifier and freshener of his talent. What is more poetical in the whole world, what is more splendid than a pure young being that expresses itself with joyous love about everything that seems to it exalted and noble, pure and beautiful as it is itself? Who has not experienced his soul reviving, his thought becoming enlightened, his whole being ennobled by the presence of a virginal soul similar to that of Cordelia, Ophelia, or Desdemona? Who has not felt that the presence of such a being sweeps poetry into his soul, and repeated together with Mr. Turgenev's hero (in *Faust*):

> Cover me with your wing
> Pacify the agitated heart
> And it will be a blessed shelter
> For the enchanted soul.

Such is the force of moral purity in poetry too. Works in which its breath blows refresh us, pacify us like nature—after all, the secret of nature's poetic effect probably lies in its purity. The graceful splendor of Count Tolstoy's works, too, depend to a great extent on the same breath of moral purity.

These two traits—a profound knowledge of the secret movements of psychic life and immediate purity of moral feeling —that now give Count Tolstoy's work a special feature will always remain the essential traits of his talent no matter what new traits may be expressed by him in his further development.

It is of course understood that his artistry too will always remain with him. While explaining the distinguishing characteristics of Count Tolstoy's works, we have not yet touched on that merit, since it comprises the appurtenance, or better, the essence of poetic talent in general, and strictly speaking is only a collective term that designates the entire conjunction of qualities characteristic in the works of talented writers. But it is worth noting that people who talk a great deal about artistry are the ones who understand least what its conditions are. We read an article somewhere that expressed surprise at the fact that the foreground of *Childhood* and *Boyhood* lacked a beautiful girl of eighteen or twenty who would fall in love passionately with some sort of handsome youth—an astounding conception of artistry! The author clearly wanted to depict childhood and boyhood, not ardent passion; and can you really fail to feel that if he had introduced these figures and that inspiration into it, the children on whom he wanted you to turn your attention would have been crowded out; their nice feelings would have ceased to interest you once passionate love appeared in the story—in short, can you really fail to feel that the unity of the story would have been destroyed, that the conditions of art would have been violated? The author could not introduce into his story of children's lives anything that would make you forget the children and turn away from them, precisely because he had to observe the laws of art. Moreover, in the same article we found something in the nature of a hint that Count Tolstoy erred in failing to present a picture of social life in *Childhood* and *Boyhood*. Isn't there a lot he has left out in these tales? They contain neither war scenes nor depictions of the Italian countryside nor historical reminiscences. In general a great deal that might have been introduced, but would have been out of place and should not have been related, is missing. After all, the author wants to transport you into the life of a child, and what does a child understand of social questions, what conceptions does he have of social life? That entire element is as foreign to the life of a child as military life, and the conditions of art would have been violated just as much if military or historical life had been described. We want literary works to describe social life as much as anyone does. But one must still understand that not every poetic idea permits social questions to be introduced into the work. One must not forget that the first rule of art is the unity of the work, and that consequently, in depicting *Childhood*, it is precisely childhood that one must describe, not something else, not social questions, nor military scenes, nor Peter the Great nor Faust, nor Indiana nor Rudin, but the child with his feelings and his concepts. And people who express such narrow demands talk about the freedom of creative art! It is amazing that they do not seek Macbeth in the *Iliad*, Dickens in Walter Scott, Gogol in Pushkin! One must understand that a poetic idea is destroyed when elements foreign to a work are introduced into it and that if Pushkin, for example, had thought of depicting Russian landowners or his sympathy for Peter the Great in his *The Stone Guest*, *The Stone Guest* would have turned out to be an absurd work as far as art is concerned. Everything has its proper place: scenes of Southern love in *The Stone Guest*, scenes of Russian life in *Onegin*, Peter the Great in *The Bronze Horseman*. Thus, too, in *Childhood* or in *Boyhood* only those elements characteristic for that age are appropriate, while patriotism, heroism, military life have their place in the *Military Tales*, a fearful moral drama in *Notes of a Billiard Marker*, the depiction of woman in *Two Hussars*. Do you remember that marvelous figure of the girl sitting by the window at night? Do you remember how her heart beats, how sweetly her breast is overcome with the premonition of love?

After saying good night to her mother, Lisa went alone to her uncle's former bedroom. She put on a white dressing jacket and, covering her long thick plait with a kerchief, extinguished the candle, opened the window, and sat down on a chair, drawing her feet up and fixing her pensive eyes on the pond now all glittering in the silvery light.

All her customary occupations and interests suddenly appeared to her in a completely new light: her capricious old mother, uncritical love for whom had become part of her soul; her decrepit but amiable old uncle; the domestic and village serfs who worshiped their young mistress; the milch cows and the calves, and all this Nature that had died and been renewed so many times and amid which she had grown up loving and beloved—her soul suddenly seemed unsatisfactory; it seemed dull, unnecessary. It was as if someone had said to her: "Litle fool, little fool, for twenty years you have been trifling, serving someone without knowing why, and without knowing what life and happiness are!" As she gazed into the depths of the moonlit, motionless garden she thought this more intensely, far more intensely, than ever before. And what caused these thoughts? Not any sudden love for the count as one might have supposed. On the contrary, she did not like him. She could have been interested in the cornet more easily, but he was plain, poor, and somehow quiet. She kept involuntarily forgetting him and recalling the image of the count with anger and annoyance. "No, that's not it," she said to herself. Her ideal had been so beautiful. It was an ideal that could have been loved on such a night amid this Nature without impairing its beauty—an ideal never abridged to fit it to some coarse reality.

Formerly, solitude and the absence of anyone who might have attracted her attention had caused the power of love, which Providence has given impartially to each of us, to rest intact and tranquil in her bosom. Now she had lived too long in the melancholy happiness of feeling within her the presence of this something, and of now and again opening the secret chalice of her heart to contemplate its riches, to be able to lavish its contents thoughtlessly on anyone. God grant she may enjoy to her grave this scanty bliss! Who knows whether or not it is the best and strongest, and whether it is not the only true and possible happiness?

"O Lord my God," she thought, "can it be that I have lost my youth and happiness in vain and that it will never be . . . never be? Can that be true?" And she looked into the depths of the sky lit up by the moon and covered by light fleecy clouds that, veiling the stars, moved toward the moon. "If that highest white cloudlet touches the moon it will be a sign that it is true," thought she. The mist-like smoky strip ran across the bottom half of the bright disk and little by little the light on the grass, on the tops of the limes, and on the pond, grew dimmer; the black shadows of the trees grew less distinct. As if to harmonize with the gloomy shadows that spread over Nature, a light wind ran through the leaves and brought to the window the odor of dewy leaves, of moist earth, and of blooming lilacs.

"But it is not true," she consoled herself. "There now, if the nightingale sings tonight it will be a sign that what I'm thinking is all nonsense, and that I need not despair," she thought. And she sat a long while in silence waiting for someone, while again all became bright and full of life and again and again the cloudlets ran across the moon making everything dim. She was beginning to fall asleep as she sat by the window, when the quivering trills of a nightingale came ringing from below across the pond and awoke her. The country maiden opened her eyes. And once more her soul was renewed with fresh joy by its mysterious union with Nature that spread out so calmly and brightly before her. She leaned on both arms. A sweet, languid sensation of sadness oppressed her heart, and tears of pure wide-spreading love, thirsting to be satisfied—good comforting tears—filled her eyes. She put both her arms on the windowsill and laid her head on them. Her favorite prayer rose to her mind, and she fell asleep with her eyes still moist.

The touch of someone's hand aroused her. She awoke. But the touch was light and pleasant. The hand pressed hers more closely. Suddenly she became alive to reality, screamed, jumped up, and, trying to persuade herself that she had not recognized the count, who was standing under the window bathed in the moonlight, she ran out of the room. . . .

Count Tolstoy possesses a real talent. That means that his works are artistic; that is, each of them very fully expresses precisely the idea that he wanted to express in that work. He never says anything irrelevant, because that would be contrary to the conditions of art; he never disfigures his works with the admixture of scenes and figures foreign to the idea of the work. Precisely therein lies one of the main demands of art. One must have a great deal of taste to appreciate the beauty of Count Tolstoy's work. But then a person who is capable of understanding real beauty, real poetry, sees a true artist in Count Tolstoy; that is, he sees a poet with a remarkable talent in him.

That talent is possessed by a young man, full of fresh forces, who still has a long road ahead of him—he will meet much that is new along that road; many new feelings are yet to stir his breast; his mind will come to grips with many new ideas—what a splendid hope for our literature! What rich new material life will provide his poetry! We predict that everything Count Tolstoy has given our literature up to now is merely a pledge for what he will accomplish in the future; but how rich and splendid is that pledge!

The Russian at the Rendez-vous

REFLECTIONS UPON READING MR. TURGENEV'S TALE *Asya*

"STRAIGHTFORWARD, accusatory stories leave a painful impression on the reader. Therefore, while recognizing their usefulness and noble aims, I am not altogether happy with the fact that our literature has taken such a gloomy direction so exclusively." This is the way many people who are apparently not stupid speak, or rather this is the way they spoke until the time when the peasant question became the sole subject of all thought and of all conversation. I don't know whether what they say is fair or not. But I was under the influence of the same idea when I began to read practically the only good new story from which one could expect a different inspiration, content of an entirely different kind than that found in straightforward stories from the very first pages. Here was neither chicanery, with violence and bribery, nor filthy rogues or official villains who explain in elegant language that they are society's benefactors, nor peasants and petty officials tormented by all these horrible and disgusting people. The action takes place abroad, far from all the base circumstances of our home life. All its characters come from the best among us, are very cultured, humane, and imbued with the most noble manner of thoughts. The tale has a purely poetic, ideal direction, and does not touch on a single one of the so-called dark sides of life. "Now, then," I thought, "I'll be able to rest and refresh myself." And I really did refresh myself with these poetic ideals until the tale came to the decisive moment. But the last pages do not resemble the first, and after reading the tale one is left with an even more disconsolate impression than that created by stories about nasty bribetakers and their cynical thefts. They do evil, but then each of us recognizes them as evil people; we do not expect the amelioration of life from them. We believe that there are forces in society that will put an end to their harmful influence, that will change our life through their noble character. That illusion is destroyed in the cruelest way in this tale, whose opening pages raised the most hopeful expectations.

Here is a man whose heart is open to all the highest feelings, whose honesty is unshakable, whose mind has appropriated everything that has given our era the designation of the era of noble intentions. But what does that man do? He creates a scene the worst bribetaker would be ashamed of. He feels the strongest and purest feeling for a girl who loves him. He cannot live an hour without seeing her. All day and all night his mind traces her beautiful likeness for him, and one would think that the time had come when his heart would drown in bliss. We see a Romeo and Juliet whose happiness no one opposes, and the minute approaches when their fate will be decided forever—all Romeo has to do is to say, "I love you; do you love me?" for her to whisper, "Yes."

And what does our Romeo do—we shall call the hero of the story Romeo, for the author does not give his name—when he appears at the assignation with his Juliet? Juliet awaits her Romeo with a shudder of expectation. She must hear from him that he loves her—that word had not been pronounced between them; now it will be spoken by him and they will be united forever. Bliss awaits them, such an exalted and pure bliss that the ardent desire for it makes the triumphant moment of decision almost unbearable for a mortal being. People would die of lesser joys. She sits like a frightened bird, shading her face from the sun of love that appears before her; she breathes rapidly, she shudders. She lowers her eyes in greater trepidation when he enters and calls her by name. She wants to look at him and cannot. He takes her hand—that hand is cold and lies death-like in his; she wants to smile, but her pale lips cannot smile. She wants to talk with him but her voice breaks. For a long time both are silent; in him too, as he himself says, his heart has melted. Now Romeo finally speaks to his Juliet. And what does he say to her? He says: "You are guilty toward me; you've placed me in unpleasant circumstances; I am dissatisfied with you; you are compromising me and I must break off my relationship with you. It is very unpleasant for me to part from you, but please go as far away from here as possible." What is this supposed to mean? How is she guilty? In that she considered him an honorable man? Did she compromise his reputation by coming to him

110   N. G. Chernyshevsky

at an assignation? That's fantastic! Every feature of her pale
face says she awaits the determination of her fate from his
words, that she has irrevocably given him her whole soul and
now only awaits his saying that he accepts her soul, her
life—and he reprimands her for compromising him! What
kind of stupid cruelty is that? What kind of base coarseness?
And the man who acted so meanly has seemed noble until
then! He fooled us, fooled the author. Yes, the poet made
too gross a mistake when he imagined that he was writing
about a respectable man. That man is more trashy than an
out-and-out rascal.

Such was the impression the completely unexpected turn
in the relationship of our Romeo to his Juliet produced on
many readers. Many people have said that the story is completely spoiled by that shocking scene, that the character of
the main figure is not maintained, that if that figure really
was what he is presented as being in the first half, then he
would not be able to act with such base coarseness, and if
he could so act, then he should have been presented to us
as a trashy person from the first.

It would be comforting to think that the author really made
a mistake, yet the sad merit of his tale lies precisely in that
the character of his hero accurately reflects society. Perhaps
the tale would have gained in its idealistic-poetic aspect if
the character was such as those people who are dissatisfied
with his coarseness at the assignation would like him to be,
if he had not been afraid to give himself up to the love that
possessed him. After the enthusiasm of the first meeting, there
would have followed several other highly poetic moments;
the quiet splendor of the tale's first half would have been
raised to an inspired enchantment in the second; and instead
of the first act of *Romeo and Juliet* with an ending à la
Pechorin, we should really have had something like *Romeo
and Juliet*, or at least something similar to one of George
Sand's novels. Whoever seeks a poetically unified impression
from the tale must really condemn the author, who after
attracting the reader with heightened, delightful expectations,
suddenly showed him the vulgarly stupid vanity of trivially
timid egoism, beginning like Max Piccolomini and ending like
some Zakhar Sidorych who plays patience for pennies.

Yet was the author actually mistaken in his hero? If he
was, then it wasn't the first time he committed that mistake.
In all the stories he has written that lead to a similar situation, his heroes extricate themselves from the situation every

time by becoming completely disconcerted before our eyes.
In *Faust* the hero tries to reassure himself that neither he
nor Vera has serious feelings for the other. He can sit with
her and dream about her, but when it comes to a decision,
even a verbal one, he conducts himself in such a way that
Vera herself has to tell him that she loves him. For several
minutes the conversation has already proceeded in such a way
that he must inevitably say it, but he, don't you see? hasn't
guessed it and hasn't dared say it to her. And when the
woman, who should have listened to the declaration, is
finally forced to make the declaration herself, he "freezes,"
don't you see? but feels that "bliss comes over his heart in
a wave"—however, "only from time and time." Strictly speaking, "he lost his head completely"—it is only a pity that he
didn't faint, and that too would have happened if he had not
opportunely come upon a tree against which he could lean.
The man has barely reassured himself when the woman he
loves and who has declared her love comes to him and asks
him what he intends to do. He . . . he "becomes disconcerted." It is no wonder that after such conduct (that man's
manner of action cannot be called anything other than "conduct") on the part of a beloved person, the poor woman
becomes ill with nervous fever; it is even more natural that
he should later begin to lament his fate.

That occurs in *Faust;* practically the same thing occurs
in *Rudin*. At first Rudin behaves somewhat more as becomes
a man than the earlier heroes do. He is so decisive that he
tells Natalya about his love himself (though he says it not
of his own will but because he is forced into that conversation); he himself asks her for an assignation. But when
Natalya tells him during the assignation that she will follow
him with or without her mother's blessing, that that does
not matter to her so long as he loves her, and when she
pronounces the words, "Know then, I shall be yours!" Rudin
can only exclaim "Oh, God!" as an answer, an exclamation
that is more confused than triumphant—and then acts so well,
that is, he is so cowardly and listless, that Natalya is forced
to ask him to an assignation herself in order to decide what
they should do. When he received the note, "he saw that
the denouement was close, and secretly his spirits fell." Natalya says that her mother told her she would rather see
her dead than let her become Rudin's wife, and she again
asks Rudin what he intends to do now. Rudin answers as
before, "My God, my God," and adds even more naïvely:

"So soon! What do I intend to do? My head is swimming, I cannot consider anything." But then he considers that one must "submit." When he is called a coward, he begins to reproach Natalya, then to lecture to her about his sense of honor; and to her remark that that is not what she should be hearing from him at that moment, he answers that he had not expected such decisiveness. The whole thing ends with the offended girl's turning away from him, practically ashamed of her love for a coward.

Yet perhaps that pitiful trait in the heroes' characters is a particularity of Mr. Turgenev's stories? Perhaps the nature of his special talent leads him to depict such figures? Not at all; it seems to us that the nature of a talent does not mean anything here. Think of any good story, true to life, by anyone you wish among today's poets, and if his story contains an ideal side, you may be sure that the representative of that ideal side behaves precisely as Mr. Turgenev's figures do.

The nature of Mr. Nekrasov's talent, for example, is totally different from Mr. Turgenev's; you may find whatever faults you like in it, but no one could say that Mr. Nekrasov's talent lacks energy and firmness. What does his hero do in the poem "Sasha"? He inculcated in Sasha the idea that "one must not be weak in spirit," for "the sun of truth shall rise over the world," and that one must act so as to achieve one's intentions. And later, when Sasha begins to act, he says that that's all in vain and leads nowhere, that he "talked nonsense." Let us remember how Beltov acts: he too prefers withdrawal to any decisive step. One could collect a large number of such examples.

Everywhere, whatever the poet's character may be, whatever his personal views of his hero's actions, the hero acts just as other respectable people do, introduced, like him, by other poets: the hero is very daring so long as there is no question of action and one need merely occupy spare time, fill an empty head or empty heart with conversation and dreams; but when the time comes to express one's feelings and desires directly and precisely, the majority of heroes begin to waver, and are stricken dumb. A few, the bravest, manage to collect all their strength and to stammer something that gives a hazy notion of their thoughts. But let someone take up their desires, and say, "You want such-and-such; very well. Begin to act. We will support you." At that reply half of the bravest heroes would faint; the other half would begin to reproach you coarsely for placing them in an uncomfortable position, to say that they did not expect such proposals from you, that they are completely dumfounded, and that they can conceive nothing, because, "How could it occur so quickly?" Moreover, they are "honorable people," and not only honorable but very peaceful, and do not want to subject you to unpleasantness; and in general, can one really fuss about everything one says merely for lack of anything to do? The best thing of all is not to undertake anything, because everything is connected with fussing and inconvenience, and nothing good can come for the time being because, as was already said, they "didn't expect and desire it at all," and so on.

That is what our "best people" are like; they are all similar to our Romeo. Whether Asya is greatly harmed by Mr. N's not knowing what to do with her and by his actual vexation when daring decision was demanded of him—whether Asya is greatly harmed thereby we cannot say. At first one thinks that she is harmed very little. On the contrary, thank heaven our Romeo's trashy weakness of character repelled the girl before it was too late. Asya will grieve for several weeks or several months, and then will forget everything and be able to give herself up to a new feeling, whose object will be more worthy of her. This is true. But the trouble is that she is not likely to find a more worthy person. That's where the sad comicality of our Romeo's relationship to Asya lies, in that our Romeo really is one of the best people of our society and that we hardly have anyone better than he.

Asya will be satisfied with her relationship to people only when she, like everyone else, learns to limit herself to beautiful discussions until the opportunity to put these discussions into action comes. As soon as that opportunity arrives, one must bite one's tongue and fold one's hands the way everyone else does. Only then will others be satisfied with her. But now, at the beginning, people will say that the girl is very nice, has a noble soul, remarkable strength of character, and is in general a girl one cannot help loving, whom one cannot help worshiping. But all that will be said only as long as Asya's character is expressed merely in words, as long as it is only assumed that she is capable of noble and decisive action. But as soon as she takes any step that justifies the expectations inspired by her character, hundreds of voices will immediately cry out:

"For heaven's sake, how can she? It's madness! To grant a young man a *rendez-vous!* Surely she's ruining herself, ruining herself completely uselessly. Surely nothing can come of that, absolutely nothing, except that she will lose her reputation! Can one risk oneself so insanely?"

"Risk one's self? That's not the worst of it," others will add. "Let her do what she likes with herself, but why subject others to unpleasantness? What sort of position did she place that poor young man in? Did he think that she would lead him that far? What can he do now when confronted with her irrationality? If he marries her, he will ruin himself; if he refuses, he'll be called a coward and he will despise himself. I don't know that it's honorable to put people who apparently have given no special cause for such absurd behavior into such unpleasant circumstances. No, that's not honorable at all. And what of the poor brother? What is his role like? What a hard pill to swallow his sister gave him! That pill won't go down all his life! She's really given him a treat, the dear sister. I won't argue that that's all very well as talk— noble intentions and self-sacrifice and God knows what other splendid things, but I'll say one thing: I wouldn't want to be Asya's brother. I'll say more: If I were in her brother's place, I'd lock her up in her room for a half a year. She must be locked up for her own good. She permits herself to be carried away by elevated feelings, don't you see? But how will others swallow what she's concocted? No, I shall not call her action noble; I shall not call her character noble because I do not call those who carelessly and boldly harm others noble."

Thus rational people will explain their opinions in a general outcry. In part we are ashamed to admit it, but it must be admitted that these opinions seem to us to be well founded. Asya really harms not only herself but also everyone who has the misfortune to be close to her through birth or circumstance; and we cannot help condemning those who do harm to all those near them for their own satisfaction.

While condemning Asya, we acquit our Romeo. What has he really done? Has he given her occasion to act irrationally? Has he incited her to an action one cannot approve? Didn't he have the right to tell her that she placed him in unpleasant circumstances in vain? You are troubled by the fact that his words are harsh; you call them coarse. But the truth is always harsh, and who would condemn me even if I let a coarse word slip out when I am mixed up in an unpleasant affair through no fault of mine and am, moreover, asked to enjoy the difficulty into which I have been dragged?

I know why you would so unfairly tend to be delighted with

Asya's ignoble behavior and to condemn our Romeo. I know
it because for a moment I was myself subject to the un-
founded impression that still remains in you. You have read
how people acted and do act in foreign countries. But take
into account that these are, after all, foreign countries. There
is a great deal done in the world in other countries, yet one
cannot after all do everything that is very convenient under
certain circumstances everywhere. For example, the familiar
form "thou" is not used conversationally in England. A manu-
facturer will say "you" to his worker, as will a landowner to
the farm hand hired by him, and a gentleman to his servant,
and where required they will employ the word "sir" to them,
that is, the equivalent of the French *monsieur*. But Russian
doesn't even have these words, and what would emerge would
be a courtesy equivalent to a master's saying to his peasant,
"Do you, Sidor Karpych, do me the favor of having a cup
of tea with me and then take care of the walks in my garden."
Would you condemn me if I spoke with Sidor without such
subtleties? Surely I would be ridiculous if I assumed an Englishman's tone.

In general, as soon as you begin to condemn what you
don't like you become an idealogue, that is, the most entertaining and, confidentially, the most dangerous man in the
world; you lose the firm support of practical reality from
under your feet. Beware of that; try to become a practical
man in your opinions. To start with, try to make peace with
our Romeo, about whom we began to speak. I am prepared
to show you the road by which I arrived at that result not
only so far as the scene with Asya is concerned but also so
far as everything in the world goes; that is, I became satisfied
with everything I saw around me. I now get angry at nothing; I am vexed by nothing (except failure in things that
are advantageous to me personally); I condemn nothing and
no one in the world (except people who destroy my personal
advantage). To put it briefly, I shall tell you how I turned
from a bilious melancholiac into a man who is so practical
and well intentioned that I wouldn't be surprised if I were
rewarded for my good intentions.

I began with the observation that one ought not to blame
people for anything at any cost, because as far I can see, even
the smartest person has his share of limitation that suffices
to make it impossible for him to stray in his thinking very
far from the society in which he was raised and lives. Even
the most energetic person has a sufficient dose of apathy to

prevent him from straying too far from routine in his actions and, as one says, following the stream wherever it leads. Ordinarily it is customary to color eggs at Easter and to eat pancakes in Lent, and everyone does so even though one person may not eat colored eggs at all, and almost everybody complains about how heavy the pancakes lie on the stomach. That is the way it is in everything, not only in trifles. It is commonly agreed that boys can be raised more freely than girls, and every father, every mother raises children according to that rule no matter how convinced they are that such a distinction is irrational.

It is agreed that riches are a good thing, and everyone would be pleased if, thanks to some fortunate circumstance, he were to receive twenty thousand rubles a year instead of ten thousand, although every intelligent person knows that those things that were unattainable at the lower income and that have now become attainable cannot bring any real satisfaction. For example, if you can give a ball for five hundred rubles on an income of ten thousand, you can give one for a thousand on an income of twenty thousand. The latter will be somewhat better than the former, but there will nevertheless be no great splendor in it and it will be called no more than a passable ball; but then the first ball would also have been passable. Thus even vanity is satisfied only a little more at an income of twenty thousand rubles than at one of ten thousand. As far as satisfaction that can be called positive is concerned, the difference is completely insignificant. A man will keep the same table, the same wine cellar, and the same seat at the opera for himself with an income of ten thousand rubles that a man of twenty thousand will. The first will be called a man of considerable means, but the second will not be called extremely rich either—there is no real difference in their circumstances. Yet through routine everyone would be very glad to have his income increased from ten to twenty thousand, though in fact he will note practically no difrence in his pleasures.

People are in general terribly given to routine. One has only to examine their thoughts a little more deeply to see that. A person will puzzle you greatly the first time with the independence of his views from those held by the society to which he belongs. He will seem to you to be a cosmopolitan, a man without class prejudices, and so on, and like his acquaintances he will quite frankly consider himself such. But look at your cosmopolitan more carefully, and he will turn

out to be a Frenchman or a Russian with all the particularities
of customs and ideas appropriate to the nation to which his
passport indicates he belongs; he will turn out to be a landowner or official, a merchant or a professor, with all the
shades of thinking appropriate to his class.

I am convinced that people who have the habit of getting
angry with each other, of accusing each other, are so numerous simply because very few make observations of a similar
nature. Only try to begin to look at people in order to verify
whether a man who at first glance seems different from others
really differs in anything important from people in his own
class; only try to occupy yourself with such observations,
and that analysis will distract you to such an extent, will
interest your mind so much, will constantly present your spirit
such calming impressions, that you will never relinquish it,
and will soon come to the conclusion that every man is like
every other and that each is made up precisely like the others.
The longer you go on, the more firmly will you become convinced of that axiom. The differences seem important only
because they appear on the surface and strike your eye, but
beneath the visible, apparent differences is hidden a total
identity.

And indeed, why should a person really prove to be a
contradiction of all nature's laws? In nature cedars and hys-
sops feed and bloom, elephants and mice move and eat, are
angry and glad according to the same laws. Beneath an external similarity of form, there is an inner identity of the
organism of monkey and whale, eagle and chicken. One need
only penetrate into the matter a little more carefully to see
that not only are various beings of one class constructed and
live according to one and the same principle but also that
various classes are similar too. One would note that the organism of mammals, birds, and fish is identical, that even
a worm breathes like a mammal, though he has no nostrils,
trachea, or lungs. Not only would the analogy to other beings
be destroyed by the nonrecognition of the identity of the
fundamental laws and motivating forces in the moral life of
every human being; the analogy to his physical aspect would
also be destroyed.

If we take two healthy people of the same age and same
temperament, the pulse of one will naturally beat a little
faster and a little stronger than the other's. But is that difference great? It is so insignificant that even science fails
to pay any attention to it. It is a different story if you compare

two people of different ages or of different circumstances. An infant's pulse beats twice as fast as an old man's, a sick man's much faster or slower than a healthy person's, the pulse of a man who has drunk a glass of champagne faster than the pulse of a man who has drunk a glass of water. But here too it is clear to everyone that the difference does not lie in the structure of the organism but in the circumstances during which the organism is observed. When the old man was an infant, his pulse beat just as quickly as the infant's with which you compared it; and a healthy person's pulse would weaken just as much as the sick person's if he came down with the same illness. And if Peter drank a glass of champagne, his pulse would quicken just as much as Ivan's.

You have practically reached the limits of human wisdom when you become convinced of the simple truth that every person is exactly like every other one. I won't talk of the consoling consequences of that conviction for your happiness in life: you will stop getting angry and vexed; you will stop being dissatisfied and accusing people; you will look benignly upon what you were formerly ready to get angry with, or forbear to complain about a person for an action that everyone would have committed him to his place. A benign peace that can be disturbed by nothing will settle in your soul, a peace that could be sweeter only if it were the Brahman contemplation of one's navel with the quiet, incessant repetition of the words *"Om mani padme hum."* I shan't mention that priceless spiritual-practical gain; I shan't even mention the financial advantage your wise condescension toward people will win. You will now meet the rascal whom you might have kicked out before. And perhaps that rascal is a man of consequence in society, and your own affairs will benefit by your pleasant relations with him. I shan't mention either the fact that you yourself will feel less constrained by false doubts and conscience in the use of those advantages that will slip into your hands. Why should you be constrained by false delicacy if you are convinced that anybody else in your place would behave precisely the same way? I shall not parade all these material advantages, since my aim is to show only the purely scientific, theoretical importance of the conviction that human nature is the same in everyone.

If all people are really alike, then where does the difference in actions arise? While rushing to seek the main truth, we have also in passing found in it the conclusion that will serve as an answer to that question. It is now clear to us that everything depends exclusively on social customs and on circumstances; that is, in the final analysis everything depends exclusively on circumstances, because social customs in their turn also arose from circumstances. Before you accuse someone, perceive first whether he is guilty of what you accuse him or whether circumstances and social customs are responsible—look carefully, for perhaps it is not his fault at all but rather his misfortune. In thinking about others, we are all too ready to consider every misfortune guilt—therein lies a real misfortune for practical life, because guilt and misfortune are two completely different things, and one requires handling of an entirely different kind than the other. Guilt requires censure or even punishment. Misfortune calls for help to the individual by removing the circumstances that are stronger than his will.

I knew a tailor who hit his pupils in the mouth with a hot iron. He may be called guilty; he may even be punished. But not every tailor hits pupils in the mouth with a hot iron; examples of that kind of rage are quite rare. But almost every artisan gets into a fight after getting drunk on a holiday, and that is no longer guilt but simply a misfortune. What is necessary here is not punishment of a particular person, but a change in the conditions of a whole class.

The harmful confusion of guilt and misfortune is all the sadder since these two things may easily be distinguished. We have already seen one indicator of the difference: rarity, exception to the rule. Misfortune is an epidemic. Premeditated arson is a crime. Among a million people, one may decide to commit it. There is another indicator, a necessary adjunct to the first. A misfortune occurs to the very man who fulfills the conditions that lead to the misfortune. A crime is practiced on others and brings an advantage to the criminal. That last indicator is very precise. A robber kills a man in order to rob him, and finds something useful to himself in it—that's crime. A careless hunter accidentally wounds someone and is himself first tormented by the woe he has created—that is no longer crime, but simply misfortune.

The indicator is a sure one, but if it is applied with some penetration, with a careful analysis of the facts, it will appear that crimes almost never occur in the world; only misfortunes do. We just mentioned a robber. Is life easy for him? If there had not been special circumstances that were very trying for him, would he have taken up that trade? Where will you find a man who would rather hide in dens during bitter cold and inclement weather, or rove over deserts, frequently to be tormented by hunger and in constant fear for his skin, awaiting the whip, who would find that more pleasant than to smoke a cigar comfortably in an easy chair or to play whist at the English Club, the way respectable people do?

It would also have been far pleasanter for Romeo to enjoy the reciprocal pleasures of happy love than to be left holding the bag and to berate himself cruelly for his vulgar coarseness with Asya. From the fact that the cruel unpleasantness to which Asya is subjected makes him ashamed of himself, rather than bringing him pleasure or utility, and that it brings upon him the bitterest of moral vexations—from that fact we see that he did not commit a crime but was the subject of a misfortune. His base behavior would have been duplicated by very many of the so-called respectable people or better people of our society. Consequently it is nothing other than a symptom of the epidemic disease rooted in our society.

The symptom of a disease is not the disease itself. And if it were only a matter of several or, better, of almost all of the "better" people offending a girl when she has greater nobility or less experience than they, then, we admit, this would have interested us very little. Forget about them, those erotic questions! They are not for a reader of our time, occupied with problems of administrative and judiciary improvements, of financial reforms, of the emancipation of the serfs. But the scene our Romeo plays with Asya, as we noted, is only the symptom of a disease that will spoil all our affairs in precisely the same base way, and we need only examine why our Romeo had this misfortune to see what all of us, so similar to him, should expect from ourselves and for ourselves in all other affairs as well.

Let us begin with the fact that the poor young man completely fails to understand the affair he is participating in. The business is perfectly clear, but he is overcome by such dull-wittedness that he cannot comprehend the most obvious facts. We absolutely cannot imagine to what such dull-wittedness can be compared. A girl who is incapable of any pretense, who has no knowledge of cunning, says to him: "I don't know what is happening to me. Sometimes I want to cry but I begin to laugh. You must not condemn me for . . . what I am doing. Ah, by the way, what is that story about Lorelei? That's her rock that can be seen, isn't it? It is said that formerly she drowned everyone, but when she fell in love

she threw herself into the water. I like that story." It seems
quite clear what feeling is aroused in her. Two minutes later
she asks him whether he had liked that lady who had been
mentioned jokingly in a conversation several days before, and
does so with such excitement that it is even reflected in the
pallor of her face. Then she asks what he likes in women.
When he remarks how nice the sparkling sky is, she says:

"Yes, it's nice! If you and I were birds, how we would soar,
how we would fly! We would drown in that blue . . . but
we are not birds."
"But you may grow wings," I answered.
"How's that?"
"Live a little and you'll find out. There are feelings that
raise you from the ground. Don't worry, you'll have wings."
"Did you have them?"
"How shall I say . . . it seems that up to the present I
have not yet flown."

The next day Asya blushes when he arrives. She wants to
run out of the room. She is sad, and finally, remembering
yesterday's conversation, says to him, "Do you remember how
you spoke about wings yesterday? I have grown wings."
Those words were so clear that upon returning home even
our unsagacious Romeo could not help arriving at the idea,
"Does she really love me?" He fell asleep with that idea, and
when he woke up the next morning he asked himself, "Does
she really love me?"
It would really be difficult not to understand that; nevertheless he fails to understand. Did he at least understand
what was going on in his own heart? Here the signs were
less clear. After the first two meetings with Asya he felt
jealous at her tender behavior toward her brother, and out
of jealousy did not want to believe that Gagin was really
her brother. Jealousy is so potent in him that he cannot see
Asya, yet he could not refrain from seeing her either, and
therefore, like a youth of eighteen he runs away from the
village where she lives to wander in the neighboring fields
for a few days. When he finally becomes convinced that Asya
is really only Gagin's sister, he is as happy as a child, and
upon returning even feels "that tears rise to his eyes out of
rapture," feels at the same time that that rapture is concentrated completely on thoughts about Asya, and finally
reaches the point where he can think of nothing but her.
It would seem that a man who has loved several times

should understand the feelings that are expressing themselves
in him by means of those indicators. It seems that a man who
understands women well could understand what is going on in
Asya's heart. But when she writes him that she loves him, her
note takes him completely by surprise; he had never, don't
you see? guessed it. Fine. It doesn't matter whether he had
guessed that Asya loved him or not. Now he knows perfectly
clearly that Asya loves him. He sees it now. Well, what does
he feel toward Asya? He positively doesn't know how to
answer that question. The poor thing! At the age of thirty,
because he is so young, he should have a tutor to tell him
when to blow his nose, when to go to sleep, how many cups
of tea to drink. In view of such stupid inability to understand things it may seem to you that you see a child or an
idiot before you. Neither one nor the other is the case. Our
Romeo is a very intelligent man who is, as we have said, under
thirty, has experienced a great deal in life, has a rich store
of observations upon himself and others. Where does his
incredible dull-wittedness come from? Two circumstances are
responsible for it, one of which really stems from the other, so
that it is all reduced to one. He is not used to understanding
anything large and living because his life was too petty and
spiritless, because all the relationships and affairs he con-
ducted were too petty and spiritless. That's the first. The
second is that he becomes shy, he retreats feebly from everything that requires broad determination and noble risk, again
because life has taught him only pale pettiness in everything.
He is like a man who played whist for pennies all his life.
Set this skillful player in a rubber where gains and losses run
to thousands of rubles rather than to change, and you will see
that he will be completely nonplused, that all his experience
will disappear, all his skill will fail him. He will make the
stupidest plays; perhaps he will not even be able to hold his
cards properly. He is like a sailor who has journeyed all his
life from Petersburg to Kronstadt and very skillfully sailed his
little boat along a path indicated by buoys, between innumer-
able shallows in the flats. What if this sailor experienced in
his glass of water were suddenly to find himself in the ocean?
Good God! Why are we analyzing our hero so harshly? In
what way is he worse than the rest of us? When we go into
society we see around us people in dress coats or dress
uniforms; these people are five and a half or six feet tall,
and some even taller; they either shave their cheeks, upper
lip, and chin or let the hair grow. And we think that we see

men before us. That is a complete mistake, an optical illusion, a hallucination, and no more. Without acquiring the habit of independent participation in civic affairs, without acquiring the sense of citizenship, a male child will become a male creature of middle age and later of old age, but he will not become a man, or at least he will not become a man of noble character.

It is better not to raise a man than to raise him without the influence of ideas on civic affairs, without the influence of that sense that rouses participation in them. If ideas and impulses that have social utility as their goal are excluded from the sphere of my observations and of the activities in which I indulge, that is, if civic motives are excluded, what will be left for me to observe? There will remain the troubled bustling of separate individuals with their personal narrow worries about their own pocketbook, their own bellies, or their own distractions. If I observe people as they are when the feeling of participation in civic activity has been removed from them, what kind of ideas will I form about people and about life.

At one time we used to like Hoffmann, and a story of his was translated into Russian that dealt with Peregrinus Tiess' accidentally acquiring the ability to see like a microscope, and what the consequences were for his conceptions of people. Beauty, nobility, virtue, love, friendship—everything sublime and elevated disappeared from the world for him. Anyone he looked at would turn out to be a base coward or a sly intriguer, every woman a coquette, all people flatterers and egotists, petty and base to the worst degree. That terrible story could have been created only in the head of a man who looks upon what is called *Kleinstädterei*, looks at people who have no sense of civic affairs, closely limited to the narrow circle of their private interests, who have no thought of anything more elevated than their penny game of preference (which, incidentally, was not yet known in Hoffmann's day).

Think what conversation becomes in any society when it ceases to deal with civic affairs. No matter how intelligent and noble the conversationalists may be, they begin to gossip and prattle if they do not talk about civic matters. Backbiting baseness or lewd baseness, in either case senseless vulgarity, is the character a conversation that parts from civic interests necessarily assumes. One can judge the conversationalists by the nature of the conversation. If even those people who have attained the highest notions fall into empty and filthy vulgarity as soon as their thoughts turn from civic interests, then it is easy to imagine what a society that lives in complete indifference to such interests must be.

Picture to yourself a man who studied life and was raised in such a society. What would the conclusions of his experiences be? What would be the results of his observation of people? He would understand everything vulgar and trivial extremely well, but beyond that he would understand nothing, because he would not have seen or experienced anything. He could read all sorts of wonderful things in books; he could find pleasure in thinking about these wonderful things. Perhaps he would even believe that they exist or should exist in the world too, not only in books. But how could you expect him to guess at them and understand them if he were suddenly to encounter them while his unprepared mind was used only to the classifications of nonsense and vulgarity? How could you expect me to say positively when I am suddenly given real champagne, "Yes, this is really no imitation," if I have been repeatedly given as champagne a wine that never saw the vineyards of Champagne, though, incidentally, it was a very good sparkling wine? If I said that, I should be a fop. My taste merely tells me that the wine is good—but haven't I drunk plenty of food wines that were imitations? How could I know that this time too I was not brought an imitation? No, no, I am a connoisseur in imitations; I can distinguish a good one from a bad; but I cannot evaluate the real wine.

We should be happy, we should be noble if it were only an unprepared point of view or inexperience of thought that prevented us from guessing and evaluating the elevated and sublime when it occurs in our life. But no, our will, too, participated in that coarse lack of understanding. It is not only concepts that have become narrow in me as a result of the base limitations among which I live. That characteristic passes into my will as well. One's breadth of decision depends upon the breadth of view. And besides, one finally cannot help acting as everyone else does. The infectiousness of laughter, the infectiousness of yawning are not exceptional instances in social physiology—the same infectiousness is found in all phenomena that exist in large groups.

Someone once wrote a fable about a healthy man who came to the kingdom of the crippled and blind. The fable goes on to relate that he was attacked by everyone because his legs and eyes were unharmed. The fable lies, since it did not tell the whole truth. The newcomer was attacked only at the beginning; but when he had become accustomed to the new place he began to close one eye and to limp himself—it already seemed to him more comfortable to look and walk that way, or at least it seemed the decent thing to do, and soon he even forgot that strictly speaking he wasn't crippled or blinded at all. If you are a fancier of sad effects, one can add that when our traveler had occasion to walk firmly and see with both eyes he could no longer do so. It turned out that the closed eye would no longer open; the crooked leg would no longer straighten itself out. From their extended constraint the nerves and muscles of the poor distorted joints lost their capacity for acting in the correct manner.

Whoever touches coal will get dirty, to his own punishment if he did so willingly, to his misfortune if unwillingly. He who lives in a pothouse cannot help smelling drunken fumes even though he doesn't drink a single glass himself. He who lives in a society that has no interests except petty day-to-day calculations cannot help being imbued with a pettiness of will. Involuntarily timidity at the thought that perhaps the time will come to take a firm stand, to take a daring step that is a long cry from the daily constitutional—such timidity will creep into his heart. That is why you try to convince yourself that the time for such an unusual action has not yet come; you will try to convince yourself until the last fatal minute that everything that varies from the customary triviality is merely a temptation. The child who is afraid of the bogeyman shuts his eyes and shouts as loud as he can that there is no bogeyman, that the bogeyman is nonsense—that is the way he encourages himself, don't you see? We are so smart that we try to convince ourselves that we fear everything that we do only because we have no strength for anything exalted; we try to convince ourselves that that's all nonsense, that in reality there is nothing like that and will not be anything like it.

But if there is? Well, then the same thing will happen to us that happened to our Romeo in Mr. Turgenev's tale. He too did not foresee anything and did not want to foresee it. He too closed both his eyes and drew back, and when the time came—well, your elbow is near but you can't bite it.

And how brief was the moment when both his fate and Asya's were being decided—only a few minutes altogether, and upon them depended a whole life, and having let them go by, nothing could any longer correct the mistake. No sooner had he entered the room, no sooner had he managed

to pronounce several unprepared, almost unconsciously heedless words, than everything was already settled: they were
parted forever, and there was no return. We don't feel sorry
for Asya at all. It would have been hard for her to hear the
harsh words of a refusal, but it was probably better for her
that a heedless man brought her to a parting. If she had
remained connected with him, it would naturally have been a
great joy for him. But we do not think it would have been
good for her to live in close association with such a man;
whoever sympathizes with Asya must be glad that the difficult, disturbing scene took place. Whoever sympathizes with
Asya is completely right: he chose a dependent being, an
offended being as the object of his sympathy.

Yet we must admit, to our shame, that we take an interest
in our hero's fate. We do not have the honor of being his
relation; there is even enmity between our families, because
his family despised everyone like us. Yet we still cannot overcome the prejudices that have been beaten into our heads
by the false books and lessons we were raised on and which
ruined our youth; we cannot overcome the trivial concepts
inculcated in us by society around us. It constantly seemed
to us (a vain dream, but nevertheless an irresistible one for
us) that he might render our society some service, since he
is a representative of our enlightenment, since he is the best
among us, since without him we should be even worse. But
the feeling that this is a vain dream about him constantly
increases in us; we feel that we shall not stay under its influence very much longer; that there are better people than
he, to wit, those he offends; that it would be better for us to
live without him—but at the moment we have not yet come
to terms sufficiently with that idea; we have not sufficiently
torn ourselves away from the dreams on which we were
raised.

Therefore we still wish well to our hero and those like him.
While we find that the decisive moment that will determine
their fate forever is approaching in reality, we still do not
want to say to ourselves: They are incapable of understanding
their situation at present; they are incapable of acting intelligently and at the same time magnanimously at present—only
their children and grandchildren, raised on other habits and
concepts will be able to act like intelligent citizens, and they
are now inadequate to the role that is given to them. We still
do not want to apply to them the prophet's words that "seeing
they see not and hearing they hear not, for their heart is

waxed gross and their ears are dull of hearing and their eyes
have closed." No; we still want to assume them capable of
understanding what is going on around them and above
them; we want to think that they are capable of following
a wise admonishment from someone who wishes to save
them; and therefore we want to give people who do not know
how, the ability to evaluate their position in time and to use
the advantages the fleeting moment offers. Against our will
our hope for the acuity and energy of people whom we beg to
understand the importance of real circumstances and to act
in accordance with common sense decreases from day to day
—but let them at least not say that they did not hear intelligent counsel nor that their situation was not explained to
them.

Among you, gentlemen (let us turn our speech to those
worthy people), there are many literate people; they know
how happiness was depicted in ancient mythology: it was
presented as a woman with a long braid unfurled before her
by the wind that is driving her. It is easy to catch her when
she is flying up to you, but if you lose her from view for a
moment she will fly past and you will try to catch her in vain:
once you've been left behind, you cannot catch her. The
happy moment cannot be brought back. You can wait forever
for the favorable concatenation of circumstance to repeat itself, just as the configuration of heavenly bodies that occurs
at the moment will not be repeated. Not to let the propitious
moment go by—that is the highest condition of life's wisdom.
There are happy circumstances for each of us, but not everyone knows how to use them, and in that art the difference between those people whose life moves successfully and those
whose lives don't lies almost exclusively. And although you
may not have deserved it, circumstances have formed in such
a propitious way that at the decisive moment your fate
depends entirely upon you. The question of eternal happiness or unhappiness then depends upon whether or not you
will understand the demands of the moment, whether you
will be able to use those conditions into which you are then
placed.

What are the means and the rules for not letting the circumstances of happiness present to you escape? What do you
mean, What are they? Is it so difficult to say what intelligence
demands should be done in any given instance? Let us assume, for example, that I have a lawsuit in which I am completely in the wrong. Let us also assume that my opponent,

128   N. G. CHERNYSHEVSKY

who is completely in the right, has become so accustomed to
fate's injustice that he believes only faintly in the possibility
that he will ever know the outcome of our suit. It has already
lasted several decades. Many times he has asked when a
decision would be forthcoming, and has repeatedly been told
"tomorrow or the following day," but each time many months
and many years passed, and the suit was still not adjudged. I
don't know why the suit has lasted so long; I know only that
for some reason the judge is friendly toward me (apparently
he thinks that I am completely devoted to him). But now
he has received an order to pass on the matter without delay.
In his friendship for me he calls me in and says: "I can no
longer delay coming to a decision in your case. Legally it
cannot end in your favor; the laws are too clear. You will
lose everything. The business will not end with the loss of
your property. The judgment of our civil court will disclose
circumstances for which you will have to answer before a
criminal court, and you know how strict they are. I don't
know what the sentence of the criminal court will be, but I
think you would be getting away far too easily if you are
sentenced only to a loss of your rights. Just between ourselves, I think you can expect a lot worse. Today is Saturday.
On Monday your case will be drawn up and decided. I cannot
delay it any longer, despite all my affection for you. Do you
know what I would advise you to do? Put the single day you
have left to use. Offer your opponent a settlement. He still
does not know that the orders I have received make an immediate decision mandatory. He has heard that the case will
be settled Monday, but he has heard that the case will be
settled soon so many times that he has given up hope. Now
he will still agree to an amicable settlement that will be very
advantageous to you from the financial point of view, not to
speak of the fact that you will thereby be spared the criminal
trial and that you will acquire the reputation of a condescending, magnanimous man who seems to have felt the voice of
conscience and humanity. Try to finish the suit by an amicable
settlement. I ask you to do so as a friend."

Each one of you will say: "What shall I do now? Shall I
rush off to my opponent for a peaceful settlement? Or shall
I lie on the couch during the single day left to me? Or shall
I berate with coarse curses the judge who is well disposed
toward me and whose friendly warning has given me the opportunity to end my litigation with honor and advantage?"

From that example the reader will see how easy it is to decide in the given case what intelligence demands.

Agree with thine adversary quickly, while thou art in the way with him; lest at any time the adversary deliver thee to the judge, and the judge deliver thee to the officer, and thou be cast into prison. Verily I say unto thee, Thou shalt by no means come out thence, till thou hast paid the uttermost farthing. [St. Matthew 5:25-26.]

N. A. DOBROLYUBOV

What Is Oblomovitis?

OBLOMOV, A Novel by I. A. Goncharov

> Where is the one who in the native lan-
> guage of the Russian soul could pronounce
> for us the mighty word "forward"? Century
> after century passes, and a half a million
> stay-at-homes, sluggards, and blockheads
> are immersed in deep slumber, but rarely is
> a man born in Rūs who is able to pronounce
> this mighty word. . . .
>
> —*Gogol*

Our public waited for Mr. Goncharov's novel for ten years.
Long before it appeared in the press it was spoken of as a work
that was something out of the ordinary. People began to read
it with the greatest expectations. And yet, the first part of the
novel, which was written as far back as 1849 and is remote
from the current interests of the present day, seemed dull to
many. At that time *A Nest of the Gentry* appeared, and everybody was charmed by its author's poetical and highly attractive talent. Many dismissed *Oblomov* from their minds; many
were even wearied by the exceedingly subtle and profound
psychological analysis that runs through the whole of Mr.
Goncharov's novel. Those people who are fond of superficial
and entertaining action found the first part of the novel tiring
because right to the very end its hero continues to recline on
the couch on which they found him at the opening of the first
chapter. Those readers who favor the accusatory trend were
dissatisfied because our official public life was not touched
upon at all in the novel. In short, the first part of the novel
created an unfavorable impression upon many readers.

There seemed to be many indications that the entire novel
would be a failure, at all events among our public which is
accustomed to regarding all poetical literature as a source of

entertainment, and to judging works of art by first impressions. This time, however, artistic truth soon prevailed. The subsequent parts of the novel obliterated the first unfavorable impression among those who had received such impressions, and Goncharov's talent, thanks to its irresistible influence, vanquished even those who were least sympathetic toward him. The secret of this success, it seems to us, lies as much in the power of the author's artistic talent as in the exceedingly rich content of the novel.

It may seem strange that we discern exceptionally rich content in a novel which by the very character of its hero contains hardly any action. But we hope to make our idea clear in the course of this essay, the main object of which is to formulate certain observations, and deductions that, in our opinion, the content of Goncharov's novel necessarily calls for.

Undoubtedly, *Oblomov* will elicit considerable criticism. Some of it will probably be of the proofreader type, which will discover some flaws in the language and style; some of it will be pathetic and contain numerous exclamations about the charm of the scenes and characters, and some of it will be of the apothecary-aesthetic type, which will carefully scrutinize the novel to see whether all the dramatis personae have been prescribed the precise and proper doses of such and such qualities, and whether these personages always take these doses in strict conformity with the prescription. We do not feel the least desire to enter into such subtleties, nor, in all probability, will the reader grieve very much if we refrain from racking our brains over the problem as to whether such and such a sentence harmonizes with the character of the hero and his position, or whether several words should have been transposed, and so on. Therefore, we do not think it will be in the least reprehensible if we engage in more general reflections concerning the content and significance of Goncharov's novel, although, of course, the *true critics* will reproach us again for having written an essay not on Oblomov, but only *in connection with* Oblomov.

We think that in the case of Goncharov more than of any other author, it is the critic's duty to formulate the general deductions he draws from the author's work. There are authors who undertake this task themselves and explain to their readers the purpose and significance of their works. Others do not express their intentions positively, but relate their story in such a way that it turns out to be a clear and correct embodiment of their ideas. The aim of every page of the works of such authors is to make the reader understand, and one would have to be very dull indeed not to understand. . . . But the fruit of such reading is more or less complete (according to the degree of talent displayed by the author) *agreement with the idea* that underlies the given work. All the rest evaporates two hours after the book is read.

With Goncharov it is entirely different. He gives you no deductions, and evidently does not set out to do so. The life that he depicts serves him not as a subject for abstract philosophy, but as a direct object in itself. He is not concerned about the reader, or about the deduction that you draw from his novel: that is your business. If you are mistaken—blame your own shortsightedness but not the author. He presents you with a living image and guarantees only that it resembles reality; the task of defining the merit of the objects depicted is yours: it is a matter of complete indifference to him. He does not display the ardor that lends the utmost strength and charm to other talents.

Turgenev, for example, talks to us about his heroes as if they were people close to his heart; he extracts their ardent sentiments from their breasts; he watches over them with tender sympathy and painful anxiety, shares the joys and sorrows of the characters he has created, and is himself carried away by the poetical environment in which he is always so fond of placing them. . . . His enthusiasm is contagious: irresistibly he captures the sympathies of his readers, rivets their thoughts and sympathies to the narrative from the very first page, and compels them to feel, to live through themselves, the scenes in which his characters appear before them. Much time may pass and the reader may forget the plot of the story, lose the connection between the details of the various incidents, forget the characteristics of individual personages and situations, and even forget everything that he has read, but he will always retain and cherish the lively and gratifying impression he obtained from reading this story.

There is nothing like this about Goncharov. His talent does not yield to impressions. He does not burst into lyrical song on seeing a rose and on hearing a nightingale; these things will strike him, he will halt, look and listen for a long time and become immersed in reflection. . . . What processes go on in his soul at such times we can never learn exactly. . . . But he begins to sketch something. . . . You look coldly upon outlines as yet indistinct. . . . Gradually they become clearer, clearer and more beautiful . . . and suddenly, as if by a miracle, a rose and a nightingale emerge from those lines in all their beauty and charm. You not only see them; you can also smell the fragrance of the rose and hear the song of the nightingale. . . . Now sing lyrical songs if the rose and the nightingale inspire you to do so; the artist has drawn them and stands aside, satisfied with his work; he will add nothing to it. . . . "It is no use adding anything," he thinks to himself. "If the image tells your heart nothing, what can words tell you? . . ."

This ability to convey the complete image of an object, to finish it like a piece of sculpture, represents the strongest side of Goncharov's talent. And this is what particularly distinguishes him among contemporary Russian writers. It serves as an easy clue to all the other features of his talent. He possesses the amazing ability at any given moment to halt a fleeting phenomenon of life in all its fullness and freshness and hold it in front of him until the artist has taken complete possession of it. We are all struck by a bright ray of life, but it instantly vanishes almost before it affects our minds. That ray is followed by others from other objects, and these also vanish as swiftly, leaving hardly any trace. And so the whole of life passes, gliding over the surface of our minds. But not so with the artist; he is able to discern something in every object that is near and dear to his heart; he is able to halt the instant something particularly strikes him.

The sphere accessible to the artist may be wide or narrow; his impressions may be livelier or more profound; his expression of them may be more passionate or more calm, according to the nature of his poetic talent and the degree to which it is developed. Often the poet's sympathies are drawn toward one particular quality of objects, and he tries to find and bring out this particular quality; he makes it his main task to express it in the fullest and most vivid manner possible, and on this he mainly exercises his artistic powers. So artists appear who merge the inner world of their souls with the world of external phenomena, and who see all life and nature through the prism of the moods that dominate themselves. Thus, some subordinate everything to the sense of plastic beauty; others depict mainly tender and attractive features; others again, in every image, in every description, reflect humane and social strivings, and so on.

But Goncharov displays none of these leanings to any marked degree. His is a different quality: a serene and all-embracing poetical world outlook. He does not devote himself to one thing to the exclusion of all others; or rather, he devotes himself to all things equally. He is not impressed by one aspect of an object, by one phase in an event; he turns an object round and examines all its sides; he waits until all the phases in an event have occurred, and then proceeds to work them up artistically. The consequence of this is, of course, that the artist's attitude toward the objects he depicts is calmer and more dispassionate; his outline of even trifling details is more distinct, and he devotes an equal amount of attention to all the particulars of his narrative.

That is why some think that Goncharov's novel is too long drawn out. Perhaps it is too long drawn out. In the first part Oblomov lies on the couch; in the second part he goes to visit the Ilyinskys and falls in love with Olga, and she falls in love with him; in the third part she realizes that she had been mistaken in Oblomov, and they part; in the fourth part she marries Oblomov's friend Stolz, and Oblomov marries the landlady of the house in which he rents his lodgings. And that is all. No external events, no obstacles (except perhaps the raising of the bridge across the Neva that put a stop to the meetings between Olga and Oblomov), no extraneous circumstances intrude into the novel. Oblomov's indolence and apathy are the sole springs of action throughout his whole story. How could this be stretched into four parts? Had another author taken up this subject he would have treated it differently: he would have written about fifty easy and amusing pages, would have invented a lovely comedy, would have ridiculed his indolent hero, would have admired Olga and Stolz, and there the matter would have ended. The story would not have been the least bit dull, although it would not have been of any particular artistic significance.

Goncharov set to work in a different way, however. He did not lose sight of a phenomenon that had once caught his eye without tracing its progress to the end, without discovering its causes, and without discerning the connection between it and all other surrounding phenomena. His aim was to elevate to a type an image that has accidentally flashed past him; to give it generic and permanent significance. Consequently, for him, there was nothing empty or insignificant in anything that concerned Oblomov. He lovingly devoted himself to everything and drew everything distinctly and in detail. Not only the rooms in which Oblomov lived, but also the house in which he only dreamed of living; not only the dressing gown he wore, but the gray frock coat and bristling

side whiskers of his valet Zakhar; not only the way Oblomov
writes a letter but also the quality of the paper and ink of
the letter the village elder wrote to him—everything is brought
in and depicted with the fullest distinctness and relief. The
author cannot even pass by a Baron von Langwagen, who
plays no role whatever in the novel; he writes an entire page
of extreme beauty about the baron, and would have written
two and even four had he not exhausted the subject in one.
This, perhaps, slows down the action, wearies the unsym-
pathetic reader, who demands that he be irresistibly carried
away by thrills. Nevertheless, this is a precious quality in
Goncharov's talent that helps him to achieve truly artistic
delineation.

When you begin to read him you find that many of the
things he writes are seemingly not justified by strict necessity;
they seem to be out of harmony with the eternal requirements
of art. But you soon begin to accustom yourself to the world
he depicts, and in spite of yourself you admit that everything
he describes is legitimate and natural; you put yourself in the
place of the dramatis personae and begin to feel that they
could not act otherwise in the places and circumstances they
found themselves and, in fact, should not have done so. The
tiny details the author constantly introduces, and draws with
such loving care and extraordinary skill, at last begin to exercise a certain charm. You transport yourself entirely to the
world into which the author carries you, and you find in it
something that is dear to you; not only the external form, but
the innermost soul of every person and of every object reveals
itself to you. And having read the whole novel you feel that
your thoughts have been enriched by something new, that
new images, new types have been deeply engraved upon
your heart. They haunt you for a long time; you feel you want
to ponder over them, you want to ascertain [their] significance
and their relation toward your own life, your own character
and inclinations. What has become of your listlessness and
weariness? Vigorous thoughts and fresh sentiments awaken
in you. You are ready to read many of the pages again, to
ponder over them and to argue about them. This, at any rate,
is how Oblomov affected us. We read *Oblomov's Dream* and
several scenes over and over again; we read the whole novel
almost right through twice, and on the second occasion we
liked it almost better than on the first. Such is the charm of
these details the author introduces into the action and which,
in the opinion of some, *drag out* the novel.

Thus, Goncharov stands before us primarily as an artist who is capable of bringing out the fullness of the phenomena of life. To depict them is his calling, his delight; his objective art is not thwarted by theoretical prejudices or preconceived ideas; it does not yield to any one set of sympathies to the exclusion of others. It is serene, sober, and dispassionate. Is this the highest ideal of artistic endeavor, or is it, perhaps, a defect that reveals the artist's dulled perception? It would be difficult to give a categorical answer to this question; at all events, it would be unfair to do so without reservations and explanation. Many dislike the poet's calm attitude toward reality and are ready forthwith to censure sharply the unattractiveness of such a talent. We realize that such censure is logical and perhaps we ourselves are conscious of a wish that the author would tickle our senses more, would thrill us more. But we are also conscious of the fact that this wish is of a somewhat Oblomov nature and that it springs from the inclination always to have a guide—even in matters of feeling.

It is unfair to ascribe dull perception to the author only because impressions do not send him into lyrical raptures but remain silently hidden in the depths of his soul. On the contrary, the more swiftly and impetuously impressions are expressed, the more often they prove to be superficial and fleeting. We see numerous examples of this at every step in people who are endowed with an inexhaustible stock of verbal and mimical fervor. If a man is able to nurse, to nurture the image of an object in his soul and then present it fully and vividly, it shows that his keen perception is combined with profound feeling. He does not express himself prematurely, but nothing in the world is lost to him. For him all that lives and moves around him, all that enriches nature and human society

> By some miraculous means
> Lives in the depths of his soul.

He reflects every phenomenon of life like a magic mirror; at any given moment, and in obedience to his will, they halt, become motionless, and assume rigid, immobile shapes. It seems as though he can halt life itself, fix its elusive moment forever and present it to us so that we may gaze at it constantly for our instruction or enjoyment.

This power, developed to its highest perfection, is of course worth everything we call the attractiveness, charm, freshness,

or vigor of a talent. But this power also varies in degree, and
moreover it can be directed toward objects of different kinds,
which is also very important. Here we disagree with the advo-
cates of so-called *art for art's sake,* who believe that the excellent delineation of a tree leaf is as important, say, as the
excellent delineation of a human character. Subjectively, this
may be right: two artists may possess talent as such to an
equal degree and only their spheres of activity may be different. But we shall never agree that a poet who wastes his talent
on exemplary descriptions of leaf buds and brooks can be as
important as an artist who is able with equal talent to reproduce, say, the phenomena of public life. We think that for
literary criticism, for literature, and for society itself, the
question of what the talent of an artist is spent on, of how it
is expressed, is far more important than that of the degree and
quality of the talent he possesses in himself, in the abstract,
as a potentiality.

How was Goncharov's talent expressed, what was it spent
on? This question can be answered by an analysis of the
content of his novel.

Apparently Goncharov did not choose a wide field for his
delineations. The story of how good-natured and indolent
Oblomov lies and sleeps, and of how neither friendship nor
love can awaken and make him get up, is, after all, not such
an important one. But it reflects Russian life; in it there appears before us the living contemporary Russian type presented with relentless severity and truth; it reflects the new
word of our social development, pronounced clearly and
firmly, without despair and without puerile hopes, but in full
consciousness of the truth. This word is—*Oblomovitis;* it is
the key to the riddle of many of the phenomena of Russian
life, and it lends Goncharov's novel far greater social significance than all our exposure novels possess. In the Oblomov
type and in all this *Oblomovitis* we see something more than a
successful production by the hand of a strong talent; we see
a product of Russian life, a sign of the times.

Oblomov is not altogether a new personage in our literature, but never has he been presented to us so simply and
naturally as he is in Goncharov's novel. Not to go too far back
into the past, we shall say that we find the generic features
of the Oblomov type already in Onegin; and then we find
them repeated several times in the best of our literary productions. The point is that this is our native, national type, which
not one of our serious artists could brush aside. But in the

course of time, as social consciousness developed, this type
changed its shape, established a different relationship with
life, and acquired a new significance. To note these new
phases of its existence, to determine the substance of its new
significance, has always been an enormous task, and the talent
who succeeded in doing it always did a great deal for the
advancement of our literature. This is what Goncharov has
done with his *Oblomov*. We shall examine the main features
of the Oblomov type, and then we shall try to draw a slight
parallel between it and several types of the same kind that
have appeared in our literature at different times.

What are the main features of the Oblomov character?
Utter inertness resulting from apathy toward everything that
goes on in the world. The cause of this apathy lies partly in
Oblomov's external position and partly in the manner of his
mental and moral development. The external position is that
he is a gentleman: "he has a Zakhar, and another three hundred Zakhars," as the author puts it. Ilya Ilyich (Oblomov)
explains the advantages of his position to Zakhar in the following way:

"Do I fuss and worry? Do I work? Don't I have enough to
eat? Do I look thin and haggard? Am I in want of anything?
Have I not people to fetch and carry for me, to do the things
I want done? Thank God, I have never in my life had to draw
a pair of stockings on. Do you think I would go to any trouble?
Why should I? . . . But I need not tell you all this. Haven't
you served me since childhood? You know all about it. You
have seen how tenderly I was brought up. You know that I
have never suffered cold or hunger, that I have never known
want, that I don't have to earn my bread and, in general, have
never done any work."

Oblomov is speaking the absolute truth. The entire history
of his upbringing confirms what he says. He became accustomed to lolling about at a very early age because he had
people to fetch and carry for him, to do things for him. Under
these circumstances he lived the idle life of a sybarite even
when he did not want to. And tell me, pray, what can you
expect of a man who grew up under the following circumstances:

Zakhar—as his [Oblomov's] nurse did in the old days—draws
on his stockings and puts on his shoes while Ilyusha, already
a boy of fourteen, does nothing but lie on his back and put up

one foot and then the other; and if it seems to him that
Zakhar has done something not in the right way, he kicks him
in the nose. If the disgruntled Zakhar takes it into his head to
complain, he gets his ears boxed by the adults. After that,
Zakhar combs Ilya Ilyich's hair, helps him on with his coat,
carefully putting his arms into the sleeves so as not to in-
commode him too much, and reminds him that he must do so
and so and so and so: on waking up in the morning—to wash
himself, and so on.

If Ilya Ilyich wants anything he has only to make a sign—
and at once three or four servants rush to carry out his wishes;
if he drops anything, if he reaches for something he needs
and cannot get at it, if something has to be brought in, or it is
necessary to run on some errand—he sometimes, like the active
boy he is, is just eager to run and do it himself, but suddenly
his mother and his father and his three aunts shout in a
quintet:

"Where are you going? What for? What are Vaska and
Vanka and Zakharka here for? Hey! Vaska, Vanka, Zakharka!
What are you all dawdling there for? I'll let you have it! . . ."

And so Ilya Ilyich is simply not allowed to do anything for
himself. Later on he found that this was much more convenient and he learned to shout himself: "Hey, Vaska, Vanka,
bring me this, bring me that! I don't want this, I want that!
Go and bring it!"

Sometimes he got tired of the tender solicitude of his parents. If he ran down the stairs, or across the courtyard, half
a score of voices would shout after him desperately: "Ah, ah!
Hold him! Stop him! He will fall and hurt himself! Stop,
stop! . . ." If he took it into his head to go out into the hall
in the winter, or open the casement window, he would again
hear cries of: "Oh, where are you going? How dare you?
Don't run, don't walk, don't open the window; you'll hurt
yourself. You'll catch cold. . . ." And Ilyusha would sadly
stay at home, tended like an exotic flower in a hothouse, and
like the latter under glass he grew slowly and listlessly. His
strength, which vainly tried to find an outlet, turned inward,
wilted and faded.

Such an upbringing is by no means exceptional or strange
in the educated section of our society. Not everywhere, of
course, do Zakharkas help little gentlemen to put on their
stockings, and so on. But it must not be forgotten that Zakharka is thus exempted from these duties by special indul-
gence, or because of higher pedagogical considerations, and
that this is quite out of harmony with the general course of
domestic life. Perhaps the little gentleman dresses himself,
but he knows that for him it is a pleasant exercise, a whim,

that he is by no means obliged to dress himself. In fact there is no need for him to do anything. Why should he trouble? Has he not people to fetch things for him and do everything he needs? . . . That is why he will never tire himself with work, whatever people may tell him about work being a necessity and a sacred duty: from his earliest years he sees that all the domestic work in his home is performed by flunkeys and housemaids, and all that Papa and Mama do is give orders and scold the servants if they don't carry out the orders properly. And so, the first conception forms in his mind—that it is more honorable to sit with folded arms than to fuss around with work. . . . And all his subsequent development proceeds in the same direction.

The effect this position of the child has upon his entire moral and intellectual development will be understood. Its internal strength necessarily "wilts and fades." Even if the child tests that strength sometimes, it is only in whims and arrogant demands that others should obey his orders. It is well known that the satisfaction of whims develops spinelessness and that arrogance is incompatible with the ability really to maintain one's dignity. Becoming accustomed to making unreasonable demands, the boy soon loses the power to keep his wishes within the bounds of the possible and practical, loses all ability to make means conform with aims, and is therefore baffled by the first obstacle that calls for the exercise of his own efforts for its removal. When he grows up he becomes an Oblomov, possessing the latter's apathy and spinelessness to a greater or lesser degree, under a more or less skillful disguise, but always with the same invariable quality— a repugnance for serious and independent activity.

An important factor here is the mental development of the Oblomovs, which, of course, is also molded by their external position. From their earliest years they see life turned inside out, as it were, and until the end of their days they are unable to understand what their relation to the world and to people should reasonably be. Later on, much is explained to them and they begin to understand something; but the views that were inculcated in them in their childhood remain somewhere in a corner and constantly peep out from there, hindering all new conceptions and preventing them from sinking deep into their hearts. . . . As a result, chaos reigns in their heads: sometimes a man makes up his mind to do something, but he does not know how to begin, where to turn. . . . This is not surprising: a normal man always wants to do only what

he can do; that is why he immediately does all that he wants
to do. . . . But Oblomov . . . is not accustomed to doing
anything; consequently, he cannot really determine what he
can do and what he cannot do—and consequently, he cannot
seriously, *actively*, want anything. . . . His wishes always
assume the form: "How good it would be if this were done,"
but how this can be done he does not know. That is why he is
so fond of dreaming, and dreads the moment when his dreams
may come in contact with reality. When they do, he tries to
shift the burden to another's shoulders; if there are no other
shoulders, why then, *perhaps* it will get done *somehow*. . . .

All these features are splendidly noted and concentrated
with extraordinary strength and truth in the person of Ilya
Ilyich Oblomov. It must not be imagined that Ilya Ilyich
belongs to some special breed of which inertness is an essential and fundamental feature. It would be wrong to think that
nature has deprived him of the ability to move of his own
volition. This is not the case at all. Nature has endowed him
with the same gifts as she has endowed all men. As a child he
wanted to run about and play snowballs with other children,
to get one thing or another himself, to run down into the
gully, to reach the nearby birchwood by crossing the canal,
climbing over fences and jumping across ditches. When everybody in the Oblomov house was taking his or her customary
afternoon nap, he would get up to stretch his legs: he "ran to
the gallery (where nobody was permitted to go because it
threatened to collapse at any moment), ran round the creak-
ing floor, climbed up to the dovecote, wandered down to the
end of the garden, and listened to a beetle droning and followed its flight with his eyes until it was far away." Sometimes he "got into the canal, grubbed about, found some
roots, peeled off the bark and ate them with the utmost relish,
preferring them to the apples and jam that Mama used to
give him."

All this might have served as the elements of a gentle and
quiet character, but not of a senselessly indolent one. Besides,
gentleness that grows into timidity and the habit of offering
your back for others to climb on is by no means a natural
characteristic of a man, but purely an acquired one, just like
insolence and arrogance; and the distance between these two
characteristics is not so great as is usually believed. Nobody
can hold his nose in the air as high as a flunkey; nobody
treats his subordinates so rudely as one who is obsequious
toward his own superiors. With all his gentleness, Ilya Ilyich

does not hesitate to kick Zakhar in the face when the latter is putting on his shoes; and if he does not do the same to others later on in life, it is only because he anticipates opposition that he would have to overcome. Willy-nilly he confines his activities to his three hundred Zakhars. If he had a hundred, a thousand times more Zakhars, he would meet with no opposition, and he would boldly kick in the face everybody who had any dealings with him. Conduct of this kind would not be evidence of a brutal nature; Oblomov himself, and all those around him, would regard it as very natural and necessary. . . . It would not occur to any of them that it is possible and necessary to behave differently. But unfortunately, or fortunately, Ilya Ilyich was born a small country squire with an estate that provided him with an income that did not exceed ten thousand rubles; consequently, he could mold the destiny of the world only in his dreams. But in his dreams he was fond of giving himself up to bellicose and heroic ambitions:

Sometimes he liked to picture himself an invincible general, compared with whom not only Napoleon but even Yeruslan Lazarevich was a nonentity; he would picture a war and its cause: for example, Africans would come pouring into Europe, or he would organize new crusades and would fight, decide the fate of nations, sack towns, show mercy, execute, perform acts of kindness and generosity.

Sometimes he would picture himself as a great thinker or artist who is followed by admiring crowds. . . . Clearly, Oblomov is not a dull, apathetic type, destitute of ambition and feeling; he too seeks something in life, thinks about something. But the disgusting habit of getting his wishes satisfied not by his own efforts but by the efforts of others developed in him an apathetic inertness and plunged him into the wretched state of moral slavery. This slavery is so closely interwoven with Oblomov's aristocratic habits that they mutually permeate and determine each other, so that it becomes totally impossible to draw any line of demarcation between them. This moral slavery of Oblomov's is, perhaps, the most interesting side of his personality, and of his whole life. . . . But how could a man enjoying the independent position of Ilya Ilyich sink into slavery? If anybody can enjoy freedom, surely he can! He is not in the civil service; he does not go into society; and he has an assured income. . . . He himself boasts that he does not have to bow and scrape and humiliate himself, that he is not like "others" who work tirelessly, fuss

and run about, and if they do not work they do not eat. . . .
He inspires the good widow Pshenitsyn with reverent love
for himself precisely because he is a *gentleman,* because he
shines and glitters, because he walks and talks so freely and
independently, because "he is not constantly copying papers,
does not tremble with fear that he might be late at the office,
because he does not look at everybody as if asking to be
saddled and ridden on, but looks at everybody and everything
boldly and freely, as if demanding obedience." And yet, the
whole life of this gentleman is wrecked because he always
remains the slave of another's will and never rises to the level
of displaying the least bit of independence. He is the slave of
every woman, of every newcomer; the slave of every rascal
who wishes to get him under his thumb. He is the slave of his
serf Zakhar, and it is hard to say which of them submits more
to the power of the other. At all events, if Zakhar does not
wish to do a thing Ilya Ilyich cannot make him do it; and if
Zakhar wants to do anything he will do it, even if his master
is opposed to it—and his master submits. . . . This is quite
natural: Zakhar, after all, can at least do something; Oblomov
cannot do anything at all. It is needless to speak of Tarantyev
and Ivan Matveyich, who do anything they like with Oblomov in spite of the fact that they are far inferior to him both
in intellectual development and in moral qualities. . . . Why
is this? Again the answer is, because Oblomov, being a gentleman, does not wish to work, nor could he even if he wanted
to; and he cannot understand his own relation to everything
around him. He is not averse to activity as long as it is in the
form of a vision and is far removed from reality: thus, he
draws up a plan for the improvement of his estate and
zealously applies himself to this task—only "details, estimates,
and figures" frighten him, and he constantly brushes them
aside, for how can he bother with them! . . . He is a gentleman, as he himself explains to Ivan Matveyich:

"Who am I? What am I? you will ask. . . . Go and ask
Zakhar, he will tell you, 'A gentleman,' he will say! Yes, I am
a gentleman, and I can't do anything! You do it, if you know
how, and help if you can, and for your trouble take what you
like—that's what knowledge is for!"

Do you think that in this way he is only shirking work,
trying to cover up his own indolence with the plea of ignorance? No, he really does not know how to do anything and
cannot do anything; he is really unable to undertake any use-

ful task. As regards his estate (for the reorganization of which
he had already drawn up a plan), he confesses his ignorance
to Ivan Matveyich in the following way:

"I don't know what corvée is. I know nothing about hus-
bandry. I don't know the difference between a poor peasant
and a rich one. I don't know what a quarter of rye, or oats is,
what its price is, in which months different crops are sown
and reaped, or how and when they are sold. I don't know
whether I am poor or rich, whether I will have enough to eat
next year, or whether I shall be a beggar—I don't know anything! . . . Therefore, speak and advise me as if I were a
child. . . ."

In other words: be my master, do what you like with my
property and leave me what share of it you think best. . . .
And that is what happened: Ivan Matveyich nearly grabbed
Oblomov's entire estate, but unfortunately Stolz prevented
him.

But Oblomov was not only ignorant of agricultural matters;
he not only failed to understand the state of his own affairs:
that would have been only half the trouble! . . . The main
trouble was that he could see no meaning in life in general.
In the Oblomov world nobody asked himself: Why life, what
is life, what is its meaning and purpose? The Oblomovs had
a very simple conception of life:

They conceived it as an ideal of repose and inaction, disturbed at times by various unpleasant accidents such as: sick-
ness, losses, quarrels and, incidentally, work. They tolerated
work as a punishment imposed on our ancestors, but they
could not love it, and they always shirked it whenever possible, deeming this permissible and right.

This is exactly how Ilya Ilyich looked upon life. The ideal
happiness that he described to Stolz consisted in nothing
more than a life of plenty, with conservatories, hothouses,
picnics in the woods with a samovar, and so on—a dressing
gown, sound sleep, and by way of a rest in between—idyllic
walks with a meek but plump wife, gazing at the peasants at
work. Oblomov's mind was so molded from childhood that he
was able, even in the most abstract arguments, in the most
utopian theories, to halt in the present and never leave this
status quo in spite of all arguments. In depicting his conception of ideal bliss Ilya Ilyich never thought of asking himself

what its inherent meaning was; he never thought of asserting its lawfulness or truth; he never asked himself where these conservatories and hothouses were to come from, who was to maintain them, and on what grounds he was to enjoy them. . . .

Failing to put such questions to himself, failing to clear up his own relation to the world and to society, Oblomov, of course, could not grasp the meaning of his own life and, therefore, found everything he had to do irksome and tedious. When he was in the civil service he could not for the life of him understand why all those documents were being written; and, failing to understand, he could think of nothing better than to resign and do no more writing. He went to school, but he could not understand the purpose of this instruction: and, failing to understand, he piled his books up in a corner and indifferently watched the dust accumulating on them. He went into society, but he could not understand why people visited each other; and failing to understand, he gave up all his acquaintances and lolled on his couch for days on end. He tried to befriend women, but he began to ask himself what could be expected of them, what one should expect of them; and after pondering over the matter, and failing to find an answer, he began to avoid women. . . . Everything bored and wearied him, and he lolled on his couch filled with utter contempt for the "human ant heap," where people worried and fussed, God knows what about. . . .

Having reached this point in explaining Oblomov's character we deem it appropriate to turn to the literary parallel we drew above. The foregoing reflections have brought us to the conclusion that Oblomov is not a being whom nature has completely deprived of the ability to move by his own volition. His indolence and apathy are the result of upbringing and environment. The main thing here is not Oblomov, but Oblomovitis. Perhaps Oblomov would even have begun work had he found an occupation to his liking; but for that he would have had to develop under somewhat different conditions. In his present position he cannot find an occupation to his liking because he sees no meaning in life in general and cannot rationally define his own relations to others. This is where he provides us with the occasion for comparing him with previous types, which the best of our writers have depicted.

It was observed long ago that all the heroes in the finest Russian stories and novels suffer from their failure to see any

purpose in life and their inability to find a decent occupation
for themselves. As a consequence they find all occupations
tedious and repugnant, and in this they reveal an astonishing
resemblance to Oblomov. Indeed, open, for example, *Onegin*,
A Hero of Our Times, Who Is To Blame?, Rudin, Unwanted,
or *Hamlet from Shchigry County*—in every one of these you
will find features almost identical with Oblomov's.

Onegin, like Oblomov, gives up society because he was

> Weary of inconstancy
> And of friends and friendship too.

And so he took to writing:

> Abandoning wild gaiety
> Onegin stayed at home,
> He picked his pen up with a yawn
> And wished to write, but diligence
> To him was loathsome; nothing
> From his pen would come.

Rudin too launched out in this field and was fond of reading
to the chosen "the first pages of the essays and works he
intended to write." Tentetnikov also spent many years writing "a colossal work that was to deal with the whole of
Russia from all points of view," but in this case too, "this
undertaking was confined mainly to thinking: his pen was
bitten to shreds, drawings appeared on the paper, and then
everything was thrust aside." Ilya Ilyich was not behind his
brothers in this respect; he too wrote and translated—he even
translated Say.

"Where is your work, your translations?" Stolz asked him
later.

"I don't know, Zakhar put them away somewhere. They
are lying in the corner, I suppose," Oblomov answers.

It appears, therefore, that Ilya Ilyich may have done even
more than the others who had set down to their tasks as de-
terminedly as he had. . . . Nearly all the brethren in the Oblomov family set to work in this field in spite of the difference
in their respective positions and mental development. Pechorin
alone looked down superciliously upon "the storymongers and
writers of bourgeois dramas"; but even he wrote his memoirs.
As for Beltov, he must certainly have written something; besides, he was an artist, he visited the Hermitage and sat behind an easel planning to paint a large picture depicting the

meeting between Biren who was returning from Siberia and
Münnich who was going to Siberia. . . . What came of this
the reader knows. . . . The same Oblomovitis reigned in the
whole family. . . .

As regards "borrowing wisdom," that is, reading, Oblomov
also differs from his brethren. Ilya Ilyich has also read something, and has not read it in the way his late father used to
read: "I haven't read a book for a long time," he would say,
"let's have a look at one." And he would pick up the first book
that came to his hand. . . . No, the ideas of modern education have affected even Oblomov: he reads intelligently, and
chooses what to read:

If he hears about some remarkable work he feels an urge to
become acquainted with it; he looks for it, asks for it, and if
it is brought to him soon he will begin to read it, and an idea
begins to form in his mind about the subject; one more step,
and the idea would be complete, but before you can look
round he is already lying on the couch, gazing apathetically
at the ceiling, while the book is lying next to him unfinished
and not understood. . . . He had cooled toward it quicker
than the desire to read it had seized him: he never took up an
abandoned book again.

Is it not the same with the others? Onegin thought of borrowing wisdom and began by

Lining his shelf with a detachment of books,

and settling down to read. But nothing came of it. He soon
got tired of reading and

His books, like his women, he deserted
And across the shelf with its dusty crew
He a black crape curtain drew.

Tentetnikov read books in the same way (because he was accustomed to having them always at hand); he read mostly
while having his dinner "with the soup, with the sauce, with
the roast, and even with the pie. . . ." Rudin also confessed
to Lezhnev that he had bought some books on agriculture, but
had not read even one to the end; he became a teacher, but
found that he knew too few facts, and concerning some relic
of the sixteenth century he was proved wrong by a teacher of
mathematics. He, like Oblomov, could grasp easily only gen-

eral ideas; as for "details, estimates, and figures," he always brushed them aside.

"But this is not yet life, it is only the preparatory school for life," mused Andrei Ivanovich Tentetnikov as he, together with Oblomov and the whole of that company, plodded through a host of useless subjects, unable to apply even an iota of them to actual life. "Real life is in the service." And so, all our heroes, except Onegin and Pechorin, go into the service; and for all of them this service is a useless and senseless burden, and all end up by resigning, early and with dignity. Beltov was fourteen years and six months short of qualifying for a clasp because, after working with intense zeal for a time, he soon cooled toward office work and became irritable and careless. . . . Tentetnikov had some high words with his chief, and, moreover, he wanted to be useful to the state by personally taking over the management of his estate. Rudin quarreled with the headmaster of the high school at which he served as a teacher. Oblomov disliked the fact that all the members of the staff spoke to the chief "not in their natural but in some other kind of voices, squeaky and disgusting." He rebelled at the idea of having to explain to his chief in this voice why "he had sent a certain document to Arkhangelsk instead of Astrakhan," and so he resigned. . . . Everywhere we see the same Oblomovitis. . . .

The Oblomovs resemble each other very closely in domestic life too:

> Sound sleep, a stroll, an entertaining book,
> A forest glade and a babbling brook,
> A dark-eyed beauty,
> Young and fresh to kiss sometimes,
> The bridle of a restive steed,
> Dinner to suit his fastidious needs,
> A bottle of light wine,
> Solitude, tranquillity,
> Holy is the life Onegin leads. . . .

Word for word, except for the steed, this is the kind of life that Ilya Ilyich regards as the ideal of domestic bliss. Oblomov does not even forget the kissing of a dark-eyed beauty:

"One of the peasant women," muses Ilya Ilyich, "with a tanned neck, her sleeves rolled up above her elbows, her sly eyes shyly drooping, just a little, only for appearance sake resisting the squire's embraces, but actually enjoying them . . .

only—the wife mustn't see, God forbid!" (Oblomov imagines
that he is already married). . . .

And if Ilya Ilyich had not been too lazy to leave St. Petersburg for his country seat, he would undoubtedly have tried to
achieve his cherished idyl. In general, the Oblomovs dream
of an idyllic, idle bliss that will cost them no effort and that
seems to say, "Take delight in me, that's all." Pechorin is
active enough, heaven knows, but even he believes that real
bliss lies in calm and sweet repose. In one passage of his
memoirs he compares himself to a starving man who "falling
asleep from exhaustion, dreams of sumptuous food and sparkling wine; he consumes the airy gifts of his imagination with
the utmost relish and feels refreshed . . . but no sooner does
he awake than his dream vanishes, and he feels twice as
hungry and desperate as before. . . ." In another passage
Pechorin asks himself: "Why did I not take the path that
destiny had opened for me and where quiet joys and spiritual
calm awaited me?" He himself believes that it was because
"his soul had accustomed itself to storms and craved for seething activity. . . ." But he is always displeased with the
struggle he is waging, and he himself is constantly saying that
he indulges in all this disgusting debauchery only because he
cannot find anything better to do. . . . And since he cannot
find anything to do and, as a consequence, does nothing and
is pleased with nothing, it shows that he is disposed more to
idleness than to activity. . . . It is the same old Oblomovitis. . . .

The attitude of all the Oblomovs toward other people, and
toward women in particular, also has certain common features. They hold all people in contempt because of the petty
labors they engage in, because of their narrow concepts and
shortsighted strivings. "They are all common laborers," is the
supercilious comment even of Beltov, the most humane of
them. Rudin naïvely imagines that he is a misunderstood
genius. Pechorin, of course, tramples everybody underfoot.
Even Onegin has two lines written about him, which read:

> He who has lived and thought grows scornful,
> And must at heart all men despise.

Even Tentetnikov, meek though he was, felt on entering
his office for the first time "as if, for some misdemeanor, he
had been degraded from the upper class to the lower," and on

arriving in the country he soon tried, like Onegin and Oblomov, to get unacquainted with all the neighbors who had hurried to make his acquaintance. And our Ilya Ilyich yields to
no one in his contempt for people: this is so easy that it requires no effort whatever. In front of Zakhar he smugly compares himself with "others"; in conversation with his friends
he expresses naïve surprise that people should worry so much,
compel themselves to go to work, to write, to read newspapers, to go into society, and so forth. In conversation with
Stolz he expresses his sense of superiority over other people
in the most categorical terms:

"They say that life is to be found in society. A nice life, to
be sure! What can you find in it? Anything that can interest
the mind and the heart? Where is the hub around which all
this turns? There's no hub. There's nothing profound that can
touch you to the quick. They are all lifeless, dormant people
are these men of the world and of society. Worse than I
am! . . ."

And Ilya Ilyich proceeds eloquently to expatiate on this subject in a way that would be worthy of Rudin himself.

In their attitude toward women all the Oblomovs behave
in an equally disgraceful manner. They are totally incapable
of loving and they have no more idea about what to seek in
love than they have about what to seek in life in general. They
are not averse to philandering with a woman as long as she
seems to them to be a doll moved by springs; nor are they
averse to enslaving a woman's heart . . . why not? This
pleases their gentlemanly natures exceedingly! But no sooner
does the affair become in any way serious, no sooner do they
begin to suspect that they are dealing not with a doll, but with
a woman who may demand that they should respect her
rights, than they turn tail and fly for their lives. The cowardice
of all these gentlemen is amazing! Onegin, who was able "early
in his life to disturb the hearts of hardened coquettes," who
sought women "without ardor and deserted them without regret," showed the white feather in front of Tatyana, showed
it twice—once when he took a lesson from her, and again
when he gave her a lesson. After all, he liked her the moment
he set eyes on her, and had she loved him less deeply he
would not have permitted himself to adopt that tone of stern
mentor toward her. But he saw that he was playing with fire
and began to talk about his spent life, his bad character, about
her falling in love with somebody else in future, and so forth.

Subsequently, he himself explains his conduct by the fact that "noticing the spark of tenderness in Tatyana, he did not wish to believe in it," and that

> His bleak and barren freedom
> He did not wish to lose.

With what beautiful phrases he covered up his own cowardice!

As we know, Beltov too dared not go to the end with Krutsiferskaya, and fled from her, although for quite different reasons if we are to believe what he says. Rudin entirely lost his head when Natalya tried to get something definite out of him. He dared not do any more than advise her to "be resigned." Next day, he wittily explained to her in a letter that he "had not been in the habit" of dealing with women like her. Such also was Pechorin, an expert in matters of the feminine heart, who confessed that he loved nothing in the world but women, and that for them he was prepared to sacrifice everything in the world. He too confesses, first, that he "cannot love women who have character: what business have they to have character?" And second, that he can never marry:

> "However passionately I might love a woman," he says, "if she makes me only feel that I must marry her—good-bye to love. My heart turns to stone and nothing warms it again. I am ready to make every sacrifice except that; I am ready to stake my life, even my honor twenty times, but I will never sell my liberty. Why do I cherish it so much? What do I want it for? What am I preparing myself for? What do I expect from the future? Absolutely nothing. It is a sort of innate fear, an inexplicable presentiment," and so forth.

Actually, it is nothing more than Oblomovitis.

Do you think that Ilya Ilyich has not in him a Pechorin and Rudin, not to speak of an Onegin element? Indeed he has, and how much of it! For example, he, like Pechorin, is determined to *possess* a woman, to compel her to make all sorts of sacrifices to prove her love. At first, you see, he had no hope that Olga would agree to marry him, and proposed to her very timidly. She answered something to the effect that he should have proposed long ago. This embarrassed him; it was not enough that Olga had accepted him, and so—what do you think? . . . He began to question her to find out whether she loved him enough to become his mistress! And he was vexed

when she said that she would never agree to anything like
that; but her explanation and the passionate scene that followed calmed him. . . . In the end his cowardice so overcame him that he was even afraid to see Olga; he pleaded in-
disposition, that the bridge was raised and he could not cross
the river, he gave Olga to understand that she might compromise him, and so forth. Why? Because she wanted him to
decide, to act, and this was not his habit. Marriage itself did
not frighten him so much as it frightened Pechorin and
Rudin; his habits were more patriarchal. But Olga wanted
him to settle the affairs of his estate before they were married;
that would have meant *sacrifice*. He would not make that
sacrifice, of course, and proved himself a true Oblomov. He
himself, however, was extremely exacting. He played Olga a
trick that one might have expected from Pechorin. He took
it into his head that he was not very prepossessing in appearance and, in general, not attractive enough to make Olga love
him very strongly. And so he began to suffer; he could not
sleep at night; and finally, mustering all his energy, he wrote
Olga a long letter in the Rudin style, in which he repeated the
old and threadbare story that Onegin had told Tatyana, that
Rudin had told Natalya, and that even Pechorin had told
Princess Mary, namely, "I am not made in such a way that you
could be happy with me. In time you will love another, more
worthy than I."

> Again and again will maiden fair
> Change her dreams and fancies. . . .
> You'll love again—but do take care,
> Learn to keep yourself in hand;
> Not everyone, like I, will understand. . . .
> And innocence may lead you to despair.

All the Oblomovs like to humiliate themselves, but they do
so in order to have the satisfaction of being contradicted, of
hearing praise from those to whom they are speaking depre-
catingly about themselves. They delight in this self-abase-
ment; all are like Rudin, concerning whom Pigasov says: "He
begins to revile himself and grovel in the mud, and you feel
sure that he will never look people in the face again. But
nothing of the kind! He soon becomes so merry that you think
he has been swilling vodka!" In the same way Onegin too,
after reviling himself in Tatyana's presence, begins to parade
his generosity. And Oblomov behaves in the same way when,
after writing Olga a lampoon about himself, he felt "not so

depressed, almost happy. . . ." And he concludes his letter
with a sermon similar to that with which Onegin concluded
his speech: "Let your relations with me," he wrote, "serve you
as a guide in your future, normal love," and so forth. Ilya
Ilyich did not, of course, continue his self-humiliation before
Olga to the end: he rushed to see what impression his letter
made upon her, he saw her weeping, he was satisfied and—
could not refrain from presenting himself before her at this
crucial moment. But she proved to him what vulgar and miserable egoism he displayed in that letter, which he had written
"out of concern for her happiness." Here his courage oozed
out completely, as indeed it does with all the Oblomovs when
they meet a woman who is superior to them in character and
intelligence.

Profound people will protest and say: "However, in spite of
the selection of apparently similar facts, there is no sense in
the parallels you have drawn. In defining character, it is not
so much outward manifestations that are important as the
motives which prompt a man to do this or the other. As regards motive, how is it possible not to see the vast difference
between Oblomov's conduct and that of Pechorin, Rudin, and
the others? . . . Oblomov does everything by inertia, because he is too lazy to move, and too lazy to resist when he is
pushed; his whole object is not to move a finger unnecessarily.
The others, however, are prompted by a thirst for activity;
they undertake everything with the greatest zeal, they are
always

> Prompted by a restless spirit,
> A yearning for a change of scene,

and suffer from other ailments that are symptoms of a strong
character. If they do nothing that is truly useful, it is because
they cannot find activities commensurate with their strength.
They, as Pechorin puts it, are like genii chained to the clerk's
desk and doomed to copy documents. They tower above the
realities of life and, therefore, have a right to hold life and
men in contempt. Their whole life is a negation, a reaction
against the present order of things; Oblomov's life, however,
consists in passive submission to existing influences, a conservative repugnance to all change, an utter lack of internal
reaction due to his nature. Can these men be compared? What!
Put Rudin on the same plane as Oblomov! . . . Denounce
Pechorin for being as much a nonentity as Ilya Ilyich! . . .

This is evidence of complete lack of understanding; it is absurd—it is a crime! . . ."

Good God! We have indeed forgotten that one must keep a sharp lookout when dealing with profound people; they are sure to draw conclusions that you did not even dream of. If you intend to bathe in the river, and a profound person standing on the bank with his hands tied boasts that he is a splendid swimmer and promises to go to your rescue if you should drown, don't dare say: "But my dear friend, your hands are tied! Had you not better first get somebody to untie your hands?" Don't dare to say that because the profound person will at once flare up and say: "Ah! You say that I can't swim! You are praising the one who tied my hands! You don't sympathize with people who rescue the drowning! . . ." And so on and so forth. . . . Profound people can be very eloquent and profuse in drawing the most unexpected conclusions. . . . And so it is in this case: they will at once jump to the conclusion that we wanted to place Oblomov on a higher plane than Pechorin and Rudin, that we wanted to justify his indolence, that we are unable to see the inherent fundamental difference between him and the preceding heroes, and so on. We hasten to explain ourselves to the profound people.

In all that we have said, we had Oblomovitis in mind rather than the personality of Oblomov and the other heroes. As regards personalities, we could not fail to see a difference in temperament of, say, Pechorin and Oblomov, Pechorin and Onegin, or Rudin and Beltov. . . . Who will deny that there is a difference in personality among men (although, perhaps, not nearly so great and as important as is usually supposed). The point, however, is that weighing heavily upon all these persons is the same Oblomovitis, which imposes upon them the indelible impress of indolence, idleness, and utter uselessness. It is highly probable that under other conditions of life, in a different society, Onegin would have been a really good fellow, Pechorin and Rudin would have performed doughty deeds, and Beltov would have proved to be a man of excellent qualities. But under other conditions of development Oblomov and Tentetnikov too, perhaps, would not have been such drones, and would have found some useful occupation. . . . But the point is that at the present time they all have one common feature—a barren striving for activity, the consciousness that they could do a great deal but will do nothing. . . . In this respect, they resemble one another to an astonishing degree:

I look back upon the whole of my past life and involuntarily ask myself: What have I lived for? What was I born for? . . . There must have been some reason; I must have had some lofty mission, because in my soul I feel that I possess boundless strength. But I failed to realize what this mission was; I allowed myself to be tempted by hollow and ungratifying passions; I emerged from the crucible hard and cold like iron, but I had forever lost the ardor of noble striving—life's finest flower.

That was Pechorin. . . . And here is how Rudin reasons about himself:

Yes, nature was bounteous with her gifts to me; but I shall die without having done anything worthy of my powers, without leaving any beneficial trace. All my wealth will be wasted: I shall not see the fruit of the seeds I have sown.

Ilya Ilyich is not behind the rest. He too "painfully felt that some good, bright element was buried within him as in a grave, perhaps dead now, or lying idle like gold in the depths of the mountains, and that it was high time that this gold served as coin. But this treasure lies buried deep down under a heavy weight of rubbish and refuse. It was as if somebody had stolen the treasure the world and life had bestowed upon him and had buried it in his own soul.

Do you see—a *treasure* was buried in his soul, but he was never able to reveal it to the world. His brothers, younger than he, "are roaming over the world

> Seeking great deeds to perform,
> Since the heritage of their wealthy sires
> Had freed them from life's petty cares. . . .

Oblomov too, when he was young, dreamed of "serving while his strength lasted, because Russia needs hands and heads to develop her inexhaustible resources. . . ." And even now, "he is responsive to universal human suffering and is capable of enjoying the pleasures of lofty thoughts"; and although he does not roam the world in quest of great deeds to perform, he nevertheless dreams of activity of world-wide importance, looks down with contempt upon the common laborer, and ardently exclaims:

> No, I shall not waste my soul
> In the ant heap labors of men. . . .

He is no more idle than all the other Oblomov brethren; he is only more candid than they—he makes no attempt to cover up his idleness even with talk in society or strolling along Nevsky Prospect.

But what causes the difference in the impression produced upon us by Oblomov and the heroes we referred to above? The heroes seem to us in their different ways to be strong natures crushed by an unfavorable environment, whereas Oblomov is a drone, who will do nothing even under the most favorable circumstances. But in the first place, Oblomov's temperament is extremely phlegmatic, and naturally, there-fore, he makes feebler attempts to carry out his plans and to resist his hostile environment than the more vigorous Onegin or jaundiced Pechorin. Actually, however, they are all equally unable to resist the forces of their hostile environment; all equally sink to the level of nonentities when real and serious activity confronts them. In what way did Oblomov's environ-ment open up for him a favorable field for activity? He had an estate he could have put in order; he had a friend who urged him to take up practical activity; there was a woman who was superior to him in vigor and clarity of views, and who loved him tenderly. . . . But tell me, which of the Oblomovs was destitute of all this, and what did they do with it all? Both Onegin and Tentetnikov pottered about on their estates; and about Tentetnikov, the peasants even said at first, "Sharp-eyed, isn't he!" But soon those same peasants tumbled onto the fact that their squire, although keen at first, under-stood nothing, and would do nothing practical. . . .

But what about friendship? What do they all do with their friends? Onegin killed Lensky; Pechorin is always quarreling with Werner; Rudin succeeded in repelling Lezhnev and failed to take advantage of Pokorsky's friendship. . . . And did not each of them meet many Pokorskys in the course of his life? What did they do? Did they combine for some com-mon cause? Did they form a close alliance to defend them-selves against their hostile environment? Nothing of the kind. . . . Everything was swept to the winds; it all ended in the same old Oblomovitis. . . . It is needless to speak of love. Everyone of the Oblomovs met a woman superior to himself (because Krutsiferskaya is superior to Beltov, and even Prin-cess Mary is, after all, superior to Pechorin), and every one of them ignominiously fled from her love, or did his best to make her dismiss him. . . . How can this be explained if not by the pressure that despicable Oblomovitis exercised upon them?

In addition to difference in temperament, there is also a great difference in age between Oblomov and the other heroes. We are not speaking of age in years: in that respect they are almost equal, Rudin was even two or three years older than Oblomov. We have in mind the time in which they appeared. Oblomov appeared at a later period and, therefore, to the younger generation, our contemporaries, he must look much older than the previous Oblomovs at his age. . . . When he was still at the university, at the age of seventeen or eighteen, he was already conscious of the same strivings, became imbued with the same ideas that inspired Rudin at the age of thirty-five. After that only two roads lay open before him: either activity, real activity—not with the tongue, but with the head and heart and hands together—or simply lying down with folded arms. His apathetic nature brought him to the latter: this is bad, but at all events there is no falsehood and pretense here. If he, like his brothers, had begun to talk loudly about what he only dares dream of now, he would have felt day after day the same annoyance that he felt on receiving the letter from the village elder, and on receiving notice to quit from his landlord. In the old days phrasemongers who talked loudly about the necessity of this or that, about lofty ambitions, and so on, were listened to with awe. Then, perhaps, Oblomov too would not have been averse to talking. . . . But nowadays all phrasemongers and schemers are confronted with the demand, "Why not try your hand at it yourself?" This the Oblomovs cannot stand. . . .

Indeed, how one feels the breath of the new life when, after reading *Oblomov*, one ponders over the circumstances that called this type into being in literature. It cannot be ascribed solely to the talent of the author and to the breadth of his views. We find talent and views of the broadest and most humane kind among the authors who portrayed the earlier types that we referred to above. But the point is that thirty years have passed since Onegin, the first of them, appeared. That which existed in embryo at that time, what was expressed only in vague hints and whispers, has now assumed firm and definite shape; it is being expressed openly and loudly. Phrases no longer count; society itself feels the need of real deeds. Beltov and Rudin, who were imbued with strivings that were truly lofty and noble, not only did not feel the urge to enter into mortal combat with the environment that was crushing them; they could not even conceive of such a combat as an early possibility. They entered a dense and unexplored forest, trod dangerous bogs, saw various snakes and reptiles creeping at their feet, and they climbed trees—partly to see if there was a road nearby, and partly to rest and to escape for a while the danger of being sucked into the bog or of being stung. The people who followed them waited to hear what they would say, and looked up to them with awe as pioneers. But these pioneers saw nothing from the heights to which they had climbed: the forest was too vast and dense. Meanwhile, in climbing the trees they scratched their faces and hurt their feet and hands. . . . They are in pain, they are weary, they must rest by making themselves as comfortable as possible among the branches. True, they do nothing for the common weal; they have seen nothing, and have said nothing; those standing below must hew and clear a road for themselves through the forest without their aid. But who would dare to cast stones at those unfortunate ones to make them drop from the height on which they have ensconced themselves with such difficulty, having the common weal in mind? They meet with sympathy; they are not even called upon to help to clear the forest; theirs was a different mission, and they have performed it. If nothing has come of it, it is not their fault.

In the past, every author could regard his Oblomov as a hero from this point of view, and he was right. To this we must add that the hope of finding a way out of the forest to the road was long cherished by the whole crowd of wayfarers, and that belief in the farsightedness of the pioneers who had climbed up the tree also lasted for quite a long time. But little by little the situation cleared and took a different turn; the pioneers have got accustomed to the tree and like it; they argue very eloquently about different ways and means of getting out of the bog and the forest; they have even found some kind of fruit on the tree and are enjoying it, throwing the rind to the ground below; they invite a few chosen ones from the crowd to join them, and these climb the tree and remain there, not to look out for the road, but only to gobble the fruit. These are the Oblomovs in the proper sense of the term. . . .

And the poor wayfarers standing below sink into the bog, they are stung by snakes and frightened by reptiles, swinging branches slash their faces. . . . At last the crowd decides to set to work, and calls those who had climbed the tree later to come down again, but the Oblomovs make no reply and go on gorging themselves with fruit. The crowd then appeals to

the former pioneers to come down and assist in the common
effort, but the pioneers merely repeat the old argument that it
is necessary to find the road, that clearing a road through the
forest would be useless toil. The poor wayfarers then see their
mistake, and say with a gesture of disgust: "Ekh! You are all
Oblomovs!" After that they set to work in real earnest: they
fell trees, use the logs to build a bridge across the bog, clear a
track, kill the snakes and reptiles that creep onto it, and give
no further thought to those wiseacres and strong characters,
the Pechorins and Rudins, upon whom they had formerly re-
posed their hopes, and whom they had so much admired.

At first the Oblomovs calmly look on at the general activity,
but later, as is their habit, they become alarmed and begin to
shout. . . . "Oh! Oh! Don't do that! Stop!" they howl when
they see the people setting to work to cut down the tree on
which they are ensconced. "Don't you realize that we may be
killed and that with us will perish those beautiful ideas, those
lofty sentiments, those humane strivings, that eloquence, that
fervor, that love for all that is beautiful and noble that have
always inspired us? Stop! Stop! What are you doing? . . ."
But the wayfarers have heard these beautiful phrases a thousand times, and they go on with their work without paying
the slightest attention to them. The Oblomovs still have a
means of saving themselves and their reputations, namely, to
climb down the tree and join the others in their work; but, as
they are in the habit of doing, they lose their heads and are
at a loss what to do. . . . "What's this, all of a sudden?" they
keep asking themselves in their despair, and go on hurling
their impotent curses at the stupid mob that had lost all respect for them.

But the crowd is right! Once it has realized that it is necessary to set to work in real earnest, it makes no difference to
it whether a Pechorin or an Oblomov stands before it. Again,
we do not say that under the given circumstances Pechorin
would act exactly in the same way as Oblomov; by virtue of
the same circumstances he may have developed in another direction. But the types great talent has created are long-lived;
even today there are people who seem to be copies of Onegin,
Pechorin, Rudin, and the others, and not in the way in which
they might have developed under other circumstances, but
exactly in the way they were depicted by Pushkin, Lermontov, and Turgenev. It is only in the public mind that they become more and more transformed into an Oblomov. It cannot
be said that this transformation has already taken place. No,

even today thousands of people spend their time talking, and thousands of others are willing to take this talk for deeds. But the fact that this transformation has begun is proved by the Oblomov type Goncharov has created. His appearance would have been impossible had society, at least some section of it, realized what nonentities all those quasi-talented natures are, which it had formerly admired. In the past they decked themselves in cloaks and wigs of different fashions and were attractive because of their diverse talents; but today Oblomov appears before us in his true colors, taciturn, reclining on a soft couch instead of standing on a beautiful pedestal, wearing a wide dressing gown instead of an austere cloak. The questions: *What is he doing? What is the meaning and purpose of his life?* have been put plainly and bluntly without being obscured by any secondary questions. This is because the time for social activity has arrived, or will soon arrive. . . . And that is why we said in the beginning of this essay that we regard Goncharov's novel as a *sign of the times.*

Indeed, look at the change that has taken place in public opinion concerning the educated and smooth-tongued drones who were formerly regarded as genuine leaders of society.

Before us stands a young man, very handsome, adroit, and educated. He moves in high society and is successful there; he goes to theaters, balls, and masquerades; he dresses and dines magnificently; he reads books and writes well. . . . His heart is stirred only by the daily events in high society; but he also has ideas about higher problems. He is fond of talking about passions,

> About age-old prejudices
> And the fatal secrets of the grave. . . .

He has some rules of honor: he can

> A lighter quit rent substitute
> For the ancient yoke of *corvée,*

Sometimes he can refrain from taking advantage of an unsophisticated young woman whom he does not love, and he does not overrate his successes in society. He stands sufficiently high above the society in which he moves to be conscious of its vapidity; he can even abandon this society and retire to his seat in the country, but he finds it dull there too, and does not know what to turn his hand to. . . . Out of idle-

ness he quarrels with his friend and thoughtlessly kills him in
a duel. . . . Several years later he returns to society and falls
in love with the woman whose love he had formerly spurned
because it would have meant surrendering his freedom to
roam about the world. . . . In this man you recognize
Onegin. But look more closely . . . it is Oblomov.

Before us stands another man with a more ardent soul, with
wider ambitions. This one seems to have been endowed by
nature with all that were matters of concern for Onegin. He
does not have to worry about his toilet and his clothes; he is
a society man without that. He does not have to grope for
words or sparkle with tinsel wit; his tongue is naturally as
sharp as a razor. He really despises men, for he is aware of
their weaknesses. He can really capture the heart of a woman,
not for a fleeting moment, but for long, perhaps forever. He
can sweep away or crush every obstacle that rises in his path.
In only one matter is he unfortunate: he does not know which
path to take. His heart is empty and cold to everything. He
has tried everything; he was sated with all the pleasures that
money could buy when still a youth. He is weary of the love
of society beauties because it has brought no solace to his
heart. Learning has also wearied him because he has seen that
it brings neither fame nor happiness; the ignorant are the hap-
piest, and fame is a matter of luck. The dangers of the battlefield too soon bored him because he saw no sense in them, and
quickly became accustomed to them. And lastly, he even
grows tired of the pure and simple-hearted love of an untamed
girl of whom he is really fond because even in her he finds no
satisfaction for his impulses. But what are these impulses?
Whither do they lead? Why does he not yield to them with
every fiber of his being? Because he himself does not understand them and does not take the trouble to think about what
he should do with his spiritual strength. And so he spends his
life jeering at fools, disturbing the hearts of unsophisticated
young ladies, interfering in the love affairs of other people,
picking quarrels, displaying valor over trifles and fighting duels
over nothing at all. . . . You remember that this is the story of
Pechorin, that he himself has explained his own character to
Maxim Maximych to some extent, almost in the same words.
. . . Please look closer: here too you will see Oblomov. . . .

But here is another man who is more conscious of the path
he is treading. He not only knows that he is endowed with
great strength; he knows also that he has a great goal before

him. . . . It seems that he even suspects what kind of goal it is and where it is situated. He is honorable, honest (although he often fails to pay his debts), ardently discusses not trifling matters, but lofty subjects, and asserts that he is ready to sacrifice himself for the good of mankind. In his mind all problems have been solved, and everything is linked up in a living harmonious chain. He enraptures unsophisticated youths with his overpowering eloquence, and hearing him speak they too feel that they are destined to perform something great. . . . But how does he spend his life? In beginning everything and finishing nothing, attending to everything at once, passionately devoting himself to everything, but unable to devote himself to anything. . . . He falls in love with a girl who at last tells him that she is willing to give herself to him although her mother has forbidden her to do so—and he answers: "Good God! Your Mama disapproves! What an unexpected blow! God, how soon! . . . There is nothing to be done, we must be resigned. . . ." And this is an exact picture of his whole life. . . . You have already guessed that this is Rudin. . . . No, even he is now Oblomov. If you examine this character closely and bring it face to face with the requirements of present-day life, you will be convinced that this is so.

The feature common to all these men is that nothing in life is a vital necessity for them, a shrine in their hearts, a religion, organically merged with their whole being, so that to deprive them of it would mean depriving them of their lives. Everything about them is superficial; nothing is rooted in their natures. They, perhaps, do something when external necessity compels them to, just as Oblomov went visiting the places that Stolz dragged him to, bought music and books for Olga, and read what she compelled him to read; but their hearts do not lie in the things they do merely by force of circumstances.

If all of them were offered gratis all the external advantages that they obtain by their work they would gladly give up working. By virtue of Oblomovitis, an Oblomov government official would not go to his office every day if he could receive his salary and regular promotion without having to do so. A soldier would vow not to touch a weapon if he were offered the same terms and, in addition, were allowed to keep his splendid uniform, which can be very useful on certain occasions. The professor would stop delivering lectures, the student would give up his studies, the author would give up writing, the actor would never appear on the stage again, and the artist would break his chisel and palette, to put it in high-flown style, if he found a way of obtaining gratis all that he now obtains by working.

They merely talk about lofty strivings, consciousness of moral duty and common interests; when put to the test, it all turns out to be words, mere words. Their most sincere and heartfelt striving is the striving for repose, for the dressing gown, and their very activities are nothing more than an *honorable dressing gown* (to use an expression that is not our own) with which they cover up their vapidity and apathy. Even the best-educated people, people with lively natures and warm hearts, are prone in their practical lives to depart from their ideas and plans, very quickly resign themselves to the realities of life, which, however, they never cease to revile as vulgar and disgusting. This shows that all the things they talk and dream about are really alien to them, superficial; in the depth of their hearts they cherish only one dream, one ideal—undisturbed repose, quietism, Oblomovitis. Many even reach such a stage that they cannot conceive of man working willingly, with enthusiasm. Read the argument in *The Economic Index* to the effect that everybody would die of starvation resulting from idleness if by the equal distribution of wealth people were robbed of the incentive to accumulate capital. . . .

No, all these Oblomovs have never converted into flesh and blood the principles with which they were imbued; they have never carried them to their logical conclusion, have never reached the borderline where words are transformed into deeds, where principle merges with the inherent requirements of the soul, disappears in it and becomes the sole spring to a man's conduct. That is why these people are always telling lies; that is why they are so bankrupt when it comes to definite action. That is why abstract views are more precious to them than living facts, why general principles are more important to them than the simple truths of life. They read useful books in order to keep themselves informed about what people are writing; they write inspiring articles in order to admire the logical construction of their own arguments; they make bold speeches in order to hear their own sonorous phrases and to win the approbation of their auditors. As regards the next step, the object of all this reading, writing, and talking—they don't want to know anything about it, or do not trouble much about it. They are constantly saying to us: This is what we know, this is what we think—as for the rest, let others worry, it is no business of ours. . . .

As long as there was no work to be done they could still fool the public with this sort of thing, they could still strut about and boast: after all, we are worrying, walking, talking, and so forth. This is what the success achieved in society by men like Rudin was based on. More than that: they could indulge in debauchery, philandering, punning, and theatricals, and to argue that they were reduced to this because there was no field for wide activities. At that time Pechorin and even Onegin must have appeared to be men endowed with boundless spiritual strength. But now all these heroes have been pushed into the background; they have lost their former significance; they have ceased to mislead us with their enigmatic natures and the mysterious disharmony between them and society, between the greatness of their strength and the insignificance of their deeds. . . .

> Now the riddle has been answered,
> A word for it has now been found.

That word is—*Oblomovitis.*

Now, when I hear a country squire talking about the rights of man and urging the necessity of developing personality, I know from the first words he utters that he is an Oblomov.

When I hear a government official complaining that the system of administration is too complicated and cumbersome, I know that he is an Oblomov.

When I hear an army officer complaining that parades are exhausting, and boldly arguing that marching at a *slow pace* is useless, and so on, I have not the slightest doubt that he is an Oblomov.

When, in the magazines, I read liberal denunciations of abuses and expressions of joy over the fact that at last something has been done that we have been waiting and hoping for for so long, I think to myself that all this has been written from Oblomovka.

When I am in the company of educated people who ardently sympathize with the needs of mankind and who for many years have been relating with undiminished heat the same (and sometimes new) anecdotes about bribery, acts of tyranny, and lawlessness of every kind, in spite of myself I feel that I have been transported to old Oblomovka. . . .

Stop the loud declamations of these people and say to them:
"You say this is bad and that is bad, but what is to be done?"
They do not know. . . . Propose some simple remedy to
them, and they will say: "What's this, all of a sudden?" They
will say this without fail, because the Oblomovs cannot
answer differently. . . . Continue the conversation with
them and ask: "What do you intend to do?" They will give
you the answer that Rudin gave Natalya:

"What is to be done? Resign ourselves to our fate, of course.
What else can be done? I know only too well how bitter, hard
and unbearable this is, but judge for yourself . . ." and so
forth.

You will get nothing more out of them because all of them
bear the brand of Oblomovitis.

Who, then, will in the end shift them from the spot to which
they are rooted by the mighty word "forward!" which Gogol
dreamed of, and for which Rūs has been longing and waiting
for so long? So far we find no answer to this question either
in society or in literature. Goncharov, who understood and was
able to reveal our Oblomovitis to us, could not, however,
avoid paying tribute to the common error that is prevalent in
our society to this day: he set out to bury Oblomovitis and
deliver a panegyric over its grave. "Farewell, old Oblomovka,
you have outlived your time," he says through the mouth of
Stolz, but what he says is not true. All Russia that has read,
or will read, *Oblomov* will disagree with him. No, Oblomovka
is our own motherland, her owners are our teachers, her three
hundred Zakhars are always at our service. There is a large
portion of Oblomov within every one of us, and it is too early
to write our obituary. Ilya Ilyich and we have not deserved
the description contained in the following lines:

He possessed what is more precious than intelligence: an
honest and loyal heart! This is natural gold; he has carried it
untarnished through life. Jostled on every side, he fell, cooled,
at last fell asleep, worn out, disillusioned, having lost the
strength to live, but not his honesty and loyalty. His heart has
never uttered a single false note, no mud has stuck to him. No
bedecked lie will ever flatter him, and nothing can divert him
to a false path; let an ocean of baseness and evil surge around
him; let the whole world poison itself with venom and turn
upside down—Oblomov will never bow down to the idol of
falsehood, his soul will ever remain pure, bright and honest.

. . . His is a soul that is crystal clear; there are few men like him; he is a pearl among the mob! You could not bribe his heart with anything, you can rely on him always and everywhere.

We shall not hold forth on this passage, but every reader will observe that it contains a great untruth. Indeed, there is one good feature about Oblomov, namely, he never tries to fool anybody, but always appears what he is—an indolent drone. But pray, in what *can he be relied on?* Only, perhaps, when nothing need be done; here he will certainly distinguish himself. But if nothing need be done we can do without him. He would not bow down to the idol of evil! But why not? Because he was too lazy to get up from his couch. And if he were dragged from his couch and forced to his knees in front of that idol he would not have the strength to get up. He cannot be bribed with anything. But what is there to bribe him for? To make him move? Well, that is a really difficult task. Mud would never stick to him! Yes, as long as he lies alone on his couch everything goes well; but as soon as Tarantyev, Zaterty, and Ivan Matveyich arrive—ugh! What awful and disgusting things begin to take place around Oblomov. They eat him out of house and home; they drink up his wine; they drive him to drink; they induce him to sign a false promissory note (from which Stolz, somewhat unceremoniously, in the Russian manner, releases him without trial or investigation); they ruin him and say his peasants are the cause o˙ it; they extort enormous sums of money from him for nothing at all. He suffers all this in silence and, for that reason, of course, never utters a false note.

No, the living must not be flattered like that, and we are still alive, we are still Oblomovs. Oblomovitis never abandoned us; it is still with us *at the present time, when,* and so forth. Which of our authors, journalists, men of education, and public leaders, which of them will not agree that Goncharov must have had him in mind when he wrote the following lines about Ilya Ilyich:

He knew the delights of lofty thoughts; his heart was responsive to universal human suffering. Sometimes, deep down in his heart, he wept bitterly over the misfortunes that mankind endured, he experienced unknowable and nameless suffering and grief, and he was conscious of a striving toward something in the remote distance, probably toward that world to which Stolz would draw him. Sweet tears roll down his cheeks. Sometimes he is filled with contempt for human vices, for falsehood, for slander, for the evil that has spread over the world, and he burns with a desire to draw mankind's attention to its sores—and suddenly ideas flare up in his mind, heave and toss in his head like the waves of the sea, and then grow into intentions and set his blood on fire—his muscles twitch, his sinews become tense, the intentions are transformed into strivings: moved by moral force, he quickly assumes two or three postures in one minute and with flashing eyes he half rises in his bed, extends an arm and looks around like one inspired. . . . Behold, the striving is materializing, it is about to become a deed. . . . And then, good Lord! What miracles, what beneficial consequences could be expected from this sublime effort! But the dawn appears, it passes away, evening sets in, and with it Oblomov's wearied strength turns to repose: the storm and excitement in his heart die down, his mind becomes more sober, his blood flows less rapidly through his veins. Silently and pensively Oblomov turns over on his back, gazes mournfully at the sky through the window and bids a sad farewell to the sun that is setting in splendor behind somebody's four-story house. How many times he has said farewell to the setting sun in this way!

Will you not agree, educated and noble-minded reader, that the above lines truly depict your own well-intentioned strivings and your useful activity? The only difference that one may find here is the stage you will reach in your development. Ilya Ilyich reached the stage of half rising in his bed, extending an arm and looking around. Others do not get so far; they reach only the stage when ideas toss about in their head like the waves of the sea (they constitute the majority); others reach the stage when their ideas grow into intentions but do not reach the degree of strivings (there are fewer of these); others again reach the striving stage (but these are extremely few). . . .

And so, following the trend of our times, when the whole of our literature, as Mr. Benediktov expresses it, is a

> . . . torment to our flesh,
> Chains of poetry and prose,

we humbly confess that much as Mr. Goncharov's praise of Oblomov may flatter our vanity, we cannot regard it as being justified. Oblomov irritates the fresh, young, and active man less than Pechorin and Rudin do, but he is a disgusting nonentity, nevertheless.

Paying tribute to his times, Mr. Goncharov provided an antidote to Oblomov in the shape of Stolz; but as regards that individual, we must repeat the opinion that we have always expressed, namely, that literature must not run too far ahead of life. Stolzes, men of an integral and active character that makes every idea a striving and translates it into deeds the moment it arises, do not yet exist in our society (we have in mind the educated section of society, which is capable of loftier strivings; among the mases, where ideas and strivings are confined to a few and very practical objects, we constantly come across such people). The author himself admits this when he says about our society:

There! Eyes have opened after slumber, brisk, wide footsteps, animated voices are heard. . . . How many Stolzes with Russian names must appear!

Many must appear; there can be no doubt about that; but for the time being there is no soil for them. And that is why all we can gather from Goncharov's novel is that Stolz is a man of action, always busy with something, running about, acquiring things, saying that to live means to work, and so forth. But what he does and how he manages to do something worth while where others can do nothing, remains a mystery to us. He settled the affairs of the Oblomov estate for Ilya Ilyich in a trice—but how? That we do not know. He got rid of Ilya Ilyich's false promissory note in a trice—but how? That we know. He went to see the chief of Ivan Matveyich, to whom Oblomov had given the promissory note, had a friendly talk with him, and after this Ivan Matveyich was called to the chief's office, and not only was he ordered to return the note but was also asked to resign. It served him right, of course: but judging by this case, Stolz had not yet reached the stage of the ideal Russian public leader. Nor could he have done so; it is too early.

For the time being, even if you are as wise as Solomon, all you can do in the way of public activity is, perhaps, to be a *philanthropic tavern licensee* like Murazov, who performs good deeds out of his fortune of ten million, or a noble landlord like Kostanzhoglo—but further than that you cannot go. . . . And we cannot understand how in his activities Stolz could rid himself of all the strivings and requirements that overcame even Oblomov, how he could be satisfied with his position, rest content with his solitary, individual, exclusive happiness. . . . It must not be forgotten that under his feet there was a bog, that the old Oblomovka was nearby, that he would have had to clear the forest to reach the high-road and thus escape from Oblomovitis. Whether Stolz did anything in this direction, what he did, and how he did it— we do not know. But until we know we cannot be satisfied with his personality. . . . All we can say is that he is not the man who "will be able to pronounce in a language intelligible to the Russian soul that mighty word: 'Forward!' "

Perhaps Olga Ilyinskaya is more capable of doing this than Stolz, for she stands nearer to our new life. We have said nothing about the women that Goncharov created, nothing about Olga or about Agafya Matveyevna Pshenitsyn (or even about Anissya or Akulina, women also with peculiar characters), because we realized that we were totally unable to say anything coherently about them. To attempt to analyze the feminine types created by Goncharov would be to lay claim to expert knowledge of the feminine heart. Lacking this quality, we can only admire Goncharov's women. The ladies say that Goncharov's psychological analysis is amazing for its truth and subtlety, and in this matter the ladies must be believed. . . . We should not dare to add anything to their comment because we are afraid of setting foot in a land that is completely strange to us. But we take the liberty, in concluding this essay, to say a few words about Olga, and about her attitude toward Oblomovitis.

In intellectual development, Olga is the highest ideal that a Russian artist can find in our present Russian life. That is why the extraordinary clarity and simplicity of her logic and the amazing harmony of heart and mind astonish us so much that we are ready to doubt even her imaginary existence and say, "There are no such young women." But following her through the whole novel, we find that she is always true to herself and to her development, that she is not merely the creation of the author, but a living person, though one that we have not yet met. She more than Stolz gives us a glimpse of the new Russian life; from her we may expect to hear the word that will consume Oblomovitis with fire and reduce it to ashes. . . . She begins by falling in love with Oblomov, by believing in him and in the possibility of his moral transformation. . . . She toils long and stubbornly, with loving devotion and tender solicitude, in an effort to fan the spark of life in this man and to stimulate him to activity. She refuses to believe that he is so incapable of doing good; cherishing her hopes in him,

her future creation, she does everything for him. She even
ignores conventional propriety, goes to see him alone without
telling anybody, and, unlike him, is not afraid of losing her
reputation. But with astonishing tact she at once discerns
every false streak in his character, and she explains to him
why it is false and not true in an extremely simple way. He,
for example, writes her the letter we referred to above and
later assures her that he had written it solely out of concern
for her, completely forgetting himself, sacrificing himself,
and so forth.

"No," she answers, "that is not true. If you had thought
only of my happiness and had believed that for it it was necessary that we should part, you would simply have gone away
without sending me any letters."

He says that he fears that she will be unhappy when she
learns that she had been mistaken in him, ceases to love him,
and loves another. In answer to this she asks him:

"Where do you see my unhappiness? I love you now and
I feel good; later I will love another, hence, I will feel good
with him. You need not worry about me."

This simplicity and clarity of thought are elements of the
new life, not the one under the conditions of which present-
day society grew up. . . . And then—how obedient Olga's
will is to her heart! She continues her relations with Oblomov
and persists in her love for him, in spite of unpleasantness,
jeers, and so on, from outside, until she is convinced of his
utter worthlessness. Then she bluntly tells him that she had
been mistaken in him and cannot combine her fate with his.
She continues to praise and pet him while she rejects him,
and even later, but by her action she annihilates him as no
other Oblomov was ever annihilated by a woman. Tatyana
says to Onegin at the end of the romance:

> I love you (why conceal it?),
> But to another my troth is plighted,
> To him forever I'll be true.

And so, only formal moral duty saves her from this empty-
headed fop; if she were free she would have flung her arms
around his neck. Natalya leaves Rudin only because he himself was obdurate from the very outset, and on seeing him off

she realizes that he does not love her and she grieves sorely
over this. There is no need to speak of Pechorin, who managed only to earn the *hatred* of Princess Mary. No, Olga did
not behave to Oblomov in that way. She said to him simply
and gently:

"I learned only recently that I loved in you what I wanted
you to have, what Stolz pointed out to me, and what he and
I conjured up. I loved the future Oblomov! You are unassum-
ing and honest, Ilya; you are tender . . . like a dove; you
hide your head under your wing—and you want nothing more;
you want to coo in the loft all your life. . . . But I am not
like that: that is not enough for me; I want something more,
but what—I don't know!"

And so she leaves Oblomov and strives toward her *something,* although she does not quite know what it is. At last she
finds it in Stolz, she joins him and is happy; but even here she
does not halt, does not come to a dead stop. Certain vague
problems and doubts disturb her; there are things she is
trying to fathom. The author did not fully reveal her emotions
to us, and we may err in our assumptions concerning their
nature. But it seems to us that her heart and mind were disturbed by the spirit of the new life, to which she was immeasurably nearer than Stolz. We think so because we find
several hints of this in the following dialogue:

"What shall I do? Yield and pine?" she asked.
"No," he answered. "Arm yourself with firmness and serenity. We two are not Titans," he continued, embracing her.
"We shall not follow the Manfreds and Fausts and challenge
disturbing problems to mortal combat, nor shall we accept
their challenge. We shall bow our heads and wait humbly
until the hard times pass, and life, happiness, will smile
again. . . ."
"But suppose they never leave us: suppose grief disturbs
us more and more?" she asked.
"Well, we'll accept it as a new element of life. . . . But no,
that cannot be; it cannot happen to us! It is not your grief
alone; it is the common ailment of mankind. You have suffered only one drop. . . . All this is frightful when a man
loses his grip on life, when he has no support. But in our
case . . ."

He did not specify the *our case,* but it is evident that it is
he who does not wish to challenge disturbing problems to

mortal combat," that it is *he* who wants to humbly bow his head. . . . She is ready for this fight; she longs for it, and is always afraid that her tranquil happiness with Stolz may grow into something that resembles the Oblomov apathy. Clearly, she does not wish to bow her head and wait humbly until the hard times pass, in the hope that life will smile again later. She left Oblomov when she ceased to believe in him; she will leave Stolz if she ceases to believe in him. And this will happen if she continues to be tormented by problems and doubts, and if he continues to advise her to accept them as a new element of life and bow her head. She is thoroughly familiar with Oblomovitis; she will be able to discern it in all its different shapes, and under all masks, and will always be able to find strength enough to pronounce ruthless judgment on it. . . .

When Will the Real Day Come?

ON THE EVE, A NOVEL BY I. S. TURGENEV

> Schlage die Trommel und fürchte dich
> nicht.
> *—Heine*

AESTHETIC criticism has now become the hobby of sentimental young ladies. In conversation with them the devotees of pure art may hear many subtle and true observations, and then they can sit down and write a review in the following style: "Here is the content of Mr. Turgenev's new novel" (follows a summary of the story). "This pale sketch is enough to show how much life and poetry, of the freshest and most fragrant kind, is to be found in this novel. But only by reading the novel itself can one obtain a true idea of that feeling for the most subtle poetical shades of life, of that keen psychological analysis, of that profound understanding of the hidden streams and currents of public thought, and of that friendly and yet bold attitude toward reality that constitute the distinguishing features of Mr. Turgenev's talent. See, for example, how subtly he has noted these psychological features" (then comes a repetition of a part of the summary, followed by an excerpt from the novel); "read this wonderful scene that is depicted with such grace and charm" (excerpt); "recall this poetical living picture" (excerpt), "or this lofty and bold delineation" (excerpt). "Does not this penetrate to the depths of your soul, compel your heart to beat faster, animate and embellish your life, exalt before you human dignity and the great, eternal significance of the sacred ideas of truth, goodness, and beauty! *Comme c'est joli, comme c'est délicieux!*"

We are unable to write pleasant and harmless reviews of this sort because we are little acquainted with sentimental young ladies. Openly confessing this, and disclaiming the role

176

of "cultivator of the aesthetic tastes of the public," we have chosen for ourselves a different task, one more modest and more commensurate with our abilities. We simply wish to sum up the data that are scattered throughout the author's work, which we accept as accomplished facts, as phenomena of life that confront us. This is not a complicated task, but it is one that must be undertaken because, what with the multiplicity of their occupations and the need for relaxation, people are rarely willing to go into all the details of a literary production, to analyze, verify and put in their proper places all the figures that combine to make this intricate report on one of the aspects of our social life and then to ponder over the result, over what it promises, and what obligations it imposes upon us. But such verification and reflection will be very useful in the case of Mr. Turgenev's new novel.

We know that the devotees of pure aesthetics will at once accuse us of wanting to thrust our own views upon the author and to set tasks for his talent. We shall therefore make the following reservation, tedious though it may be to do so. No, we have no wish to thrust anything upon the author; we say at the very outset that we do not know what object the author had in view, or what views prompted him to write the story that constitutes the contents of the novel *On the Eve*. The important thing for us is not so much what the author *wanted* to say, as what he *said*, even unintentionally, simply in the process of truthfully reproducing the facts of life. We prize every talented production precisely because it enables us to study the facts of our own lives which, without these facts, are so little exposed to the gaze of the ordinary observer.

To this day there is no publicity in our lives except official publicity; everywhere we encounter not living but official persons, persons who are serving in one sphere or another; in government offices we meet clerks, at balls we meet dancers, in clubs—card players, in theaters—hairdressers' clients, and so forth. Everybody hides his spiritual life as far away from the public gaze as possible; everybody looks at us as much as to say: "I have come here to dance, or to show my coiffure. That being the case, be satisfied with the fact that I am going about my business, and please don't take it into your head to question me about my feelings and my ideas." And indeed, nobody makes any attempt to make anybody confess, nobody is interested in anyone; everybody in society goes his own way, regretting that he must come together with others on official occasions as, for example, a first night at the opera, an official banquet, or a meeting of some committee or other. Under these circumstances, how is a man, who does not devote himself exclusively to the observation of social habits, to study and learn what life is? On top of all this there is the variety, even opposites, in the different circles and classes of our society! Ideas that have become banal and out of date in one circle are still hotly debated in another; what some regard as inadequate and weak others regard as excessively sharp and bold, and so forth.

We have no other way of knowing what is defeated, what is victorious, or what is beginning to permeate and predominate in the moral life of society but literature, and mainly through its artistic productions. The author-artist, although not troubling to draw any general conclusions about the state of public thought and morality, is always able to grasp their most essential features, throw a vivid light upon them, and place them before the eyes of thinking people. That is why we think that as soon as it is recognized that an author-artist possesses talent, that is, the ability to feel and depict the phenomena with lifelike truth, this very recognition creates legitimate ground for taking his productions as a basis for the discussion of the milieu, the epoch, which prompted the author to write this or that production. And here the criterion of the author's talent will be the breadth of his conception of life, the degree to which the images he has created are permanent and comprehensive.

We have deemed it necessary to say this in order to justify our method, namely, to interpret the phenomena of life on the basis of a literary production, without attributing to the author any preconceived ideas or aims. The reader perceives that we regard as important precisely those productions in which life is expressed as it is and not according to a program previously drawn up by the author. We did not discuss *A Thousand Souls*, for example, because, in our opinion, the whole social side of this novel was forcibly adjusted to a preconceived idea. Hence, there is nothing to discuss here except the degree of skill the author displayed in composing his work. It is impossible to rely on the truth and living reality of the facts delineated by the author because his inner attitude toward these facts is not simple and truthful. We see an entirely different attitude of an author toward his subject in Mr. Turgenev's new novel, as indeed we see in most of his novels. In *On the Eve* we see the inescapable influence of the natural course of

social life and thought, to which the author's own thoughts
and imagination were involuntarily adjusted.

In expressing the view that the main task of the literary
critic is to explain the phenomena of reality that called a
given artistic production into being, we must add that in the
case of Mr. Turgenev's novels this task acquires a special
meaning. Mr. Turgenev may be rightly described as the
painter and bard of the morality and philosophy that have
reigned among the educated section of our society during the
past twenty years. He very soon divined the new requirements, the new ideas that were permeating the public mind,
and in his works he, as a rule, devoted (as much as circumstances would permit) attention to the question that was
about to come up next and that was already beginning
vaguely to stir society.

We hope to trace the whole of Mr. Turgenev's literary
activity on a future occasion, and so we shall not deal with
it at length now; we shall only say that it is to this sensitive-
ness that the author displays toward the living strings of
society, to this ability of his to respond forthwith to every
noble thought and honest sentiment which is only just beginning to penetrate the minds of the best people, that we
largely ascribe the success Mr. Turgenev has always enjoyed
among the Russian public.

It goes without saying that his literary talent too has contributed a great deal to this success, but our readers know
that Mr. Turgenev's talent is not of the titanic kind, which
by sheer poetic expression alone captivates you, thrills you,
and compels you to sympathize with a phenomenon, or an
idea, with which you were not in the least inclined to sympathize. Not a turbulent and impulsive power but, on the contrary, gentleness and a kind of poetic moderation are the characteristic features of his talent. That is why we believe that
he could not have roused the general sympathy of the public
had he dealt with questions and requirements that were
totally alien to his readers or that had not yet arisen in society.
Some readers would have noted the charm of the poetical descriptions in his novels, the subtlety and profundity with
which he portrayed different individuals and situations; but
there can be no doubt that this alone would not have been
enough to make the author's success and fame permanent.
Even the most attractive and talented narrator must, if he
fails to display this responsive attitude toward modern times,

share the fate of Mr. Fet, whom people praised at one time, but of whose work only about a dozen of his best poems are remembered by only about a dozen admirers. It is his responsive attitude toward modern times that has saved Mr. Turgenev and has guaranteed him permanent success among the reading public. A certain profound critic once rebuked Mr. Turgenev for having in his works so strongly reflected "all the vacillations of public thought." We, on the contrary, regard this as the most vital feature of Mr. Turgenev's talent; and we believe that it is this feature of his talent that explains the sympathy, almost enthusiasm, with which all his productions have been received up till now.

Thus, we may boldly assert that if Mr. Turgenev touches upon any question in a story of his, if he has depicted any new aspect of social relationships, it can be taken as a guarantee that this question is rising, or soon will rise, in the mind of the educated section of society; that this new aspect is beginning to make itself felt and will soon stand out sharply and clearly before the eyes of all. That is why, every time a story by Mr. Turgenev appears, our curiosity is roused and we ask: What sides of life are depicted in it? What questions does it touch upon?

This question arises now, and in relation to Mr. Turgenev's new novel it is more interesting than ever. Up to now Mr. Turgenev's path, in conformity with the path of our society's development, has proceeded in one, fairly clearly defined, direction. He started out from the sphere of lofty ideas and theoretical strivings and proceeded to introduce these ideas and strivings into coarse and banal reality, which had digressed very much from them. The hero's preparations for the struggle, his sufferings, his eagerness to see the triumph of his principles, and his fall in face of the overwhelming power of human banality have usually been the centers of interest in Mr. Turgenev's stories.

It goes without saying that the background of this struggle, that is to say, the ideas and aspirations, was different in each story, or was expressed more definitely and sharply with the progress of time and change of circumstances. Thus, the unwanted man's place was taken by Pasynkov; Pasynkov's place was taken by Rudin; Rudin's place was taken by Lavretsky. Each of these persons was bolder and more perfect than his predecessor, but the substance, the basis of their characters and their entire existence was the same. They introduced new ideas into a certain circle; they were educators and propagandists—even though it was for one woman's soul, but propagandists nevertheless. For this they were highly praised and, indeed, in their time they were evidently greatly needed; and their task was extremely difficult, honorable, and beneficial. It is not surprising that they were so popular, that their spiritual sufferings roused so much sympathy and their fruitless efforts so much pity. It is not surprising that nobody at that time even thought of observing that these gentlemen were splendid, noble, and intelligent, but, at bottom, idle people. Depicting them in various situations and conflicts, Mr. Turgenev himself usually treated them with moving sympathy; it was evident that his heart ached for their sufferings, and he always roused the same feeling among the bulk of his readers. When one motive for this struggle and suffering began to look inadequate, when one feature of nobility and exaltation of character began to show signs of banality, Mr. Turgenev was able to find other motives and other features, and thereby again strike at the heart of his readers, and again rouse admiration and sympathy for himself and for his heroes. The subject seemed to be inexhaustible.

Lately, however, demands entirely different from those which Rudin and all his fraternity roused have made themselves heard fairly distinctly in our society. A radical change has taken place in the conceptions of the majority of educated people in relation to these personages. It is now not a question of changing the particular motives, or the particular principles, underlying their strivings, but of the very substance of their activities. During the period in which all these enlightened champions of truth and virtue, these eloquent martyrs to exalted convictions, were parading before us, new people have grown up, for whom love of truth and honest strivings are no longer a novelty. The conceptions and ideals for which, in the past, the best people had to fight, to hesitate over and to suffer at a mature age, these new people imperceptibly and steadily imbibed in their childhood.[1]

---

[1] We have already been rebuked once for our partiality for the young generation, and our attention has been drawn to the banalities and trivialities to which the majority of its representatives devote themselves. It has never occurred to us to defend all young people indiscriminately, for this would not have been in conformity with our object. Banality and triviality are characteristics of all ages and of all times. We did speak, and we speak now, of chosen people, the best people, not of the crowd; for Rudin, and all the men of his type, belong not to the crowd, but to the best people

As a consequence, the very character of education in our present young society has assumed a different hue. The conceptions and strivings that, in the past, were the hallmarks of the progressive person, are now regarded as the primary and essential attributes of the most ordinary education. You will hear a high-school boy, a mediocre cadet, and sometimes even a seminary student a little above the average, expressing convictions that formerly Belinsky, for example, was obliged to defend in heated controversy. And the high-school boy, or cadet, expresses these convictions—which were formerly arrived at with such difficulty and struggle—quite calmly, without any particular ardor or smugness, as if any other convictions were impossible and even quite inconceivable.

Nobody among respectable people now expresses astonishment and admiration on meeting a man who belongs to the so-called progressive trend; nobody looks into his eyes with mute awe; nobody shakes hands with him mysteriously and gives him a whispered invitation to meet a close circle of the chosen in his home to discuss the point that injustice and slavery are fatal for the state. On the contrary, anybody who reveals a lack of sympathy for publicity, unselfishness, emancipation, and so forth, arouses instinctive astonishment and contempt. Today even those who dislike progressive ideas must pretend to like them in order to gain admission to decent society. Clearly, under such circumstances, the former sowers of the seeds of good, people of the *Rudin* type, lose a considerable part of their former credit. They are respected as old teachers, but rarely is anybody with an independent mind disposed to listen again to those lessons that were learned so eagerly in the past, in the period of childhood and initial development. Now something different is needed; it is necessary to go further.[2]

---

of our times. Incidentally, we shall not be wrong in saying that the level of education has, after all, risen lately, even among the bulk of society.—N. D.

[2] This view may seem to be contradicted by the extraordinary success that has attended the publication of the works of some of our authors of the forties. A particularly striking example of this is Belinsky, whose works, in an edition of 12,000 copies, it is said, were quickly sold out. In our opinion, however, this very fact serves to confirm our view. Belinsky was a progressive among progressives; none of his contemporaries went further than he, and where 12,000 copies of the works of Belinsky can be sold out in several months the Rudins can find positively nothing to

"But," we may be told, "society has not yet reached the limit of its development; further mental and moral improvement is still possible. Consequently, society needs leaders, preachers of the truth, and propagandists, in short, men of the Rudin type. Let us assume that everything of the past has been accepted and absorbed by the public mind, but that does not preclude the possibility that new Rudins, the preachers of new and higher trends, will appear, who will fight and suffer again, and again rouse sympathy for themselves in society. This subject is indeed inexhaustible and may constantly bring fresh laurels for a writer like Mr. Turgenev."

It would be a pity if observations such as these found confirmation at the present time. Luckily, we think, they are refuted by the latest trend in our literature. Speaking abstractly, it cannot be denied that the view that ideas in society are in a constant process of movement and change and, consequently, that there is a constant need for preachers of these ideas, is quite correct; but we must also bear in mind that society does not live exclusively for the purpose of arguing and exchanging ideas. Ideas and their gradual development are of importance only because, engendered by already existing facts, they always precede changes in actual reality. A certain state of affairs creates a need in society; this need is recognized; following the general recognition of this need an actual change must take place in the direction of satisfying this generally recognized need. Thus, after a period of *recognition* of certain ideas and strivings a period must arise in society in which these ideas and strivings are *carried out;* reflection and talk must be followed by action.

The question now arises: What has our society done during the past twenty to thirty years? So far, nothing. It studied, developed, listened to the Rudins, sympathized with them in their setbacks in the noble struggle for convictions, prepared for action, but did not do anything. . . . So much that is beautiful has accumulated in the minds and hearts of men; so much that is absurd and dishonest has been discovered in the present order of society; the number of people who "regard themselves as standing above surrounding reality" is

do. Belinsky's success proves not that his ideas are new for our society and call for much effort to disseminate, but that they are now precious and sacred for the majority and that their advocacy now no longer calls for heroism or exceptional talent on the part of the new men.—*N. D.*

growing year after year, so that soon everybody, perhaps, will be standing above reality. . . . One would think that there were no grounds for wishing that we should continue for- ever to proceed along the painful road of discord, doubt, and abstract grief and consolation. It would seem to be clear that now we need, not people who will "raise us still higher above surrounding reality" but who will raise, or teach us how to raise, reality itself to the level of the rational demands that we have already recognized. In short, we need men of action and not of abstract, and always somewhat Epicurean, argu- ment.

This was recognized, although vaguely, by many on the appearance of *A Nest of the Gentry.* On this occasion too Mr. Turgenev's talent, together with his true sense of reality, helped him to emerge from a difficult situation in triumph. He succeeded in depicting Lavretsky in such a way that it seemed out of place to treat him with irony, although he actually belongs to the type of idlers that we look upon with ridicule. The drama in his situation is no longer the struggle against his own impotence, but his collision with concepts and cus- toms, the fight against which is enough to daunt even a bold and energetic man. He is married, but has left his wife; he falls in love with a pure, angelic woman who is convinced that it is a heinous crime to love a married man. Nevertheless, she loves him, and his claims continuously and frightfully tor- ture her heart and conscience. A situation like this cannot help giving rise to deep and bitter reflection, and we remember how painfully our hearts throbbed when Lavretsky, in bid- ding farewell to Lisa, said to her: "Oh, Lisa, Lisa! How happy we could have been!" And when she, already at heart a nun resigned to her fate, answers: "You can see for yourself that happiness depends not on us but on God." In reply to this he says: "Yes, because you . . ." but he does not finish what he wants to say. . . .

We remember that readers and critics of *A Nest of the Gentry* admired many other things in that novel; but what interests us most in it is this tragic collision of Lavretsky, whose passivity, precisely in this case, we cannot but excuse. Here it seems as though Lavretsky, as if contradicting one of the generic features of his type, is scarcely even a propagan- dist. Beginning with his first meeting with Lisa, when she is going to morning prayers, he throughout the story timidly yields to her unshakable conviction and never dares to enter into a cool argument with her in order to shake those convictions. But this too, of course, is due to the fact that in such a case propaganda is the very thing Lavretsky and his entire fraternity fear most. In spite of all this, it seems to us (at least it seemed to us when we were reading the novel), that the very situation in which Lavretsky finds himself, the very collision that Mr. Turgenev chose for this novel, and that is so familiar in Russian life, should [serve as powerful propaganda and] prompt in the mind of every reader a number of thoughts concerning the significance of an entire complex of concepts that govern our lives. From various published and spoken comments we now know that we have not been altogether right; Lavretsky's situation was either differently interpreted or quite misunderstood by many readers. That there is something genuinely and not artificially tragic about him was understood, however, and this, together with its artistic merits, gained for *A Nest of the Gentry* the unanimous admiration of the whole of the Russian reading public.

After *A Nest of the Gentry* there were grounds for apprehension concerning the fate of Mr. Turgenev's new work. The path of creating exalted characters who are compelled to resign themselves to the blows of fate has become very slippery. Amidst the admiration expressed for *A Nest of the Gentry* voices were heard expressing dissatisfaction with Lavretsky, from whom much more was expected. The author himself deemed it necessary to introduce Mikhalevich into his story in order to rebuke Lavretsky for his indolence. And Ilya Ilyich Oblomov, who appeared at the same time, definitely and bluntly explained to the entire Russian public that it is now far better for a man who lacks will and energy to refrain from making people laugh; that it is far better for him to remain lying on his couch than to make a lot of fuss and noise and bother, to argue and beat the wind for whole years and decades. The people who read *Oblomov* recognized his kinship with those interesting personages the "unwanted men," and realized that these men were indeed already unwanted, that they were of no more use than good old Ilya Ilyich. "What will Mr. Turgenev create now?" we asked ourselves, and we sat down to read *On the Eve* with the utmost curiosity.

On this occasion too the author's feeling for reality did not fail him. Realizing that the former heroes had already done their work and could no longer win the sympathies of the best section of our society as they had done in the past, he decided to abandon them, and sensing in several fragmentary mani-

186 N. A. Dobrolyubov

festations the spirit of the new demands on life, he stepped
onto the road along which the progressive movement is pro-
ceeding at the present time. . . .

In Mr. Turgenev's new novel we meet with situations and
types that differ from those we have been accustomed to finding in his previous works. The social demand for action, for
real action, incipient contempt for dead, abstract principles
and passive virtue are expressed in the whole structure of the
new novel. Everybody who reads this essay has undoubtedly
read *On the Eve;* hence, instead of summarizing the story
we shall make only a brief sketch of its principal characters.

The heroine of the story is a girl of a serious turn of mind,
possessing an energetic will and a heart filled with humane
strivings. Her development has been very peculiar owing to
special domestic circumstances.

Her father and mother were very narrow-minded but not
vicious; her mother was even favorably distinguished for her
kindness and soft heart. From her childhood Helena was free
from the yoke of that domestic despotism which crushes so
many beautiful characters in the bud. She grew up alone,
without friends, absolutely free; no formalism restricted her.
Nikolai Artyomich Stakhov, her father, was a rather dull-
witted person, but he regarded himself as a philosopher of the
skeptical school and kept himself aloof from domestic life, at
first only admiring his little Helena, who revealed unusual
abilities at an early age. While she was little, Helena worshiped her father. But Stakhov's relations with his wife were
not altogether satisfactory. He married Anna Vassilyevna for
her dowry; he had no feeling toward her whatever; he treated
her almost with contempt and left her for the society of
Augustina Christianovna, who fooled and fleeced him. Anna
Vassilyevna, a sick and sensitive woman, after the type of
Maria Dmitriyevna in *A Nest of the Gentry,* meekly bore her
lot but could not refrain from complaining about it to everybody at home and, incidentally, even to her daughter. Thus,
Helena soon became her mother's confidante, one to whom to
pour out her woes, and involuntarily she became the judge
between her and her father. Owing to Helena's impressionable
nature this greatly influenced the development of her inner
strength. The less she could do practically in this matter, the
more work she found for her mind and imagination. Compelled from her earliest years to watch the relationships between those she loved, participating with both heart and
mind in the explanation of these relationships and in passing

judgment upon them, Helena early trained herself to think independently and to form a conscious opinion about everything around her.

The domestic relationships of the Stakhovs are very briefly sketched in Mr. Turgenev's novel, but this sketch gives us profoundly true indications that explain a great deal in the early development of Helena's character. She was an impressionable and clever child; her position between her mother and father early prompted her to serious reflection and early raised her to an independent, authoritative role. She placed herself on the level of her elders and put them before the bar of her judgment. Her reflections were not cold, however; her whole soul merged with them, because the matter affected people who were extremely close and extremely dear to her, whose relationships were bound up with her most sacred sentiments and her most vital interests. That is why her reflections directly affected the disposition of her heart. She ceased to worship her father and acquired a passionate attachment to her mother, whom she regarded as an oppressed and suffering being. Her love for her mother, however, did not rouse the contrary feeling of hostility toward her father, who was neither a villain, a positive fool, nor a domestic tyrant. He was just an ordinary mediocrity, and Helena cooled toward him instinctively, and later, perhaps, consciously decided that there was nothing lovable about him. But soon she observed that her mother too was a mediocrity, and passionate love and respect for her gave way in her heart to a mere sense of pity and condescension. Mr. Turgenev very aptly describes her attitude toward her mother when he says that she "treated her mother as if she were an ailing grandmother." The mother admitted to herself that she was beneath her daughter; the father, however, as soon as his daughter began to surpass him in intellect, which was not a very difficult matter, cooled toward her, decided that she was queer, and dropped her.

Meanwhile Helena's feelings of sympathy and humanity grew and expanded. Of course, the pain she felt at the sight of the suffering of others was originally caused in her childish heart by the downtrodden appearance of her mother long before she began to understand what the trouble was about. This pain was always with her; it accompanied her at every step she took in her development; it gave an exceptionally pensive bent to her thoughts, and it gradually called forth and determined active aspirations in her, all of which she

directed toward a passionate and irresistible quest for the
good and happiness of all. This yearning was still vague, her
strength was still feeble when she found fresh sustenance
for her reflections and dreams, a new object for her sympathy
and love; we refer to her strange acquaintance with the
beggar girl Katya. She befriended this girl when she was
over nine years of age, clandestinely met her in the park,
brought her sweetmeats, gave her shawls and ten-kopek
pieces (Katya would not take toys), sat with her for hours
eating the girl's stale bread with a sense of joyous humility;
she listened to the stories the girl told, learned her favorite
song, and with concealed awe and fear heard her threaten
to run away from her wicked aunt and go and live *in God's
full freedom;* and she herself dreamed of putting a knapsack
on her back and running away with Katya. Katya soon died,
but Helena's acquaintance with her necessarily left deep
traces upon her character. A new side was added to her pure,
human, sympathetic disposition, a side that cultivated in her
contempt for, or at all events stern indifference to, the
superfluous luxuries of the life of the rich, a feeling that
always penetrates the soul of a person, who is not entirely
spoiled, at the sight of helpless poverty.

Soon Helena's whole soul longed to do good, and at first
this desire was satisfied with the customary acts of charity
that were accessible to her. "The poor, the hungry, and the
sick held her attention, stirred and pained her; she saw them
in her dreams, she questioned all her acquaintances about
them." Even "all ill-treated animals, the emaciated back-
yard dogs, kittens condemned to death, young sparrows that
had fallen from their nests, and even insects and reptiles
found a protector in Helena; she herself fed them and never
felt disgust for them." Her father called all this "banal sentimentality," but Helena was not sentimental, for sentimentality is characterized precisely by an abundance of sentiment
and words accompanied by a complete absence of effective
love and sympathy. Helena always tried to express herself in
action. She could not tolerate empty caresses and tenderness
and, in general, attached no value to words that were unac-
companied by deeds, and respected only practical and useful
activity. She was not even fond of poetry, and had no judgment of art.

But the active strivings of the soul mature and grow strong
only if there is scope and freedom for them. One must test
one's strength several times, suffer reverses and collisions,

learn to know what various efforts cost and how various obstacles have to be overcome in order to acquire the courage and determination necessary for an active struggle, in order to appraise one's strength and be able to find commensurate work for it. Notwithstanding the freedom of her development, Helena could not find sufficient outlets for her strength and was unable to satisfy her strivings. Nobody prevented her from doing what she wanted to do, but there was nothing to do. She was not restricted by the pedantry of systematic education and was therefore able to educate herself without acquiring the multitude of prejudices that are inseparable from systems, courses, and routine education in general. She read a great deal and with interest, but reading alone could not satisfy her; the only effect it had upon her was that her power of reasoning developed more than her other powers, and her intellectual requirements even began to outweigh her feelings. Nor could the giving of alms, tending pups and kittens, and protecting flies from spiders satisfy her. When she grew older and wiser she could not fail to see how shallow this activity was, and moreover, these occupations called for very little effort and could not fill her life. She wanted something greater, something loftier, but what it was she did not know; even if she did know she could not set to work at it. This explains why she was always in such a state of agitation, why she was always expecting and looking for something, and that is why her very appearance became so peculiar:

Her whole being, the expression on her face, her *attentive and somewhat timid, clear but unsteady gaze, her smile which seemed to be strained, and her low uneven voice* expressed something nervous, electrical, something *impulsive and hasty*. . . .

Clearly, she is still beset by vague doubts about herself; she has not yet determined her role. She has realized what she does not need, and remains proud and independent amidst the habitual circumstances of her life; but she does not yet know what she needs, and above all she does not understand what she must do to achieve what she needs, and that is why her whole being is strained, uneven, and impulsive. She is waiting, living on the eve of something. . . . She is ready for vigorous, energetic activity, but she is unable to set to work by herself, alone.

This timidity, this virtual passivity of the heroine combined
with her abundance of inner strength and her tormenting
thirst for activity astonishes us and makes us think that there
is something unfinished about Helena's personality, her lack
of activity reveals precisely the living connection between
Mr. Turgenev's heroine and the whole of the educated section of our society. In the way Helena's character is conceived, at bottom, it is an exceptional one, and if she were
indeed presented everywhere as expressing her views and
strivings she would have been alien to Russian society and
would not have had that intimate meaning for us that she
has now. She would have been a fictitious character, a plant
unskillfully transplanted to our soil from some foreign land.
But Mr. Turgenev's true sense of reality did not permit him
to make the practical activities of his heroine fully coincide
with her theoretical concepts and the inner promptings of
her soul. Our public life does not yet provide an author with
the materials for this. At present we observe throughout our
society only an awakening desire to get down to real work,
a realization of the banality of the various beautiful toys, of
the lofty phrases and inert forms with which we have amused
and fooled ourselves for so long. But we have not yet emerged
from the sphere in which we were able to sleep so peacefully,
and we do not yet know very well where the exit is; if anybody does know, he is still afraid to open the door.

This difficult and painful transitional state of society inevitably leaves its impress on works of art that are produced
under these conditions. There may be individual strong
characters in society, individuals may achieve a high level
of moral development, and so such personalities appear in
literary productions. But all this remains only in the portrayal of the characters of these persons; it is not carried
over into life; the possibility of its existence is assumed, but
it is not seen in real life. Olga, in *Oblomov*, appeared to us to
be an ideal woman whose development had gone far beyond
the rest of society; but where is her practical activity? She
seems to be capable of creating a new life and yet she lives
amidst the same banality in which all her women friends live
because she cannot get away from this banality. She likes
Stolz because he is an energetic and active character, and yet,
notwithstanding all the skill displayed by the author of
Oblomov in depicting characters, he reveals to us only Stolz's
abilities, but gives us no opportunity to see how he applies

them; he has no firm ground under his feet and floats before our eyes in a sort of mist.

In Mr. Turgenev's Helena we now see another attempt to create an energetic and active character, and it cannot be said that the author's portrayal of this character is unsuccessful. If we have rarely met women like Helena, many of us, of course, have observed even in the most ordinary women the embryo of one or other of the essential features of Helena's character, the possibility of development of many of her strivings. As an ideal personage, constituted of the finest elements that are developing in our society, Helena is intelligible and close to us. Her strivings are defined for us very clearly; she seems to serve as an answer to the questions and doubts of Olga, who, while living with Stolz, is yearning and longing for something she herself cannot define. The portrait of Helena explains this longing, which inevitably overcomes every decent Russian, no matter how good his own circumstances may be. Helena is thirsting to perform good deeds; she is looking for the means to create happiness around herself, because she cannot conceive of herself enjoying peace of mind, let alone happiness, if she is surrounded by suffering, unhappiness, poverty, and the humiliation of her fellow men.

But what activities commensurate with these inner demands could Mr. Turgenev provide for his heroine? It is difficult to answer this question even in the abstract, and it is probably still less possible for a Russian author of the present day to create such activities in his art. There is no scope for such activities, and the author is, willy-nilly, obliged to compel his heroine to display her lofty strivings in a shallow way, by giving alms and saving abandoned kittens. She is unable, and afraid, to undertake activities that call for great strain and struggle. All around her she sees one thing oppressing another, and precisely because of her humane and sympathetic disposition she tries to keep aloof from everything in order to avoid oppressing others herself. At home her influence is not felt at all; her father and mother are like strangers to her; they stand in awe of her authority, but she never offers them advice or instruction, or makes demands of them. She has a companion living in the house, a young, good-natured German girl named Zoya, but Helena keeps aloof from her, scarcely ever speaks to her, and their relations are very cold. There is also the young artist Shubin, about whom we shall speak in a moment; Helena annihilates him with her withering criticism, but she never dreams of exercising any influence over him, although this would have been extremely beneficial for him.

There is not a single instance throughout the story where the yearning to do good induces Helena to intervene in the affairs of those around her and to exercise her influence in any way. We do not think that this is due to a casual oversight on the author's part. No, up to very recently we saw, not among women but among men, a special type who towered and shone above society and took pride in standing aloof from the surrounding milieu. "It is impossible to keep pure in this environment," they said, "and besides, this environment is so shallow and banal that it is far better to keep out of it." And they did indeed keep out of it; they did not make a single vigorous attempt to improve this banal environment. Their self-exclusion from it was regarded as the only honest way out of their situation, and was glorified as an act of heroism. Naturally, having such examples and concepts before him, the author had no better means of depicting Helena's domestic life than by describing her as standing entirely aloof from that life. As we have said, however, in the story Helena's impotence is attributed to a special cause, which springs from her feminine, humane sentiments: she dreads all collisions, not because she lacks courage but because she is afraid that she may offend or harm somebody. Having never experienced a full and active life, she still imagines that her ideals can be achieved without a struggle, without causing anybody any harm. After one incident (when Insarov heroically threw a drunken German into a pond), she made the following entry in her diary:

No, he will stand no nonsense, and he has the courage to take up the cudgels on another's behalf. But why that anger, those quivering lips and that venom in his eyes? But perhaps it cannot be otherwise? Perhaps a man, a fighter, cannot remain meek and mild?

This simple idea had only just entered her mind, and then only in the form of a question she is unable to answer.

In this state of indefiniteness, of inaction, in spite of a continuous yearning for something, Helena lives until she reaches the age of twenty. Sometimes she feels exceedingly depressed; she realizes that she is wasting her strength, that her life is empty. She says to herself: "If I got a place as a serving maid I would feel much better, I am sure." This feeling of depression is intensified by the fact that she meets with no sympathy from anybody; she can find no one to support her. Sometimes it seems to her that she wants something that nobody else wants, that nobody in all Russia is thinking about. . . . She becomes frightened, and the need for sympathy grows stronger, and she longs intensely and agitatedly for another soul that would understand her, that would respond to her innermost sentiments, that would help her and teach her what to do. A desire arises within her to surrender herself to somebody, to merge her being with somebody, and the lone independence in which she stands among those immediately around her becomes repugnant to her:

From the age of sixteen she lived her own life, but it was a lonely life. Her soul flared up and died down alone; she beat her wings against the bars like a bird in a cage; but there was no cage, nobody restricted her, nobody restrained her; nevertheless, she struggled and pined. Sometimes she did not understand herself; she even feared herself. Everything around her seemed to her to be either senseless or unintelligible." How is it possible to live without love? But there is no one to love," she mused, and these thoughts, these sensations frightened her.

It is in this state of mind and heart that she comes upon the scene in the story, in the summer, at a country house in Kuntsevo. In a short space of time three men appear before her, one of whom attracts her whole soul. Incidentally, there is a fourth man, introduced casually, but not one of the unwanted type, whom we shall also count. Three of these gentlemen are Russians; the fourth is a Bulgarian, and him Helena regards as her ideal. Let us look at all these gentlemen.

One of these young men, who, in his own way, is passionately in love with Helena, is the artist Pavel Yakovlevich Shubin, a handsome and graceful youth of about twenty-five, good-natured and witty, merry and ardent, carefree and talented. He is a distant relative of Anna Vassilyevna, Helena's mother, and therefore stands very close to the young girl and hopes to win her affections. But she always looks down superciliously upon him, regards him as a clever but spoiled child who can never be taken seriously. Shubin, however, says to his friends, "There was a time when she liked me," and indeed there is much about him that is likable. It is not surprising that for a moment Helena attached more importance to the good sides of his character than to the bad ones; but she soon discerned the *artistic* side of this character; she realized that everything about him was ephemeral, that there was nothing constant and reliable about him, that his entire makeup was a mass of contradictions: indolence crushed his talent, and waste of time later called forth fruitless contrition, caused spleen and roused self-contempt, which, in its turn, served to console him for his failures and fostered his pride and conceit. Helena realized all this instinctively, without tormenting perplexity, and therefore, her decision regarding Shubin was absolutely calm and dispassionate. "You think that everything about me is pretense, you do not believe that I have repented, you do not believe that I can weep sincerely!" said Shubin to her one day in an outburst of despair. She does not answer, "I do not believe." She says simply, "But I do believe you have repented, Pavel Yakovlevich, and I believe your tears, but it seems to me that your repentance amuses you, and so do your tears." Shubin shuddered as he heard this simple verdict, which must indeed have stabbed deeply into his heart. He had never imagined that his impulses, contradictions and sufferings, his tossing from one side to another, could be interpreted and explained so simply and truthfully. After hearing this explanation he even stopped making himself an "interesting person." And indeed, as soon as Helena has formed an opinion about him he ceases to interest her. She does not care whether he is present or not, whether he remembers or has forgotten her, whether he loves or hates her. She has nothing in common with him, although she is not averse to praising him sincerely when he does something worthy of his talents. . . .

Another begins to occupy her thoughts. He is of an entirely different type. He is uncouth, oldish; his face is not handsome, and it is even funny in a way, but it expresses a thoughtful and kindhearted character. Moreover, according to the author, "his entire uncouth figure bears the *impress of decency.*" This is Andrei Petrovich Bersenev, a close friend of Shubin. He is a philosopher, a scholar, reads the history of the Hohenstaufens and other German books, and he is modest and capable of self-sacrifice. In answer to Shubin's exclamation: "We want happiness, happiness! We shall win happiness for ourselves!" he says skeptically, "As if there is

nothing higher than happiness!" and then comes the following dialogue between them:

"For example?" Shubin asked, and halted.
"Well, take this, for example. We two, as you say, are
young, we are good fellows. All right, let's admit that it is so.
Both of us want happiness. But is the word 'happiness' the one
that will unite, inflame us two, induce us to extend a hand to
each other? Is it not a selfish word? What I want to say is:
Is it not a word that disunites us?"
"But do you know any words that unite?"
"Yes. Quite a number. And you know them, too."
"What words are these? Tell me."
"Well, take the word 'art,' since you are an artist. Then
there are 'country,' 'science,' 'freedom,' 'justice.' "
"And 'love'?" Shubin asked.
"And 'love' is a uniting word, but not the love that you are
now yearning for, not love that means pleasure, but love that
means sacrifice."
Shubin frowned.
"That's all right for the Germans. I want love for myself. I
want to be Number One."
"Number One," Bersenev echoes. "But I think that the entire mission of our lives is to make ourselves Number Two."
"If everybody behaves as you advise," said Shubin with a
plaintive grimace, "nobody will eat pineapples; everybody will
leave them all for others."
"That shows that pineapples are not essential. But don't be
afraid; there will always be people who will even take bread
out of another's mouth."

This conversation shows what noble principles Bersenev
professes, and how his soul is capable of what is called self-
sacrifice. It expresses sincere readiness to sacrifice his happiness for the sake of one of those words he calls "uniting
words." Consequently, it was inevitable that he should win
the sympathy of a girl like Helena. But it at once becomes
evident why he cannot capture her soul, fill her whole life.
He is one of the heroes of passive virtue, a man capable of
bearing a great deal, of sacrificing a great deal, of acting in a
noble manner in general when opportunity occurs, but he will
not be able and will not dare to undertake broad and bold
activity, a free struggle, an independent role in any cause.
He wants to be Number Two because he thinks that this is
the mission of every living being; and indeed his role in the

story to some extent reminds one of Bizmenkov in *The Superfluous Man,* and still more of Krupitsyn in *Two Friends.* Although in love with Helena, he becomes the mediator between her and Insarov, with whom she has fallen in love; he generously helps them, nurses Insarov when he is sick, renounces his own happiness for the sake of his friend, although not without some heartache, and even not without complaint.

He has a kind and loving heart, but everything goes to show that he will always do good not so much because of the promptings of his heart as because he thinks it his *duty* to do good. He holds that one must sacrifice one's happiness for the sake of one's country, of science, and so forth, and thereby condemns himself to remain an eternal slave and martyr to an idea. He draws a line between his happiness and his country, for example; he, poor fellow, cannot rise sufficiently to be able to understand that the good of his country is inseparably bound up with his own happiness, and to be unable to conceive of happiness for himself apart from the well-being of his country. On the contrary, he seems to be afraid that his personal happiness may hinder the well-being of his country, hinder the triumph of justice, the achievements of science, and so forth. That is why he is afraid to wish for happiness for himself, and owing to the nobility of his principles he decides to sacrifice his happiness for the sake of his ideas and, of course, thinks that this is an act of magnanimity on his part.

Clearly, such a man is capable only of passive nobility. He cannot merge his soul with any great cause; he cannot forget the whole world for the sake of a favorite idea; that idea cannot inflame him and he cannot fight for it as if he were fighting for his own joy, his own life, his own happiness. . . . He does what duty bids him; he strives for what he regards as just on principle; but his actions are listless, cold, and hesitant, because he is always doubting his strength. He finished his course at the university with distinction, he loves science, and he is constantly studying and wishes to become a professor. What could be simpler? But when Helena asks him about his professorship he deems it necessary to display praiseworthy modesty: "I, of course, know only too well how much I still lack to be worthy of such a lofty . . . I want to say that I am too little prepared for it, but I hope to obtain permission to go abroad. . . ." Exactly like the introduction to an academic speech: "I hope, ladies and gentlemen, that you will kindly excuse the dryness and colorlessness of my exposition," and so forth.

And yet the professorship about which Bersenev speaks in this way is the object of his cherished dreams! When Helena asks him whether he will be quite content with his position when he is appointed to a university chair he answers:

"Quite, Helena Nikolayevna, quite! What higher calling can there be? Think of it! To follow in the footsteps of Timofei Nikolayevich . . . The very thought that I shall engage in such activities fills me with joy and embarrassment. . . . Yes, embarrassment which . . . which springs from the consciousness of my own weakness."

The same consciousness of his weakness first induces him stubbornly to refuse to believe that Helena has grown to love him, and then to grieve that she has grown indifferent toward him. This same consciousness can be discerned when, in recommending his friend Insarov, he mentions among his other merits the fact that he does not borrow money. The same consciousness can even be discerned in his reflections about nature. He says that nature awakens in him a sort of disquietude, anxiety, and even melancholy, and he asks Shubin:

"What can this mean? Does the consciousness of our utter imperfection, of our lack of clarity grow stronger in her presence, before her face, or is that which she gives us inadequate for us, while the other . . . what I mean to say is . . . she lacks what we need?"

Most of Bersenev's reflections run in this air-beating romantic style. And yet, in one passage of this story we are told that he argued about Feuerbach. It would have been extremely interesting to hear what he had to say about Feuerbach! . . .

And so, Bersenev is a very good Russian nobleman, trained in the principles of duty, who later plunges into scholarship and philosophy. He is far more practical and reliable than Shubin, and if he were led along some road he would go willingly and straight ahead. But he is incapable of leading not only others but even himself: by his very nature he lacks initiative; he failed to acquire it during his upbringing and he failed to acquire it in later life. At first Helena feels an attraction for him because of his kindness and the serious subjects

he discusses with her. She is even ashamed of her own ignorance, because he is always bringing her books that she cannot read. But she cannot become completely attached to him,
she cannot surrender her soul, her fate, to him; she instinctively realizes even before she meets Insarov that Bersenev
is not the man she needs. And indeed, we may confidently
assert that Bersenev would have been scared had Helena
thrown herself upon his neck, and he would certainly have
fled on various extremely noble pretexts.

Incidentally, living in a wilderness, as it were, Helena was
for a moment enchanted with Bersenev and already asked herself whether he was not the man for whom her soul had been
yearning for so long, the man who was to relieve her of all
her perplexities and point out to her the path of activity. But
Bersenev himself introduces Insarov to her, and the enchantment vanishes. . . .

Strictly speaking, there is nothing extraordinary about
Insarov. Bersenev and Shubin, Helena, and even the author
of the novel himself, describe him in negative terms: he never
tells lies, he never breaks a promise, he does not borrow
money, he is not fond of talking about his achievements, he
never puts off the execution of a decision once adopted, his
deeds never contradict his words, and so forth. In short, he
has none of the features for which any man with claims to
respectability should bitterly reproach himself. But in addition to this, he is a Bulgarian whose soul is filled with a passionate desire to liberate his country, and to this idea he devotes himself entirely, openly and confidently; it represents
the ultimate goal of his life. He does not think that his personal happiness can come into collision with his life's object;
such an idea, so natural for the Russian nobleman-scholar
Bersenev, would never enter the head of this simple Bulgarian. On the contrary, he is striving for the liberation of
his country because to him it means ensuring his own peace
of mind, the happiness of his whole life; if he could have
found satisfaction in anything else he would not have concerned himself about his enslaved country. But he cannot
conceive of himself separately from his country:

"How can one be content and happy when one's countrymen are suffering?" he thinks. "How can a man remain calm
while his country is enslaved and oppressed? What pleasure
can he find in any occupation if that occupation does not lead
to the alleviation of the lot of one's poor countrymen?"

Thus, he pursues his cherished cause quite naturally, without posing, without any fanfare, as naturally as eating and drinking. For the time being he can do little in the way of putting his idea into execution, but that cannot be helped. At present he has little to eat and sometimes even starves, but for all that the food, although scanty, is essential for his existence. So it is with the liberation of his country: he studies at the Moscow University in order to become thoroughly educated and to become intimate with the Russians, and throughout the story he is content for the time being with translating Bulgarian songs into Russian, compiling a textbook of Bulgarian grammar for Russians and a Russian grammar for Bulgarians, keeps up a correspondence with his fellow countrymen, and intends to return to his country in order to prepare for an insurrection on the very first outbreak of an Eastern war (the action of the story takes place in 1853). This, of course, is meager sustenance for Insarov's active patriotism, but he does not regard his stay in Moscow as real life, and does not consider his feeble activities satisfactory even for his personal strivings. He too lives *on the eve* of the great day of liberation of his country, in which his being will be illumined by the consciousness of happiness, life will become full and will be real life. He looks forward to this as to a festival, and this explains why it never enters his head to entertain any doubts about himself, or coolly to calculate and weigh how much he will do, and to the level of which great man he will rise. It is a matter of total indifference to him whether he will be a Timofei Nikolayevich or an Ivan Ivanych; whether he will be Number One or Number Two does not worry him. He will do what his nature prompts him to do; if his nature is such that no better will be found, he will be Number One; he will march at the head; if men stronger and bolder than he are found, he will follow them, and in both cases he will remain true to himself. Where he will stand and how far he will go will be determined by circumstances; but he wants to go, and he cannot help going, not because he is afraid of failing to perform some duty but because he would die if he were unable to go.

It is this that constitutes the enormous difference between him and Bersenev. Bersenev is also capable of making sacrifices and of performing heroic deeds, but in this he resembles a generous girl who consents to marry a man she hates in order to save her father. She looks forward to the wedding with smothered pain and unwilling submission to her fate,

and would be glad if something happened to prevent it.
Insarov, however, looks forward to his feats of heroism, to
the day when he can engage in his self-sacrificing activities
with eagerness and impatience, like a young man in love
looking forward to the day of his wedding with the girl he
loves. Only one anxiety disturbs him, and that is that something may happen to put off the wished-for day. Insarov's
love for the freedom of his country lies not in his mind, not
in his heart, nor in his imagination: it permeates his whole
being, and whatever else penetrates his being is transformed
by the power of this feeling, submits to it and merges with it.
That is why, notwithstanding his quite ordinary abilities,
notwithstanding the lack of brilliance in his nature, he is
immeasurably superior to, charms and influences Helena
ever so much more than brilliant Shubin and clever Bersenev, although both are also noble and loving characters.
Helena makes the following extremely apt observation concerning Bersenev in her diary (on which the author did not
spare his profundity and wit):

Andrei Petrovich may be more learned than he [Insarov],
he may even be more intelligent, but I don't know why it is—
he looks so small in his presence.

Is it necessary to relate the story of how Helena and
Insarov were drawn together, the story of their love? We
think not. Our readers probably remember this story well,
and besides it cannot really be told. We are afraid to touch
this tender poetical creation with our cold rough hands; in
fact, we are afraid to offend our readers' feelings, which,
undoubtedly, have been stirred by the poetry of Turgenev's
narrative, with our dry and unfeeling account of it. Mr. Turgenev, the bard of pure and ideal feminine love, peers so
deeply into the young virgin soul, understands it so fully
and depicts its finest moments with such inspired emotion,
with such an ardor of love, that we actually feel in this story
the quiver of her maidenly breast, her tender sighs, her moist
glance, every throb of her agitated heart, so that our own
hearts melt and stop beating from deep emotion, tears of
happiness rise to our eyes more than once, and something
bursts from our breasts as if we were sitting beside an old
friend after a long separation, or had returned home to our
native land after a sojourn in foreign parts. This feeling is
both sad and joyful: it conjures up bright recollections of

childhood, gone never to return; the proud and joyous hopes of youth, the ideal, harmonious dreams of a pure and mighty imagination as yet untamed or degraded by the trials of mundane experience. All this has passed never to return; but the man is not yet lost who can return to these bright dreams if only in recollection, to this pure and youthful intoxication with life, to these grand and ideal plans, and then shiver at the sight of the sordidness, banality, and pettiness in which his present life is passing. And blessed is the one who can rouse such recollections in others, who can awaken such sentiments in another's soul. . . .

Mr. Turgenev's talent has always been distinguished for this; his stories always create this pure impression of their general construction, and therein, of course, lies their essential importance for society. This importance is inherent in *On the Eve* because of its portrayal of Helena's love. We are certain that our readers will be able, without our aid, to appreciate the charm of those passions, those tender and languorous scenes, those subtle and profound psychological details with which the love of Helena and Insarov is depicted from beginning to end. Instead of relating the story we shall recall Helena's diary, her waiting for Insarov to come to say good-bye, the scene in the chapel, Helena's return home after that scene, her three visits to Insarov, especially the last,[3] then her parting from her mother and her country, her departure, and lastly, her last stroll with Insarov along the Canal Grande, her visit to the opera to hear *La Traviata*, and her return. This last episode strongly impresses us by its strict truthfulness, and by the infinite sadness of its charm; we think

---

[3] There are people whose imaginations are so sordid and corrupted that in this charming, pure, and profoundly moral scene, so full of the passionate merging of two loving beings, they see only material for voluptuous scenes. Judging everybody by themselves, they even howl that this scene may have a bad influence upon morals because it rouses impure thoughts. But let them howl. After all, there are people who feel only sensuous excitement at the sight of a statue of Venus of Milo; and on seeing a picture of the Madonna they say with a lascivious smirk: "She's . . . fit for . . . you know. . . ." But art and poetry are not for such people, nor is true morality. Everything in their minds is transformed into something disgustingly impure. But give these scenes to an innocent, purehearted maiden to read; you may be sure that she will gain from this reading nothing but the brightest and most noble thoughts.—*N. D.*

it is the most touching, the most charming passage in the
whole story.

We shall leave our readers to enjoy the recollection of the
entire development of the story while we return to Insarov's
character, or rather to the relationship in which he stands
to the Russian society around him. We have already seen that
here he does almost nothing to achieve his principal aim; only
once do we see him go off on a journey of sixty versts to
Troitsky Posad, to reconcile his compatriots who had quarreled
among themselves, and at the end of his stay in Moscow
it is mentioned that he traveled all over the city clandestinely
visiting various personages. But it goes without saying that
he has nothing to do while living in Moscow. To do anything
real he must go to Bulgaria. And he does go, but death in-
tercepts him on the road, and so we see no activity on his
part in the story. From this it is evident that the purpose of
the story is not to depict for us an example of civic, that is,
public heroism, as some critics try to assure us. Here there
is no reproach aimed at the Russian young generation, no
indication as to what a civic hero should be. Had this been
the author's object, he should have brought his hero face to
face with his cause—with parties, with the people, with the
alien government, with those who share his views, with the
enemy force. . . . But the author did not wish and, as far
as we are able to judge from his previous works, was unable
to write a heroic epic. His object was entirely different: from
all the Iliads and Odysseys he borrowed only the story of
Ulysses' sojourn on the island of Calypsos, and further than
that he does not go. After making us understand and feel
what Insarov is, and in what environment he finds himself,
Mr. Turgenev devotes himself entirely to describing how
Insarov is loved, and what came of this love. At the point
where love must at last make way for real civic activity he
cuts the life of his hero short and ends his tale.

What then is the significance of the *Bulgarian's* appearance
in this story? Why a Bulgarian and not a Russian? Are there
no such characters among Russians? Are Russians incapable
of loving passionately and persistently, incapable of recklessly
marrying for love? Or is this only a whim of the author's
imagination, and it is useless seeking any particular meaning
in it? As much as to say: "Well, he went and took a Bulgarian, and that's all there is to it. He might just as well have
taken a gypsy, or a Chinese, perhaps. . . ."

The answers to these questions depend upon one's views

concerning the entire meaning of the story. We think that the Bulgarian's place here could indeed have been taken by a man of some other nationality, by a Serb, a Czech, an Italian or a Hungarian, but not by a Pole or a Russian. Not a Pole, because a Pole is entirely out of the question. But why not a Russian? That is the question at issue, and we shall try to answer it to the best of our ability.

The point is that the principal personage in *On the Eve* is Helena, and it is in relation to her that we must examine the other personages in the story. She expresses that vague longing for something, that almost unconscious but irresistible desire for a new way of life, for a new type of people, which the whole of Russian society, and not only its so-called educated section, now feels. Helena so vividly expresses the finest strivings of our present society, and she brings out the utter hollowness of the common everyday life of this society in such prominent relief, that one involuntarily feels like drawing a detailed parallel. Here all would be in their place: Stakhov, who is by no means malicious, but is featherbrained and stupidly puts on airs; Anna Vassilyevna, whom Shubin calls a hen; the German companion toward whom Helena is so cold; dreamy but sometimes profound Uvar Ivanovich, who is disturbed only by the news of the counterbombardment; and even the mean footman, who reports Helena to her father when everything is over. . . . But parallels of this kind, while undoubtedly revealing a playful imagination, become overstrained and ludicrous when they go into great detail. We shall therefore refrain from going into details and confine ourselves to a few observations of a most general nature.

Helena's development is not based on deep learning or on wide experience of life; the finest, the ideal side of her character blossomed, grew, and matured at the sight of the meek sufferings of the person who was dear to her, at the sight of the poor, the sick and the oppressed, whom she found and saw everywhere, even in her dreams. Is it not with impressions like these that all the best characters in Russian society grew and were molded? Is it not in the character of every truly decent person [in this country] to hate all violence, tyranny, and oppression, and to wish to help the weak and the oppressed? We do not say *"activity* in protecting the weak from the strong," because this is not the case; we say *desire*, which is exactly the case with Helena. We too are glad to perform a good deed when it concerns only the positive side, that is, when it does not call for a struggle, when

no outside opposition is anticipated. We give alms, arrange
theatrical performances for charitable purposes, and even
sacrifice part of our fortunes if need be; all on the condition,
however, that the matter ends here, that we shall not have
to encounter and combat all sorts of unpleasantness for the
sake of some poor or wronged person. We have the "desire
actively to do good," and we have the strength to do it; but
fear, lack of confidence in our strength and, lastly, our ignorance of what is to be done, constantly check us and, without
knowing why, we suddenly find ourselves outside social life,
cold and alien to its interests, exactly like Helena and all
those around her. And yet the *desire* still seethes in everybody's breast (we mean in the breasts of those who do not
strive artificially to suppress it), and we are all seeking,
thirsting, waiting . . . waiting for someone to tell us what
is to be done. It is with the anguish of perplexity, almost of
despair, that Helena writes in her diary:

Oh, if only somebody said to me: this is what you must do!
Be good—that is not enough. Do good . . . yes, that is the
main thing in life. *But how is one to do good?*

Who in our society, conscious of possessing a loving heart,
has not, in his torment, put this question to himself? Who has
not confessed to himself that all the forms of activity in which
his desire to do good has manifested itself, as far as it was
possible, have been insignificant and pitiful? Who has not felt
that there is something different, something more lofty, that
we could have done, but did not do because we did not
know how to proceed about it? Who can solve our doubts?
We long for this solution, we seek it eagerly in the bright
moments of our existence, but we cannot find it anywhere.
It seems to us that everybody around us is either tormented
by the same perplexity that torments us, or has crushed his
own feelings in his heart and confines himself to pursuing
only his petty, selfish, animal interests. And so life passes, day
after day, until it dies in a man's heart, and day after day
a man waits and hopes that the next day will be better, that
his doubts will be solved tomorrow, that somebody will tell
us how to do good. . . .

Russian society has been longing and waiting like this for
quite a long time; and how many times have we, like Helena,
erred in thinking that the one we had been waiting for had

arrived, and then cooled off? Helena became passionately attached to Anna Vassilyevna, but Anna Vassilyevna turned out to be a spineless nonentity. . . . At one time Helena felt well disposed toward Shubin in the same way as our society at one time became enthusiastic about art, but it turned out that Shubin lacked real content; there were only sparkle and whims about him; and absorbed in her searching, Helena could not stop to admire trinkets. For a moment she was interested in serious learning, in the person of Bersenev, but serious learning turned out to be modest, beset by doubt, learning that was waiting for a Number One to lead him. What Helena needed was a man without a number, a man who was not waiting for a lead, an independent man, who irresistibly strove toward his goal and carried others with him. At last such a man appeared in the person of Insarov, and in him Helena found her ideal; in him she found the man who could tell her how to do good.

But why could not Insarov have been a Russian? After all, he does nothing in the story; he merely intends to do something; this much a Russian could have done. Insarov's character could have been encased in a Russian skin, particularly in the way it expresses itself in the story. In the story his character expresses itself in that he loves strongly and resolutely; but is it impossible for a Russian to love in this way?

All this is true; nevertheless the sympathies of Helena, of the girl as we understand her, could not turn toward a Russian with the same justification and with the same naturalness as they turned toward this Bulgarian. All Insarov's charm lies in the grandeur and sacredness of the idea that permeates his whole being. Thirsting to do good, but not knowing how, Helena is instantly and profoundly captivated by the mere relation of his aims, even before she has seen him. "Liberate one's country," she says; "these are words that one even fears to utter—they are so grand!" And she feels that she has found the word her heart has been longing for, that she is satisfied, that no higher goal than this can be striven for, and that her whole life, her whole future will be filled with activities if only she follows this man. And so she tries to study him; she wants to peer into his soul, to share his dreams, to learn the details of his plans. He has only one idea: his country and its freedom, an idea that is constantly with him and has merged with his being; Helena is satisfied, she is pleased with the clarity and definiteness of his aim,

the serenity and firmness of his heart, with the grandeur of
the very idea, and soon she herself becomes the echo of this
idea that inspires him.

When he talks about his country [she writes in her diary],
he seems to grow and grow; his face becomes handsomer; his
voice becomes like steel, and it seems as though there is not
a man in the world before whom his eyes would droop. And
he not only talks; he has done things, and will do things. I
will ask him about it. . . .

Several days later she writes again:

But it is strange, though, that up till now, until I was
twenty, I have never loved anybody! It seems to me that D
(I will call him D, I like that name: Dmitri) has such a serene
soul because he has devoted himself entirely to his cause, to
his dream. Why should he worry? Whoever devotes himself
to a cause entirely . . . entirely . . . entirely, knows little
worry, he has nothing to answer for. It is not what *I want;* it
is what *it* wants.

Realizing this, she wants to merge herself with him in such
a way that *not she* should want, but that *he,* and *that* which
inspires him, should want. We can fully understand her position; and we are sure that the whole of Russian society, even
if it is not yet carried away by the personality of Insarov as
she is, will understand that Helena's feelings are real and
natural.

We say that society will not be carried away, and we
base this statement on the assumption that *this* man Insarov
is, after all, an alien to us. Mr. Turgenev himself, who has
so thoroughly studied the finest part of our society, did not
find it possible to make him *our man.* Not only did he bring
him from Bulgaria but he also refrained from making his hero
sufficiently endearing to us even as a man. This, if you look
at it even from the literary standpoint, is the main artistic
defect in the novel. We know one of the principal reasons
for this, one over which the author had no control, and therefore we are not blaming Mr. Turgenev for this. Nevertheless, the pale sketch of Insarov affects the impression we
obtain from the story. The grandeur and beauty of Insarov's
idea are not brought out with full force, so that we are not
imbued with it sufficiently to compel us to exclaim with proud
inspiration: We shall follow you! And yet this idea is so

sacred, so exalted. . . . Far less humane, even utterly false ideas, vividly brought out in artistic images, have exercised a feverish effect upon society; the Charles Moores, the Werthers, and the Pechorins had a crowd of imitators.

Insarov will have no such imitators. True, it was difficult for him to express his ideas fully, living as he did in Moscow and doing nothing; he could not indulge in rhetorical outpourings! But from the story we learn little about him even as a man; his inner world is inaccessible to us; what he does, what he thinks, what he hopes for, what changes his relationships undergo, his views on the course of events, on life that is sweeping past our eyes, are concealed from us. Even his love for Helena is not fully revealed to us. We know that he loves her passionately, but how he becomes imbued with this passion, what it is about Helena that attracts him, how deep this passion is, when he becomes aware of it and decides to go away—all these inner details about Insarov's personality, and many others that Mr. Turgenev is able to depict with such subtle poetic skill, are kept from us.

As a living image, as a real personality, Insarov is extremely remote from us, and this explains why *On the Eve* produces upon the public such a faint and partly even unfavorable impression compared with Mr. Turgenev's previous stories, which portray characters whom the author had studied down to the minutest detail, and for whom he had felt such a lively sympathy. We realize that Insarov must be a good man and that Helena must love him with all the ardor of her soul because she sees him in real life and not in a story. But he is near and dear to us only as a representative of an idea, which attracts us, as it did Helena, like a flash of light and lights up the gloom of our existence. That is why we understand how natural are Helena's feelings toward Insarov; that is why we ourselves, pleased with his indomitable loyalty to an idea, fail to realize at first that he is depicted for us only in pale and general outline.

And yet some want him to be a Russian! "No, he could not be a Russian!" exclaims Helena herself in answer to a regret that had arisen in her own heart that he was not a Russian. Indeed, there are no such Russians; there should not and cannot be such, at all events at the present time. We do not know how the new generations are developing and will develop, but those that we see in action today have not by any means developed in such a way as to resemble Insarov. Every individual's development is influenced not only by his private relationships but also by the entire social atmosphere in which it is his lot to live. One social atmosphere will develop heroic trends, another will develop peaceful inclinations, a third irritates, a fourth soothes. Russian life is so well arranged that everything in it induces calm and peaceful slumber, and every sleepless person seems, and not without good reason, to be a troublesome character and absolutely unwanted by society. Indeed, compare the conditions under which Insarov's life begins and passes with those met with in the life of every Russian.

Bulgaria is enslaved; she is groaning under the Turkish yoke. We, thank God, are not enslaved by anybody; we are free; we are a great people who more than once have decided with our arms the destinies of kingdoms and nations; we are the masters of others, but we have no masters. . . .

In Bulgaria there are no social rights and guarantees, and Insarov says to Helena: "If only you knew what a bounteous land my country is, and yet she is being torn and trampled upon. We have been robbed of everything: our church, our rights, our land; the vile Turks drive us like cattle, we are slaughtered. . . ." Russia, on the contrary, is a well-ordered state; she has wise laws that protect the rights of citizens and define their duties; here justice reigns and beneficent publicity flourishes. Nobody is robbed of his church, and religion is not restricted in any way; on the contrary, the zeal of preachers in admonishing the errant is encouraged; far from anybody's being robbed of rights and land, these are even granted to those who hitherto have not possessed them; nobody is driven like cattle.

"In Bulgaria," says Insarov, "every peasant, every beggar, and I—we all want the same thing, we all have the same goal." There is no such monotony in Russian life, in which every class, even every circle, lives its own separate life, has its own separate goal and aspirations, has its own appointed place. With the good social order prevailing here each one need be concerned only with the pursuit of his own welfare, and for this purpose there is no need whatever to merge with the whole nation in one common idea, as they do in Bulgaria.

Insarov was still an infant when a Turkish Aga kidnaped his mother and afterward murdered her, and then his father was shot because he wanted to avenge his mother by stabbing the Aga. Which Russian could ever gain such impressions in his life? Can anything like this be conceived of in Russia? Of course, criminals may be found anywhere, but if, in this country, an Aga kidnaped and afterward killed another man's wife, the husband would not be allowed to avenge her because we have laws, before which all are equal and which punish crimes irrespective of persons.

In short, Insarov imbibed hatred for enslavers and discontent with the present state of things with his mother's milk. There was no need for him to exert himself, to resort to a long series of syllogisms to be able to determine the direction of his activities. Since he is not lazy, and no coward, he knows what to do and how to behave. There is no need for him to take up many tasks at once. And besides, his task is so *easily understood,* as Shubin says: "All you have to do is to kick the Turks out—that's not much!" Moreover, Insarov knows that he is doing right not only in his own conscience but also before the court of humanity: his idea will meet with the sympathy of every decent man. Try to picture something like this in Russian society. It is inconceivable. . . . Translated into Russian, Insarov would turn out to be nothing more than a robber, a representative of the "antisocial element," with whom the Russian public are so familiar from the learned investigations of Mr. Solovyov, which have been published in the *Russian Herald.* Who, we ask, could love such a man? What well-bred and clever girl would not flee from him in horror?

Is it clear now why a Russian could not have taken the place of Insarov? Characters like his are of course born in Russia in no small number, but they cannot develop as freely and express themselves as frankly as Insarov does. A contemporary Russian Insarov will always remain timid and dual-natured; he will lie low, express himself with various reservations and equivocations . . . and it is this that reduces confidence in him. Sometimes he may even prevaricate and contradict himself, and it is well known that people usually prevaricate for their own gain, or out of cowardice. What sympathy can one feel toward a covetous man and a coward, especially when one's soul longs for action and seeks for a great mind and a strong hand to lead it?

True, minor heroes appear among us who somewhat resemble Insarov in courage and in sympathy for the oppressed. But in our society they are ludicrous Don Quixotes. The distinguishing feature of a Don Quixote is that he does not know what he is fighting for or what will come of his efforts, and these minor heroes display this feature to a remarkable degree. For example, they may suddenly take it into their heads that it is necessary to save the peasants from the tyranny of the squires and simply refuse to believe that there is no tyranny here at all, that the rights of the squires are strictly defined by the law, and must remain inviolable as long as these laws exist; that to rouse the peasants against this tyranny means not liberating them from the squires, but making them, in addition, liable to a penalty under the law. Or, for example, they may set themselves the task of protecting the innocent from miscarriages of justice, as if the judges in this country administer the law according to their own arbitrary will.

Everybody knows that in this country everything is done according to the law, and that to interpret the law one way or another it is not heroism that is needed, but skill in legal quibbling. And so our Don Quixotes simply beat the air. . . . Or they may suddenly take it into their heads to eradicate bribery, and what a torment they will make of the lives of poor officials who take ten kopeks or so for some little service rendered! Our heroes who will set out to protect sufferers will make the lives of these poor officials unbearable. It is, of course, a noble and lofty task, but do these unwise people deserve our sympathy?

We are not referring to those cold slaves to duty who act in this way simply in their official capacity; we have in mind Russians who really and sincerely sympathize with the oppressed, and are even ready to fight in their defense. But it is these who turn out to be useless and ludicrous, because they fail to understand the general character of the environment in which they are operating. How can they understand it when they themselves are in it, when their tops, so to speak, are pushing upward, while their roots are, after all, embedded in this very soil? They want to alleviate their neighbors' sufferings, but these sufferings spring from the very milieu in which both the sufferers and the would-be alleviators of suffering live. What can be done here? Turn this whole milieu upside down? If so, they will have to turn themselves upside down. Get into an empty packing case and turn it upside down with yourself inside it! What efforts you will be compelled to exert! If you stand outside the packing case, however, you can easily turn it over with just one push. Insarov's advantageous position is that he is not inside the packing case; the oppressors of his country are the Turks, with whom he has nothing in common. All he has to do is go up and push them as hard as his strength will allow.

The Russian heroes, however, belonging, as a rule, to the

educated section of society, are themselves vitally connected
with what must be overthrown. They are in a position that
a son of a Turkish Aga, for example, would be in if he took
it into his head to liberate Bulgaria from the Turks. It is
difficult even to conceive of such a situation; but even if it
occurred, if this son of an Aga wanted to avoid appearing
like a stupid and ludicrous fellow, he would have to renounce
everything that connects him with the Turks—his faith, his
nationality, his relatives and friends, and the material advantages of his social position. It must be admitted that this
is frightfully difficult, and determination of this kind requires
a somewhat different upbringing from that which the son of
a Turkish Aga usually receives.

It is not much easier for a Russian to be a hero. This explains why likable and energetic characters in this country
content themselves with petty and unnecessary bravado and
fail to rise to real and serious heroism, that is, renouncing
the entire complex of concepts and practical relationships that
bind them to their social milieu. Their timidity in face of the
host of enemy forces is reflected even in their theoretical
development; they are afraid, or are unable, to delve down
to the roots, and setting out, for example, to punish evil,
they merely attack some minor manifestation of it and wear
themselves out frightfully before they have time even to look
for the source of this evil. They are reluctant to put the ax
to the tree on which they themselves grew, and so they try
to assure themselves, and others, that all the rot is only on
the surface, that it is only necessary to scrub it off and all
will be well. Dismiss a few corrupt officials from the service,
appoint trustees over a few squires' estates, and expose the
tapster at one tavern who is selling diluted vodka, and justice
will reign supreme, the peasants all over Russia will live in
bliss, and the tavern licensing system will become a splendid
thing for the people. Many sincerely believe this, and do
indeed waste all their strength on efforts of this kind, and
for this they quite seriously regard themselves as heroes.

We were told about a hero of this type who, it was said,
was a man of extraordinary energy and talent. While still a
student at the high school he started a row with one of the
tutors because the latter was appropriating the paper intended
for the use of the students. The affair took a bad turn; our
hero managed to get into trouble also with the school inspector and the headmaster, and was expelled. He began to prepare to enter the university and meanwhile gave private

lessons. At the very first house at which he gave these lessons
he saw the mother of his pupils slap the face of her house-
maid. He flared up, raised a scandal in the house, called the
police, and formally charged the mistress with cruelly ill-
treating her servant. A lengthy investigation ensued, but, of
course, he could not prove anything and barely escaped
severe punishment for laying false information and for slander.
After that, he could get no more private lessons.

With great difficulty, thanks to somebody's special inter-
cession, he obtained a situation in the government service.
One day he was asked to copy a decision of an extremely
absurd nature. Unable to restrain himself, he challenged this
decision. He was told to hold his tongue, but he persisted in
his protest. After that, he was told to clear out.

Having nothing to do, he accepted the invitation of an
old school chum of his to stay in the country with him during
the summer. When he arrived in the village and saw what
was going on there he began to tell his friend, his friend's
f-ather, and even the steward of the estate and the peasants
that it was illegal to compel the peasants to perform *corvée*
for more than three days, that it was outrageous to flog them
without trial and sentence, that it was dishonorable to drag
peasant women into the house at night, and so forth. The
upshot was that the peasants who had agreed with what he
had said were flogged, and the old squire ordered the car-
riage to be brought round for him and asked him to leave
and never show his face in those parts again if he wanted to
keep a whole skin.

Pulling through the summer somehow, our hero entered
the university in the autumn, and he succeeded in doing so
only because, at the examinations, he was given innocuous
questions to answer that gave him no scope for argument.

He took up medicine and really studied hard; but during
his practical course, when a professor expounded the in-
tricacies of the science at the bedside of a patient, he could
never restrain himself from interrupting when the professor
revealed the obsolescence of his views, or quackery; as soon
as the latter said anything of that nature he at once butted
in and tried to prove that he was talking nonsense.

As a result of all this, our hero was not allowed to remain
on as a post-graduate student, was not sent abroad for further study, but was appointed to a hospital in some remote
district. No sooner did he arrive there than he exposed the

superintendent and threatened to lodge a complaint against him. One day he caught the superintendent red-handed and lodged a complaint, but for this he received a reprimand from the head doctor. When he received this reprimand, he of course protested very loudly and was soon dismissed from the hospital. . . .

After that he received an appointment to go with some expedition or other, and here he took up the cudgels on behalf of the soldiers and quarreled with the chief of the expedition and with the official in charge of the food supplies. As his protests were unavailing, he sent a report to headquarters complaining that the men were being starved owing to the malpractices of the official and that the chief of the expedition was conniving at this. When the party reached its destination an investigator arrived and interrogated the soldiers. The latter stated that they had no complaints. Our hero became indignant, was disrespectful to the General Staff doctor, and a month later was reduced to the rank of orderly. He remained in this post for two weeks, but unable to stand the deliberately brutal treatment to which he was subjected, he shot himself.

An extraordinary case, a strong and impulsive character, is that not so? And yet, look what he perished for. There was nothing in his actions that would not represent the direct duty of any honest man in his place; but he must possess considerable heroism to act in this way; he must have self-sacrificing determination to die for the sake of doing good. The question arises: Since he possessed this determination, would it not have been better to have exercised it for some bigger cause, so that something really useful might have been achieved? The whole trouble is, however, that he did not realize the necessity and the possibility of such a cause, and he did not understand what was going on around him; he refused to see the conspiracy that went on around him; he refused to see what went on before his very eyes, and imagined that every manifestation of evil that he noticed was nothing more than an abuse, which could only be a rare exception, of the system which in itself was splendid. Holding views such as these, the Russian hero can, of course, do nothing more than confine himself to petty details without thinking of the general, whereas Insarov always subordinated the particular to the general, convinced that the particular, too, "will not get away." Thus, in answer to Helena's question as to whether he avenged his father's murder, he said:

"I did not search for the murderer. I did not search for him, not because I could not kill him—I would have done that with a clear conscience—but because there is no time for private vengeance when the liberation of a nation is at stake. One would have hindered the other. But the murderer will not get away. His time will come too."

It is this love for the general cause, this premonition that gives him the strength coolly to bear private wrong, that makes the Bulgarian Insarov far and away superior to all the Russian heroes, who have no conception whatever of a general cause.

Incidentally, even of such heroes there are very few in this country, and most of these do not hold out to the end. Far more numerous among the educated section of our society is another category of men—those who indulge in reflection. Among these there are also many who, although able to reflect, understand nothing, but of these we shall not speak. We wish to point only to those men who really have bright minds, men who after a long period of doubt and searching attained the integrity and clarity of ideas Insarov attained without exceptional effort. These people know where the root of evil lies and they know what must be done to put a stop to evil; they are deeply and sincerely imbued with the idea they attained at last. But they no longer possess the strength for practical activity; they have strained themselves to such an extent that their characters seem to have sagged and become enfeebled. They welcome the approach of the new way of life, but they cannot go out to meet it, and they cannot satisfy the fresh sentiments of a man who is thirsting to do good and is looking for a leader.

None of us finds ready-made the humane concepts for the sake of which one must subsequently wage a life-and-death struggle. That is why we all lack that clarity, that integrity of views and actions that are so natural in, say, Insarov. In his case, the impressions of life that affect his heart and rouse his energy are constantly reinforced by the demands of his intellect, by the whole theoretical education he has received. With us, it is entirely different. An acquaintance of ours, a man of progressive opinions, and also burning with desire to do good, but one of the meekest and most innocuous men in the world, told us the following about his development to explain his present inactivity:

"As a boy" [he said], "I was of a very kind and impression-able nature. I used to weep bitterly when I heard of some misfortune; I suffered at the sight of another's suffering. I re-member that I could not sleep at night; I lost my appetite and could not do anything when anybody was sick at home. I re-member that I used to be driven into a sort of frenzy at the sight of the tortures to which a relative of mine subjected his son, my chum. All that I saw and all that I heard developed in me a feeling of grave discontent. Very early in life, my soul became troubled with the question: 'Why is everybody suffer-ing like this? Is there no way of alleviating this suffering into which everybody seems to be plunged?' I hungrily sought an answer to these questions. And soon I found an answer, a rational and systematic one. I went to school. The first maxim that I was given to copy was the following: 'True happiness lies in a clear conscience.' When I asked what conscience is, I was told that it punishes us for bad behavior and rewards us for good behavior.

"From that time onward all my attention was concentrated on the task of learning what behavior was good and what was bad. This was not a difficult matter. The code of morality al-ready existed in the copybook maxims, in parental admoni-tions, and in a special textbook: 'Respect your elders,' 'Don't rely on your own strength, for you are nothing.' 'Be content with what you have; don't strive for more,' 'By patience and obedience will you win universal love,' and so forth—this is what I wrote in my copybook. I heard the same thing at home, and from all those around me. From various textbooks I learned that there can be no perfect happiness on earth. In so far as happiness is possible at all, it is achieved in well-ordered states, and my country is the most well-ordered state in the world. I learned that Russia is now not only great and bounteous, but also that the most perfect order reigns here, that it is only necessary to obey the laws and the behests of one's elders, and also to be moderate, and the greatest well-being awaits every man, no matter of what station and rank.

"I was overjoyed at all these discoveries, and eagerly clutched at them as the best solution for my doubts. I took it into my head to verify them with my inexperienced mind, but much of this was beyond my powers. What I was able to verify in this way turned out to be correct. And so, trustfully and enthusiastically I devoted myself to this newly discovered system, directed all my strivings toward it, and at the age of twelve I was already a little philosopher and a stern supporter of law. I reached the conviction that a man is himself to blame for all the misfortunes that beset him—either he was not cautious, nor careful enough, or was not content with little, or was not sufficiently imbued with respect for law and

the will of his elders. I did not yet have a clear conception of
what the law, as such, was, but it was personified for me in
every superior and every elder. This explains why, in that
period of my life, I always supported my teachers, my superiors, and so forth, and was a favorite with my superiors
and elders.

"One day my classmates nearly threw me out of the window. A teacher, addressing the whole class, said: 'You pigs!'
There was a frightful uproar when the class was over, but I
defended the teacher and argued that he had a perfect right
to say what he did. On another occasion one of our classmates
was expelled for being rude to a superior. Everybody was
sorry for him because he was one of the best boys in the class.
But I maintained that he had fully deserved his punishment,
and expressed astonishment at the fact that a clever boy like
him could not understand that obedience to elders is our first
duty and the first condition of happiness. And so, day after
day, my conception of law became more firmly fixed and I
gradually grew accustomed to regarding most people only as
instruments for the execution of orders from above. At the
same time, I broke off living connection with the human soul;
the sufferings of my fellow men ceased to trouble me; and I
stopped seeking means for alleviating them. 'It's their own
fault,' I said to myself, and I became conscious of a feeling
akin to anger and contempt toward people who were unable
calmly and contentedly to enjoy the benefits of our public
order. Everything that was good in my nature was turned to
a different purpose, the purpose of supporting the rights of
our elders over us. I felt that in this lay self-sacrifice, the re-
nunciation of one's independence; I was convinced that I was
doing this for the public good, and I regarded myself almost
as a hero. I know that many remain at this stage, but others
change slightly and assure everybody that they have changed
completely. Happily, I did indeed have to alter my course
rather early.

"At the age of fourteen I was already an elder to some people—in the classroom and at home—and, of course, I was a
very bad one. I could do everything that was demanded of
me, but I did not know what I should demand, or how. On top
of all this, I was stern and aloof. Soon, however, I became
ashamed of this and began to put my previous conceptions
about elders to the test. The occasion for this was provided
by an incident that reawakened living sensations in my deadened soul. Being an elder brother, and clever, I used to give
lessons to one of my sisters. I was given the right to punish
her for laziness, disobedience, and so forth. One day her mind
wandered for some reason and she would not understand
what I was telling her. I ordered her to go down on her knees.
She at once collected her thoughts and, assuming an attentive

air, asked me to repeat what I had said. But I insisted that
she should first carry out my order—go down on her knees.
She was obstinate, and refused. I then caught her by the arm,
pulled her off her seat, and placing my elbows on her
shoulders pressed down with all my might. The poor girl sank
down on her knees and shrieked, for, as her knees bent, she
sprained her ankle. I was frightened, but when my mother
began to scold me for treating my sister in this way, I coolly
argued that it was her own fault, that had she obeyed my
order at once, nothing would have happened. In my heart
of hearts, however, the incident pained me, the more so that
I was very fond of my sister.

"It was then that the thought entered my mind that elders
too may be wrong and do stupid things, and that it was necessary to respect the law as such and not as it is interpreted by
various individuals. I then began to criticize the actions of
people, and I jumped from conservative irresponsibility into
the *opposition légale*. For a long time, however, I attributed
all evil solely to particular abuses, and these I attacked not
in the interests of the urgent requirements of society, not out
of sympathy for the sufferings of my fellow human beings,
but simply for the sake of the positive law. At that time, of
course, I would have argued very heatedly against cruelty to
Negroes, but, like a certain Moscow publicist, I would have
strongly condemned John Brown for wanting to liberate the
Negroes contrary to the law. I was very young then, however,
probably younger than that esteemed publicist.

"My thoughts roamed and wandered; I could not halt here,
and after much reflection I at last realized that even laws may
be imperfect, that they are of relative, transient, and particular importance, and should change with the passage of
time and upon the demands of circumstances. But again, what
inspired me to reason in this way? The supreme, abstract law
of justice, and not the promptings of the living feeling of love
for my fellow men; not my consciousness of those direct and
imperative needs to which the life that is passing before us is
pointing. And what do you think? I took the final step: from
the abstract of justice I passed to the more real demand of
the good of mankind; at last I reduced all my doubts and
speculations to one formula: man and his happiness. But this
formula had already been engraved in my soul during my
childhood, before I began to study various sciences and to
write copybook maxims. Needless to say, I understand it
better now and can prove it more thoroughly; but at that time
I felt it more, it was bound up with my whole being, and I
think I was ready to do more for it then than I am now. Now I
try not to do anything that contradicts the law that I now
recognize, I try not to deprive people of happiness, but I confine myself to this passive role. If, however, my childish senti-

ments and dreams had developed unhindered and had grown
strong, I might have been able to rush in search of happiness,
to bring it nearer to people, to destroy everything that hindered it; but those sentiments and dreams were being crushed
and deadened for some fifteen years. I am returning to them
only now, and I find them pale, thin, and weak. I must revive
them completely before I can put them into action; but who
knows whether I shall succeed in reviving them! . . ."

We think that this narrative contains features that are by
no means exceptional. On the contrary, they may serve as
a general indication of the obstacles the Russian encounters
in his path of independent development. Not all become attached to copybook maxims to an equal degree, but nobody
escapes their influence, and they have a paralyzing effect
upon all. To rid himself of them a man must spend a great
deal of his strength and lose a great deal of self-confidence
in this constant struggle with this ugly confusion of doubts,
contradictions, compromise, twists and turns, and so forth.

Thus, whoever among us has retained strength for heroism
need not be a hero; he sees no real goal before him, he does
not know how to set about his task and, consequently, he
can only play the Don Quixote. He who knows what to do
and how to do it has put all that was in him into the effort
of knowing, and therefore cannot take a practical step toward
activity. Consequently, he refrains from all intervention, as
Helena does in the domestic sphere. Even then Helena is
bolder and freer than the others, because it was only the
general atmosphere of Russian life that affected her; as we
have said already, she escaped the impress of the routine of
school education and discipline.

This is what explains the fact that the best of the people
that we have seen in our present-day society so far are capable
only of understanding the desire to do good that consumes
Helena and of sympathizing with her, but they are not
capable of satisfying that desire. And these are the progressives, these are the men we call "public figures"; the majority
of intelligent and impressionable people, however, flee from
civic glory and devote themselves to various muses. Take
even Shubin and Bersenev in *On the Eve*. They are splendid
characters; both can appreciate Insarov, and even follow him
with all their heart and soul; if only they had had a slightly
different development and a different environment they too
would not sleep. But what can they do here in this society?
Reshape it after their own fashion? But they know of no

fashion, and they have no strength. To patch up something
in it, cut off and cast aside little bits of the sordid side of the
social order? But is it not a repulsive task to draw the teeth
of the dead? And besides, what is the use? Only heroes of
the type of those gentlemen like the Panshins and Kurnatovskys are capable of doing that.

Incidentally, here we can say a few words about Kurnatovsky, who is also one of the finest representatives of the educated section of Russian society. He is a new species of
Panshin, only without social and artistic talents, and more
businesslike. He is very honest and even generous. In proof
of his generosity Stakhov, who is thinking of him as a husband for Helena, mentions the fact that as soon as he was
able to live comfortably on his salary he at once renounced
in favor of his brothers the annuity his father had granted
him. In general, there is a great deal of good in him; even
Helena admits this in describing him in a letter to Insarov.
The following is her judgment, from which alone we can
obtain some idea of Kurnatovsky; he takes no part in the
action of the story. Helena's narrative is so complete and to
the point, however, that we need nothing more, and so,
instead of paraphrasing her letter to Insarov, we shall quote
it in full:

Congratulate me, dear Dmitri, I have a fiancé. He dined
with us yesterday. Papa made his acquaintance, at the English
Club I think it was, and he invited him home. He did not
come yesterday as my fiancé, of course, but dear kind Mama,
to whom Papa had expressed his hopes, whispered into my ear
what sort of guest he was. His name is Yegor Andreyevich
Kurnatovsky. He is a senior secretary in the Senate. I'll first
of all describe him. He is short, shorter than you are, and well
built. He has regular features, close-cropped hair and long
side whiskers. His eyes are small (like yours), brown and
restless, his lips are broad and flat. There is always a smile in
his eyes and on his lips, a sort of official smile, it looks as if it
were on duty. He is modest in his demeanor, speaks distinctly;
in fact everything about him is distinct. He walks, laughs, and
eats as if it were some formal business. "How closely she has
studied him!" you must think as you are reading this. Yes, I
did study him in order to be able to describe him to you. And
besides, why should not one study one's fiancé? There is
something like iron about him . . . something dull and empty,
and at the same time, honest. Indeed, they say he is very
honest. You, too, are like iron, but not in the way he is. He
sat next to me at table, and Shubin sat opposite to us. At

first they discussed certain commercial undertakings. They
say that he is an expert in these matters and that he had
nearly resigned the service in order to take over a large fac-
tory. What a chance he missed! Then Shubin began to talk
about the theater. Mr. Kurnatovsky stated, without false
modesty, I must confess, that he understood nothing about
art. This reminded me of you. . . . But I thought to myself:
No, Dmitri and I don't understand art in a different way. It
seemed as though Mr. Kurnatovsky wanted to say: "I don't
understand anything about art, nor is it necessary, but it is
permitted in a well-ordered state." Incidentally, he seems
rather indifferent toward St. Petersburg and to *comme il faut.*
Once he even called himself a proletarian. "We are the common laborers," he said. I thought to myself: If Dmitri had said
that I would not have liked it, but let him say it if he wants
to! Let him brag! He was very polite to me, but all the time
it seemed to me that a very, very condescending high official
was talking to me. When he wants to praise anybody he says
about him that he *has rules*—this is his favorite expression. He
must be self-confident, diligent, and capable of self-sacrifice
(you see, I am unbiased), that is, he is capable of sacrificing
his own profit, but he is a great despot. Woe to the one who
falls into his hands! At dinner the discussion turned to
bribery. . . .

"I fully realize," he said, "that in many cases the people
who take bribes are not to blame. They cannot do otherwise.
But once they are caught they must be crushed."

I exclaimed: "What, crush an innocent person!"

"Yes, for the sake of the principle."

"What principle?" inquired Shubin. Kurnatovsky looked
confused, or surprised, I am not sure which, and said that that
needed no explanation. Papa, who, it seems to me, worships
him, interjected and said that of course there was nothing
to explain, and to my disappointment the subject was then
dropped.

Bersenev came in the evening and had an awful argument
with him. I have never before seen our good Andrei Petrovich so excited. Mr. Kurnatovsky did not at all deny the
benefits of learning, universities, and so forth . . . but yet,
I can understand Andrei Petrovich's indignation. The other
one seems to look upon all this as some kind of gymnastics.

When dinner was over, Shubin came up to me and said:
"This man and another one" (he cannot utter your name)
"are both practical men, but look at the difference between
them. The other has a real, living ideal, created by life itself,
but this one has not even a sense of duty: he is simply an
honest official, and his practicalness has no content." Shubin
is a clever man and I took note of his wise words for your
sake. But what can there be common between you two? You

believe, but he does not, because one *cannot believe* only in oneself.

Helena grasped Kurnatovsky's character at once and commented on it not quite favorably. But study this character closely and call to mind the business people of your acquaintance who are honestly striving for the common good. Probably many of them will be worse than Kurnatovsky; whether any will be found better than he it is hard to say. But why is this? Precisely because life, our environment, does not make us either clever, honest, or active. We must borrow wisdom, honesty, and vigor for activity from foreign books that, moreover, must be brought into harmony with the Code of Laws. It is not surprising that this difficult task chills the heart, kills all the living spirit in a man, and transforms him into an automaton that steadily and unfailingly performs what it is supposed to do. And yet, we repeat, these are the best. Beyond them commences a different stratum.

On the one hand, we have the utterly somnolent Oblomovs who have entirely lost even the charm of eloquence with which they enchanted young ladies in the past; on the other, we have the active Chichikovs who are unslumbering and tireless in their heroic pursuit of their narrow and sordid interests. Still further in the distance loom the Bruskovs, Bolshovs, Kabanovs, and Ulanbekovs, and all this evil tribe claims a right to the life and will of the Russian people. . . . How can you expect heroism here? And if a hero is born, where is he to obtain the light and wisdom to enable him to expend his strength in the service of virtue and truth instead of wasting it? And even if he at last acquires this light and wisdom, how can he, weary and broken, display heroism? How can a toothless squirrel nibble its nuts? No, better not give way to temptation, better choose some abstract specialty that is remote from life and bury yourself in it and suppress that ignoble feeling of instinctive envy of people who are alive and know what they are living for.

This is exactly what Shubin and Bersenev do in *On the Eve.* Shubin flies into a rage when he hears of Helena's marriage to Insarov and begins to rave:

"Insarov . . . Insarov . . . What's the use of false humility? Suppose he is a fine fellow, suppose he does stand up for himself, but are we such downright rotters? Take me, am I a rotter? Did God leave me destitute of everything?" and so forth. . . .

And then, poor fellow, in the next breath he turns to art:
"Perhaps," he says, "I, in time, will become famous for my
work. . . ." And indeed, he begins to develop his talent and
eventually becomes a splendid sculptor. And Bersenev, kind,
self-sacrificing Bersenev, who so sincerely and gladly nursed
Insarov when he was sick, who so generously served as the
intermediary between him, his rival, and Helena—even Bersenev, that man with a heart of gold, as Insarov expressed it,
cannot refrain from bitter reflections when he finally becomes
convinced of the mutual love between Insarov and Helena.

"Let them!" he says. "It was not for nothing my father
used to say to me: 'We two are not sybarites, not aristocrats,
my boy. We have not been pampered by fate and by nature.
We are not even martyrs. We are just toilers, toilers, toilers.
And so put on your leather apron, toiler, and sit down at your
bench in your gloomy workshop! And the sun, let it shine for
others. We, too, in our lowly lives have our pride and our
happiness!' "

What venomous envy and despair these unjust reproaches
breathe—envy of whom and of what, no one can say! . . .
Who is to blame for all that has happened? Is it not Bersenev
himself? No, Russian life is to blame. "If we had sensible
people among us," as Shubin said, "this girl would not have
left us, this sensitive soul would not have slipped through our
fingers like a fish into the water." But sensible and foolish
people are made by life, by its general structure at a given
time and in a given place. The structure of our life proved to
be such that Bersenev could find only one means of salvation:
"To drown his mind with fruitless learning." This is what he
did and, according to the author, scholars highly praised his
essays: "On Certain Specific Features of Ancient German Law
in the Matter of Juridical Punishment" and "On the Significance of the Urban Principle in Civilization." It is a good thing
that he found salvation at least in this. . . .

But Helena found no resource in Russia after she met
Insarov and conceived of a different life. That is why she
could neither remain in Russia nor return home after her husband's death. The author understood this perfectly well, and
preferred to leave her fate unknown rather than bring her
back to her father's house and compel her to live for the rest
of her life in sad loneliness and idleness in her native Moscow.
Her mother's appeal, which reached her almost at the moment
she lost her husband, failed to soften her repugnance for this

banal, colorless, and inactive life. "Return to Russia? What for? What shall I do in Russia?" she wrote to her mother, and went off to Zara to be swallowed up by the waves of insurrection.

What a good thing it was that she took this decision! Indeed, what awaited her in Russia? Could she have an object in life, or even life itself here? Return to the unfortunate cats and flies? Give to beggars money that she herself did not earn, but obtained God knows how? Rejoice at Shubin's successes in his art? Discuss Schelling with Bersenev, read the *Moscow News* to her mother, and see *rules* parading in the public arena in the shape of various Kurnatovskys and nowhere see real deeds performed, or even feel the breath of a new life . . . and gradually, slowly and painfully wilt, wither, and die? . . . No, once having tasted a different life, having breathed a different air, it was easier for her to rush into danger, however grave, than to condemn herself to this painful torture, to this slow execution. . . . And we are glad that she escaped from our life and did not confirm by her own example that hopelessly mournful and heart-rending prophecy of the poet that is so invariably and ruthlessly confirmed by the fate of the finest, the chosen characters in Russia:

> Remote from nature and the sun,
> Remote from light and art,
> Remote from life and love
> Your youth flashes by,
> Your living feelings die,
> Your dreams fade away.
> And your life will pass unseen
> In a deserted, nameless land,
> In an unchartered land—
> And vanish like a cloud of smoke
> In the dull and foggy sky,
> In autumn's boundless gloom. . . . [Tyutchev]

It remains for us now to sum up the various features scattered through this essay (for the incompleteness and incoherence of which we ask our readers to excuse us) and draw a general conclusion.

Insarov, being consciously and completely engrossed by a great idea of liberating his country and being ready to play an active part in this, could not develop and reveal his talents in present-day Russian society. Even Helena, who was able to love him so fully and merge herself completely with his

ideas, could not remain in Russian society, even among her
near and dear ones. And so, there is no room among us for
great ideas and great sentiments? . . . All heroic and active
people must fly from us if they do not wish to die of idleness,
or perish in vain? Is that not so? Is this not the idea that runs
through the novel that we have reviewed?

We think not. True, we lack an open field for wide activity;
true, our life is spent in petty affairs, in scheming, intriguing,
scandalmongering, and meanness; true, our civic leaders are
hardhearted and often thickheaded; our wiseacres will not do
a thing to achieve the triumph of their convictions; our liberals
and reformers base their schemes on legal subtleties and not
on the groans and cries of their unhappy fellow men. All this
is true, and all this is seen to some extent in *On the Eve*, as
well as in dozens of other novels that have appeared recently.
Nevertheless we think that *today* there is already room for
great ideas and sentiments in our society and that the time
is not far distant when it will be possible to put these ideas
into practice.

The point is that, bad as our present way of life is, the appearance of types like Helena has proved to be possible. And
not only have such characters become possible in life; they
have already been grasped by the artists' mind; they have
been introduced into literature; they have been elevated to a
type. Helena is an ideal personage, but her features are
familiar to us; we understand and sympathize with her. What
does this show? It shows that the basis of her character—love
for the suffering and the oppressed and a desire to do good,
and weary search for the one who could show how good can
be done—all this is at last being felt in the best section of our
society. And this feeling is so strong and so near to realization
that it is no longer, as before, dazzled either by brilliant but
sterile minds and talents, by conscientious but abstract learning, by official virtues, or even by kind, generous, but passive
hearts. To satisfy our feeling, our thirst, something more is
needed; we need a man like Insarov—but a Russian Insarov.

What do we need him for? We ourselves said above that we
do not need liberating heroes, that we were a nation of rulers,
not of slaves. . . .

Yes, we are safeguarded against outside dangers; even if we
were obliged to wage an external struggle we need not worry
about it. We have always had sufficient heroes to perform
deeds of valor on the battlefield, and the raptures that even at
the present day our young ladies go into at the sight of an

officer's uniform and mustaches is irrefutable proof that our society knows how to appreciate these heroes. But have we not many internal enemies? Is it not necessary to wage a struggle against them? And is not heroism needed for such a struggle? But where are the men among us who are capable of action? Where are the men of integrity who have been from childhood imbued with a single idea, who have merged themselves with that idea so thoroughly that they must either achieve this triumph or perish in the attempt? There are no such men among us, because up to now our social environment has been unfavorable for their development. It is from this environment, from its banality and pettiness, that we must be liberated by the new men whose appearance is so impatiently and eagerly awaited by all that is best, all that is fresh in our society.

It is as yet difficult for such a hero to appear; the conditions for his development, and particularly for the first manifestations of his activity, are extremely unfavorable, and his task is far more complicated and difficult than Insarov's. An external enemy, a privileged oppressor can be attacked and vanquished far more easily than an internal enemy, whose forces are spread everywhere in a thousand different shapes, elusive and invulnerable, harassing us on all sides, poisoning our lives, giving us no rest, and preventing us from surveying the battlefield. This internal enemy cannot be combated with ordinary weapons; we can liberate ourselves from him only by dispelling the raw, foggy atmosphere of our lives in which he was born, grew up, and gained strength, and by surrounding ourselves with an atmosphere in which he will be unable to breathe.

Is this possible? When will it be possible? Of these two questions a categorical answer can be given only to the first. Yes, it is possible, and for the following reasons. We said above that our social environment suppresses the development of personalities like Insarov. But now we may add the following: this environment has now reached the stage when it itself can facilitate the appearance of such a man. Eternal banality, pettiness, and apathy cannot be the lawful lot of man, and the people who constitute our social environment and who are fettered by its conditions have long ago realized the harshness and absurdity of these conditions. Some are dying of ennui; others are striving with all their might to go away, to escape from this oppression. Various ways of escape have been invented; various means have been employed to infuse some animation into the deadliness and rottenness of our lives, but they have all proved to be feeble and ineffective. Now, at last, concepts and demands are appearing, such as those that we saw in the case of Helena; these demands meet with sympathy in society; nay, more, efforts are being made to put them into effect. This shows that the old social routine is passing away. A little more vacillation, a few more powerful words and favorable factors, and active men will appear.

Above, we hinted that in our society the determination and energy of a strong character are killed at their birth by that idyllic admiration of everything in the world, by that proneness for indolent self-satisfaction and somnolent repose with which every one of us, when still a child, meets everything around us; and every effort is made—by means of various counsels and admonitions—to inculcate them into us. Lately, however, things have changed very much in this respect too. Everywhere, and in all things, we observe the growth of self-realization; everywhere the unsoundness of the old order of things is understood; everybody is waiting for reform and rectification, and nobody now lulls his children to sleep with songs about the inconceivable perfection of the present state of things in every corner of Russia. On the contrary, today everybody is waiting, everybody is hoping, and children are now growing up imbued with hopes and dreams of a brighter future, and are not forcibly tied to the corpse of the obsolete past. When their turn comes to set to work, they will put into it the energy, consistency and harmony of heart and mind of which we could scarcely obtain even a theoretical conception.

Then a full, sharp, and vividly depicted image of a Russian Insarov will appear in literature. We shall not have to wait long for him; the feverishly painful impatience with which we are expecting his appearance in real life is the guarantee of this. We need him; without him our lives seem to be wasted, and every day means nothing in itself, but is only the eve of another day. That day will come at last! At all events, the eve is never far from the next day; only a matter of one night separates them.